Better Dressmaking

Better Dressmaking

Margaret McCrirrick

B.T. BATSFORD LTD, LONDON
VAN NOSTRAND REINHOLD, AUSTRALIA, MELBOURNE

McCrirrick, Margaret.
    Better dressmaking.

    Index
    Simultaneously published, London: B.T. Batsford.
    Bibliography
    ISBN 0 442 25009 6

    1. Dressmaking.   I. Title.

646.4

First published 1979
© Margaret McCrirrick 1979
ISBN 0 7134 1092 2 (U.K.)

Filmset in 'Monophoto' Apollo by
Servis Filmsetting Ltd, Manchester

Printed by The Anchor Press Ltd, Tiptree, Essex
for the publishers, B.T. Batsford Ltd
4 Fitzhardinge Street, London W1H 0AH
and Van Nostrand Reinhold
17 Queen Street, Mitcham, Victoria 3132

Contents

Acknowledgments

I would like to express my thanks to the following people for permission to reproduce copyright illustrations: Coats Domestic Marketing Division for photo no. 7 in chapter 4, and figure 25; Pfaff Sewing Machines for the photographs in chapter 5, nos. 8 and 22;Elna Sewing Machines (Tavaro s/a Geneva) for the photographs in chapter 5, nos. 9–18; British Enkalon Ltd for the photograph in chapter 7, no. 30; Barrow Hepburn Leathercraft Ltd for the photographs in chapter 24, nos. 71 and 72; Lace Productions (1948) Ltd, for the diagrams in chapter 24, figure 323; Simplicity Patterns Ltd for their 'Pick-A-Knit Rule' in chapter 25, figure 328; and my thanks for their help, advice and suggestions to: John Lewis & Co Ltd, (chapters 8 and 21); Horrockses Ltd for advice on terry fabrics, (chapter 24); Barrow Hepburn and Gomshall and Associated Tanneries for advice on leather (chapter 24); A.C. Gill Ltd, and the British Lace Federation for advice on lace (chapter 24); Singer Sewing Machines, Elna Sewing Machines, Bogod Machine Co. Ltd (Bernina), Husqvarna, Pfaff (Britain) Ltd and Necchi (Great Britain) Ltd for information for chapter 5; Perivale-Gutermann Ltd, Coats Domestic Marketing Division, (especially for her time and interest to Mrs Barbara Walters), Scovil Dritz Sewing Aids Division, Leisure Arts and A.E. Arthur Ltd for information for chapters 4 and 6; Ells and Farrier for information on beads for chapter 22; Lightning Fasteners Ltd, Aero Zipps (Textron) Ltd and Newey Goodman Ltd for information for chapter 14. Lastly, my thanks to my friend, Richard Green, for his excellent photography and endless patience.

1   The Successful Garment

The aims of this book are to help the amateur dress-maker produce more professional-looking garments, to make dressmaking more pleasurable by removing some of the difficulties and to help the student think out the subject in as logical a way as she would with any other subject of study. Successful dressmaking requires not only practical skill and a flair for fashion but also a reasoned, intelligent approach based on sound knowledge, experience and thoughtful experiment.

What makes a successful garment? It might be a good idea to stop reading at this point and make your own list of priorities, later to be compared with the author's. A successful garment suits the wearer in colour and style, reflects her personality and flatters her figure. An experienced dressmaker should be able to advise the wearer on choice of style and fabric and should be able to adapt patterns sufficiently to highlight good figure points and disguise bad ones. Garments should be fashionable, but not slavishly so. Remember that fashion consists mainly in a line or silhouette such as the New Look with its tight waists and billowing calf length skirts, the 'A' line or the shift. A garment which follows fashion's line, adapted to suit the figure and made in a colour which becomes the wearer, will be far more successful than one which follows rigidly every detail of the latest fashion. It will not, moreover, be in danger of being just a 'uniform'.

The garment must be suitable for the occasion it is meant for, and if regular wear is required it should be easily maintainable. Where long or regular travel is involved, for example, crease-resisting fabric should be used. It should have character and immediate eye appeal, and not be a dull copy of many others. A good example of this is to be seen in the original use of mix and match fabrics, so often thoughtlessly planned as, for example, in a dress of one fabric with its partner used for collar and cuffs, when the two fabrics should have formed the basis of the design, emphasizing unusual seaming or line. Decoration should never look as though it were added as an afterthought. In other words, the garment must appear well planned. Fit is important, so the garment must hang well and not be too tight or too roomy.

Pattern and fabric must be consistent. The author has often been asked which one should buy first, pattern or fabric. The answer is that it does not matter so long as one is bought with the other in mind. Buying or drafting the pattern first is more economical as the exact amount of fabric can be bought, but buying fabric when the bargain or the mood takes you can be stimulating, particularly to those who design their own clothes. Qualities to consider when buying fabric are its weight, bulk, drapability or stiffness and its feel, as these have more influence on the success of the completed garment than the pattern or the colour. Complicated styles need plain fabrics to emphasize style lines, but a plain fabric made into a plain style will probably produce a dull garment. Stripes and checks need planning for and grain lines may need changing to make the necessary impact (see chapter 22, photos 52 and 53).

The real crux of the matter is, however, that the garment must be so *well constructed* that it does not look home-made. You are complimented when someone remarks, 'Surely you didn't make that yourself, did you?', but are not so flattered when told that it is obvious you made it yourself. Why is this? It ought to be a compliment. Another good exercise is to make a list of the features that readily give away the home-made garments you see on others – maybe some of these give you away too. The author's list is:

1 *Facings*   Seam showing instead of underneath.
2 *Collars*   Badly set, outside seam showing, sometimes curled up at the corners.
3 *Darts*   Not pointing to the fullest part and poking at the ends.
4 *Bulk*   Not trimmed away where several layers of fabric lie together, giving a lumpy effect.
5 *Hems*   The most frequent give-away – not straight, stitches showing or not sewn with a

light enough touch, bulk at the stitching line, often because a double turning was taken where a single one was needed.

6 *Inaccurate machining* Imperfect topstitching is often seen.

7 *Zips* Clumsily inserted, visible where they should be inconspicuous, possibly machined where handstitching would have made them less obvious.

8 *Patch pockets* Inaccurately machined on where the stitching should have been invisible.

9 *Support* Garment not properly supported, interfacing missing or too stiff, lack of support for seams which require it (see chapter 11), sagging pleats and pockets.

10 *Pressing* The amateur's greatest bugbear. Insufficient pressing during construction, bad pressing giving ridges of turnings at seams, hems, etc.

Many workers make constructional errors because they know only one or two methods of working a process instead of being familiar with several possibilities, and consequently choosing the wrong method. There are many methods of doing most things, such as seams and seam finishes (chapter 11) and methods of fixing hems (chapter 20), but the skill lies as much in the choice as in the execution of the method.

Some suggestions in this book will be hotly disputed. That is good, because better dressmaking needs experience, thought and debate. All the practical advice given is born of the author's personal experience, but she does not claim to have the best solution all the time. A good dressmaker must think and be selective, must experiment and practise, and must argue with other good dressmakers. If a suitable process does not exist she must invent another. The only criterion of her success is that it works!

2 Patterns

To make or to buy?

If you have been dressmaking for some years, feel you are moderately experienced and are able to handle the more difficult trade patterns well, you may well be considering whether the time has come to launch out into the second stage of dressmaking, that is, designing your own clothes and making your own patterns. Before deciding whether or not you wish to embark upon what is by no means a simple or brief course in pattern cutting, whether at a class or on your own from books, here are some points for you to consider – the pros and cons of buying or making.

The advantages of buying

Paper patterns were made for use by the general public as far back as the middle of the last century, when they could be hired. The pattern companies came into existence in this century. Simplicity Patterns Ltd, for example, was founded in 1927 and has been developing and improving the paper pattern ever since. It is certain, therefore, that any good brand of paper pattern that you buy is backed up by many more years' experience than you will ever obtain. There is almost no possibility of error – the number of hands through which a pattern passes in its production is guarantee of that. All patterns of reputable companies are tested out on actual fabric to ensure that they are workable. Since the paper pattern industry formed its Measurements Standard Committee sizing has been universal, and much progress has also been made with the clothing industry to see that sizes in ready-made clothes also correspond in many cases. It is helpful to know, for example, that if you have made a successful dress from the patterns of one major company, you will obtain a similar fitting when making a coat of another. The patterns which are made in a range of figure types, for example 'Miss Petite', 'Misses', 'Half Sizes', have evolved out of a great deal of patient research into average sizes and are always being reviewed.

Sewing 'primers' or instruction sheets are prepared with as much expertise as is given to the pattern, and you may be sure that difficult construction points are described and diagrammed simply for you. The general sewing guides issued with some patterns are also of value and help to keep your sewing ideas and methods up to date. Often some indication is given on the front of the packet as to the degree of difficulty involved. Pattern catalogues are useful because in them different types of patterns are grouped together under such headings as 'evening wear' or 'designer patterns'. The sketches themselves can also be stimulating even to the person who is subsequently going to make her own pattern.

That bought patterns are good value for money is beyond doubt. Time is money for most people. This is particularly true of the more difficult pattern cutting operations. Dolman styles, for example, which are so quick and easy to construct, often coming under the 'very easy' heading in the book, are among the most difficult and time consuming to cut.

Above all, the quality paper pattern can be very much up-to-date, appearing in the catalogue a few weeks after the first hint of change by the couture world. Dozens of new designs are added to the ranges each month to keep pace with changes of fashion and season, and unless you follow fashion carefully your own ideas may very probably be less than up-to-date. The pattern companies know what fabrics will be in production six or eight months ahead of time. They also know what trimmings and haberdashery requirements are planned to reach the shops and incorporate all these ideas in their patterns.

Lastly, reflect that for a pound, or two at the most, plus the price of the fabric you can produce a dress from one of the world's top designers. What value for money, indeed.

The disadvantages of buying

If you have used paper patterns for any length of time, you will probably have discovered the pitfalls for yourself. Over the years the major companies have ironed out most of the problems from their patterns, but many a dressmaker has made cutting mistakes through trying to economize with a cheaper 'multi-size' pattern. They are unbelievably difficult to understand and frequently the instructions accompanying them are far from watertight. Many of the patterns issued by women's magazines are also difficult. The fit is sometimes of a low standard, the instructions unclear and the designs untempting and unexciting, the latter presumably because it is vital to their financial success to produce something that will appeal to all ages and types of their readership. The result is frequently just a piece of clothing rather than a fashionable garment.

The instructions accompanying paper patterns must always be used thoughtfully, and one of the principal drawbacks of these patterns is that they do not encourage the user to bring her experience to bear on the task. For example, fitting is scarcely ever mentioned. The user is told to start construction by stitching all the darts. What bad practice! – darts, like every other part, must be tacked for fitting.

Turnings are a standard 1·5cm ($\frac{5}{8}$in) all round – too small for main seams or to allow for fitting, and too much for inside collar seams, for instance. Processes are described with no reference to the type of fabric being used: there are, for example, many ways of neatening seams, turning hems and attaching interfacings, but frequently one method only is given which cannot possibly be suited to all the different types of fabric listed on the pattern back as suitable for the style. One of the aims of this book is to give guidance on all these matters, so that the dressmaker who knows how to do the basic processes will also be led to think *how to choose the right one*.

The guidance given on choice of fabric for the design is in itself frequently misleading and breaks one of the first principles of design, namely that a designer should always work with a particular fabric in mind to achieve a unified result. A long list of fabric suggestions usually indicates one of two things – that the design is uninteresting in its use of fabric or that it simply will not look good in some of the materials suggested.

Illustrations can be misleading. One must remember that while showing style lines and features clearly, proportions are often not clearly drawn – the aim of the illustrator for the catalogue and the pattern cover is, after all, to sell the pattern. How often has your completed garment just not looked like the picture? The dressmaker who cuts her own patterns to her own sketches rarely falls into this trap, as she has learned to be realistic. Necklines on commercial patterns frequently come out lower than is illustrated, and experienced dressmakers have learned to cut these higher at first, altering later if necessary. It is a pity that more guidance is not given on the styles which will best suit different figure types – quite unsuitable styles are often made in pattern sizes to fit women who should never be seen in them.

Another sore point with users of commercial patterns is the waste of material when the amount stated is bought. The reason for this is obvious and the mistake can be avoided by making trial layouts. Consider that the pattern may have three views, six sizes and be suitable for fabric in three different widths. To illustrate the most economical layout for each of these possibilities would require 54 illustrations, an expensive proposition for the pattern manufacturer and a confusing one for the user!

The principal misgiving about commercial patterns is the fit. Young people frequently complain that garments are too loose and the elderly that they want more room to sit in! This is hardly surprising, considering that a woman who quite correctly buys a size 14 because she is 1·6m (5ft 6in) tall and has a 91cm (36in) bust may be a plump, shapeless middle-aged matron, a shapely teenager with narrow back and very prominent bust or an elderly lady with a flat chest and a rounded stooping posture. In some cases the only real answer to this problem is to have such a masterly grasp of the art of pattern alteration and its implications that you can virtually re-cut the pattern or – much the best way – to design your own and cut it to fit first time!

Making your own patterns

Here, then, is the crux of the matter. Many of the disadvantages of buying patterns we have considered are relatively minor and need only experience and good reference books to overcome, but some are so basic that the only satisfactory solution is the custom-made pattern intended for one wearer only and designed with one fabric in mind. Never be tempted to learn pattern cutting purely as a money saver because, as we have seen, it simply isn't worth it from this angle. Neither are you ready to learn until you have fully mastered the principles of fitting, the basic sewing techniques, the problems of layout and so on. As much as one may criticize pattern primers for their inadequacies, remember that if you cut your own pattern you will not have a primer at all. The road to success is long and as with your first attempts at dressmaking, the price of learning may be some early disappointments.

The fit of a custom-made pattern does not compare in any way with the fit of the commercial pattern. Every contour of the body is taken into account. The three size 14 ladies described above need three totally different patterns, with the bust measurement properly distributed in the right places and the size of the bust dart related to the actual prominence and shape of the figure rather than merely to its measurement. Very few individuals have hip measurements corresponding exactly to the standard pattern bust/hip ratio, but with individually drafted patterns this does not present a problem.

Pattern cutting develops the understanding of construction techniques. Once a dressmaker has learned the theory behind collar cutting, for example, and why certain shapes of collar set in certain ways, she will also be better able to choose the best method for mounting that collar. Planning and cutting unusual openings will force her to work out their implications in fabric and so the knowledge of construction techniques grows with every fresh pattern idea she incorporates in her designs.

Frequently to design and cut your own pattern is the only way to get exactly what you want. How often have you searched the catalogues and not found just what you had in mind? 'If only that blouse had the other collar . . .' or 'If only that dress had a jacket to match . . .' – these are the problems we have all met.

Lastly, the most important reason for cutting your own patterns is the creative one. The garment you made yourself can give so much more pleasure than the one you bought, and so much more again if you designed it yourself as well. It is absolutely unique, designed for the fabric, designed for the individual figure, designed for the occasion and a complete expression of yourself. If you do not feel sufficiently experienced to launch out yet on your own designs, the time will inevitably come when you will.

Methods of making patterns

There are four principal methods:

(a) Flat pattern cutting from a block.
(b) Modelling on a stand (or even on to a person).
(c) Drafting by direct measurement for parts of patterns only, e.g. cuffs, shirt-style collars, waistbands, pockets and also for circular skirts.

(d) Taking a pattern from a finished garment.

Since this is not a pattern cutting or modelling book, it is not proposed to go into any great detail on the first two methods. Good books are available on both methods and classes for teaching them are given. We shall attempt here only to outline the methods so that the reader may decide whether or not she wishes to follow them up at length. Both methods are used by couture houses and commercial pattern companies. Method (c) is simple enough to be of use to those who do not wish to embark on making their own patterns in a big way and some details will therefore be given, while method (d) will be described in more detail as it is not often taught in classes and is well within the scope of the average dressmaker.

Flat pattern cutting

The method is based on the adaptation of five basic blocks – front bodice, back bodice, front skirt, back skirt and sleeve. These are made to fit the individual figure from a large number of body measurements. The blocks are drafted according to the rules, fitting toiles (see chapter 3) made and corrected and the corrections transferred back to the draft. This is then permanently made in thick paper or card and used as a basis for adaptations, the basic principle for shaping being the use, size and positioning of darts. In order to be successful no effort must be spared at obtaining a perfect fit of the basic blocks – several fittings may be necessary – since all patterns depend for their success on the fit and accuracy of these blocks. Unfortunately the making of the block is one of the most confusing and difficult parts for the novice to master – probably simply because she is a beginner. It can become tedious and uninteresting, but she should be encouraged to press ahead, because as soon as the blocks are produced she may start the interesting work safe in the knowledge that she will not have to go through the block-making process again unless she suffers a drastic change of figure. It is possible to circumvent the tediousness of the block-making process by use of the pattern companies' shell patterns, made and fitted as a base, but the true fit of the block drafted pattern is never obtained in this way. Patterns from shell blocks will fit more like trade patterns.

Practice in pattern cutting is necessary and there is no short cut to perfection – practice, practice and more practice are needed. To save paper and space this may be done in part in quarter or one-fifth scale with accurately scaled down blocks. Some examination bodies demand this type of work to be done as part of the syllabus.

Modelling

While all garments can in fact be cut flat, there are certain styles for which modelling on the stand is preferable. These are complicated styles with many pleats or folds, drapery or bias cuts. Asymmetric styles can often be better judged for appearance on the stand, and in many garments some parts can be modelled while the rest is cut flat. For example, a plain, fairly tailored style, cut flat, may be completed with a draped or bias collar modelled on to the garment on the stand. The method was first introduced in a big way about 1935 by the French couturier, Madame Grès, for her silk jersey dresses in large patterned fabrics and is still used for these purposes by designers today. Her original methods are now often modified by the application of certain basic principles of flat cutting, such as measuring the parts of a garment to make sure they conform to body measurements while still on the stand. This saves time and material.

There are many advantages of the method. Some designers feel more free to express themselves when working in this way, and certainly it has the advantage that the design may be seen coming to life and its success or not judged early in the process. It is invaluable for draped or bias styles since one can tell immediately exactly how much material needs to be incorporated in a fold or drape and how much ease or lack of it is required in a bias cut. It helps the worker understand the full implications of the grain in any particular style and trains her in the fitting process. A little modelling experience is valuable to even the most hesitant of flat pattern cutters as it is the quickest way to understand the full implications of the flat method, and also develops her skill in handling fabric, as a light touch is required when modelling.

Modelling is usually done in mull or calico and a pattern made from the toile thus made, but it is also possible to work directly in the garment fabric. This is particularly desirable when working with plaids, stripes or large patterns or when working on the bias. One can see immediately the exact effect of the pattern in the first instance and of the hang of the garment in the second. This method is, however, extremely extravagant on material as pieces larger than necessary must be cut for each part of the garment and then cut to shape on the stand creating much wastage.

The general principles are that pieces of muslin or light calico are cut to approximately the right shape for each part of the garment and moulded on to the stand in the right shape, using darts, seams and drapes in accordance with the rules of grain. When all the pieces are pinned on they are marked up with balance marks while still on the stand, removed, laid flat on the table, lines trued up, tacked together and refitted on to the stand for final checking. This toile is then taken apart and used for a pattern or the garment cut directly from it. While, as with flat pattern cutting for most people there is no substitute for practice with the help of good books or teachers, the following elementary instructions are given for a simple bodice and skirt to introduce the reader to the system and whet the appetite for developing her interest. She may find she is amongst the number of beginners whose natural flair for fashion and handling fabric can lead them far in the practice of modelling without a great deal of formal instruction.

Start with the *back bodice*, as it is easier than the front.

Fabric needed: a rectangle, warpways measurement 8cm (3in) longer than nape to waist, weftways, about 28cm (11in). This will fit a dress stand up to about 97cm (38in) bust. The centre back (CB) edge should be a selvedge.

Figure 1 (a) With 5cm (2in) above the nape and 2·5cm (1in) below waist, pin the selvedge down the CB of the stand.

(b) Always keeping the weft grain horizontal, smooth across from the CB at about the level of midway down the armhole and pin.

(c) Smooth upwards around the neck, pinning from CB to neck point, trimming neck turnings to about 1·5cm (½in) and clipping in to neck line to enable fabric to lie flat.

(d) Smooth across the shoulder, pinning, and folding in a 13mm (½in) dart about midway across.

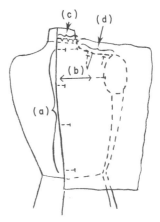

Figure 1

Figure 2 (e) Following grain down from mid-armhole pin, measure out to underarm exactly 5cm (2in) and pin underarm, checking that there is just a little ease at this point across back (about 1·5cm ($\frac{1}{2}$in)).

(f) From underarm point, follow straight grain down precisely to waistline, move inwards on weft grain 2·5–4cm (1–1$\frac{1}{2}$in) and pin side waist.

(g) This should leave about 2·5cm (1in) to be smoothed into back waist dart. Pin along waist.

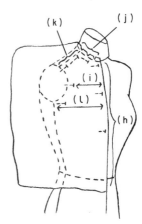

Figure 3

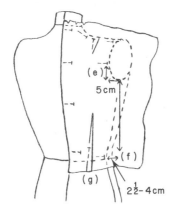

Figure 2

Survey the general effect and make adjustments according to eye and experience of good fit if necessary. Fit should have a little ease across the back but be a good close fit around the waist. Mark in all seam lines *lightly* with pencil – they may have to be trued up later.

Front bodice. Fabric needed: a rectangle 15cm (6in) longer than neck to waist measurement, and about 33cm (13in) across. Centre front (CF) should be a selvedge.

Figure 3 (h) With 12·5cm (5in) above neck and 2·5cm (1in) below waist, pin the selvedge down the CF of the stand.

(i) Following principles in (b) pin front armhole.

(j) Following principles in (c) pin front neck.

(k) Smooth shoulder into position and pin along.

(l) Still keeping weft grain horizontal, smooth fabric firmly across widest point of bust to underarm, release fabric slightly to allow 1·5–2cm ($\frac{1}{2}$–$\frac{3}{4}$in) ease across bust and pin underarm point.

Figure 4 (m) Following straight grain accurately down from bust point, make a mark at waist line. This mark is the inside fold of the waist

dart. Arrange and pin waist dart taking in about 4cm (1$\frac{1}{2}$in) fabric.

(n) Smoothing from side waist up the side seam, take up the spare fullness arranging it in side dart pointing towards bust point. Making sure that lower edge of fabric lies exactly 2·5cm (1in) below waistline all the way from CF to side seam and that side seam will be correct length for stand, pin this dart.

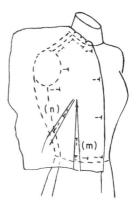

Figure 4

Figure 5 (o) To true up side seam, follow straight grain down from underarm point to side dart and continue this straight line down to waist. (The part below dart will not be on straight grain because of the dart.) Pin waist point, in from this line about 2·5–4cm (1–1$\frac{1}{2}$in) (same as back).

Survey the general effect of these last two darts and adjust relative amounts of fullness in them if necessary. Bust should have 1·5–2cm ($\frac{1}{2}$–$\frac{3}{4}$in) ease around widest point, and front waist should have 1·5cm ($\frac{1}{2}$in) ease, not a close fit as at back. Mark in all seam lines lightly with pencil.

Trim side and shoulder seams to 2·5cm (1in), front

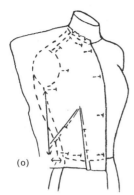

Figure 5

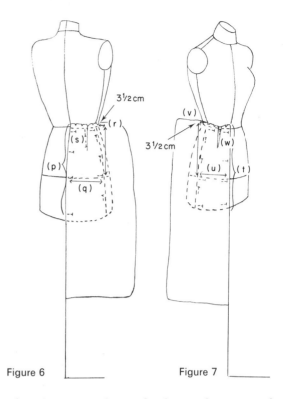

Figure 6   Figure 7

and back, pin bodice parts together at these seams. Trim armholes to 1·5cm ($\frac{1}{2}$in).

Remove the toile from the stand, making sure all darts are marked; unpin and lay flat on the table. True up seam lines to match and if necessary true armhole shapes to the shape you will know from experience of patterns to be satisfactory. Re-mark, place balance marks, tack toile up and replace on stand for final check.

A plain skirt is easy to model. The method is the same for both front and back. Two pieces of fabric are required: warpways – length as desired; weftways – $\frac{1}{4}$ hip measurement plus 8cm (3in) for each piece. CB and CF should be selvedges.

Figure 6 Back skirt. (p) pin CB (selvedge) from waist to bottom of stand, allowing 2·5cm (1in) above waist.

(q) Keeping weft grain horizontal, smooth across firmly from CB to side at hip line, release fabric a little to allow about 1·5cm ($\frac{1}{2}$in) ease, and pin at side seam.

(r) Following straight grain up from side hip point to waist, move in on straight (weft) grain at waist for 3·5cm (1$\frac{1}{2}$in) to shape side seam, and pin at waist. Pin side seam also.

(s) Arrange waist dart to take in spare fullness. Dart should be about 15cm (6in) long, centre fold of dart should be on straight grain, dart should be about halfway between side seam and CB, and there should be about 1cm or $\frac{1}{2}$in ease left at waist. Pin along waist.

Figure 7 (t), (u), (v) and (w) of the front skirt – proceed in exactly the same way as for back skirt, except that dart should be only 10cm (4in) long.

Mark all lines lightly in pencil, take toile off stand, lay flat on the table, true up all lines, add balance marks, tack toile up and replace on stand for final check.

Sleeves can be modelled by the same principles on a bought arm attachment for the stand or on one that can be made at home (see p. 30). Principles to watch when modelling sleeves are that straight grain runs down from shoulder to the back of the hand and weft grain across the crown of the sleeve.

The art of modelling may be proceeded further in classes or with a good modelling book. Small scale models can also be bought for further practice with economy of fabric.

Direct measurement drafting

A very limited number of patterns can be drafted in this way, without blocks, the best known example being that of the circular skirt, instructions for which are given in figure 8. Direct drafting of collars and cuffs is given in chapter 16. Frills and flounces and pockets are cut from direct measurement patterns also.

Taking a pattern from a garment

In the fashion trade this operation is done when wholesale houses buy toiles from couture houses or fashion collections. Rather than taking the toile to pieces it is copied and an identical toile made for the pattern of the wholesale garment. There are two methods of doing this, simplified from the fashion trade methods, suitable for the home dressmaker.

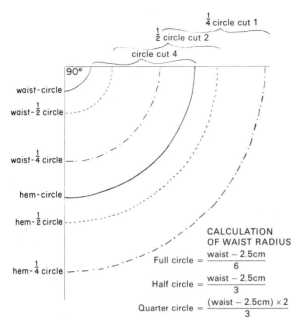

$\frac{1}{4}$ circle cut 1

$\frac{1}{2}$ circle cut 2

circle cut 4

90°

waist-circle

waist-$\frac{1}{2}$ circle

waist-$\frac{1}{4}$ circle

hem-circle

hem-$\frac{1}{2}$ circle

hem-$\frac{1}{4}$ circle

CALCULATION
OF WAIST RADIUS

$$\text{Full circle} = \frac{\text{waist} - 2.5\text{cm}}{6}$$

$$\text{Half circle} = \frac{\text{waist} - 2.5\text{cm}}{3}$$

$$\text{Quarter circle} = \frac{(\text{waist} - 2.5\text{cm}) \times 2}{3}$$

Figure 8   Drafting circular skirts by direct measurement

These patterns may be cut on straight grain or cross according to fabric or effect required. Placed to fold or not according to width of fabric used and length of skirt.

Method 1   Establish the CB and CF of the garment by measurement or by folding in half. Trace tack down the garment using a fine needle and pure silk thread to avoid damaging it, following exactly the straight grain down CB and CF. Similarly place lines of trace tacking down the garment (right hand side only, unless asymmetrical) at regular intervals, about 5cm (2in) apart. The exact amount can be varied according to the complications of the style. These trace tacks are followed by horizontal lines, starting at underarm level and working rows above and below. These lines serve to accentuate the grain and allow it to show through the mull used for making the copy.

Prepare a stand so that the garment fits closely, and place mull over the garment grain for grain, starting at CB and CF. The amount taken up in pleats, folds and darts if complicated should be measured previously and noted so that it may be copied precisely.

Mark out the mull as if for modelling and complete by laying flat, truing up, and so on as for modelling. Tack up the new toile and fit back on to the stand to ascertain that a correct copy has been obtained.

Method 2   It is also possible to take the pattern of a very simple garment by flat cutting. The garment should be marked up in the same way, the amount in darts, etc. measured and noted and then the lines measured and transferred to squared pattern paper.

It is important for ease of copying that the lines of trace tacking should be at the same intervals as the lines on the squared paper.

Both these methods are made extremely difficult to carry out accurately if the garment being copied does not have a clear, evident grain structure.

Shell patterns

Sometimes known also as 'basic patterns', these are issued by all the major pattern companies principally as an aid to fitting, but they do in fact have a variety of advantages and uses. They consist of a simple dress with a natural neck-line, a choice of short or long semi-fitted sleeves, plainly set-in, bodice having standard fitting darts i.e. from side seam, to shape bust and at waistline, and plain straight skirt darted to fit at waist, or 'A' line. There are also shell patterns of plain shift style dresses without waist seam. They include detailed sewing and fitting instructions and usually charts for the recording of fitting alterations and figure deviations.

When made up and fitted these patterns establish the fitting problems that will be met with in all patterns of the same make and size, and thus if a permanent record is made of the fitting alterations necessary the theory is that the same alterations should be made on all other patterns. While undoubtedly a good idea and a blessing to home dressmakers, the theory is a little naïve since the fit of any particular garment depends on factors other than the pattern and the figure. Different types of material call for closer or looser fits even when made in the same style, and there is therefore no real substitute for fitting each garment at the right stages in its own construction. Use of the shell pattern does, however, give the hesitant fitter much good practice and enables her to master the principles of fit more easily than with complicated styles. As a learning exercise alone they are worth the cost and time.

They have other advantages. When making garments for somebody other than oneself and where the number of fittings that may be arranged is limited for some reason, commencing with a shell pattern can reduce the number of alterations and hence the number of fittings needed in the actual garment. A dressmaker who regularly makes dresses for the same client finds the making of a shell for each client a time-saving operation. It is also valuable for dressmakers to keep sets of shell patterns made up in different standard sizes for new clients to try on so that they themselves may see and comment upon the fit. Thus their preference for a close fit, for example, or for 'plenty of room to move' may be established before the first garment is ever started. When a figure type falls between one or two categories of pattern e.g. 'Miss Petite' or 'Misses', the making of shells in both sizes will enable the dressmaker to ascertain which pattern really does suit the figure best and will require the least number of alterations.

Shell patterns may also be used as basic blocks for pattern cutting. This has already been dealt with in the section on flat pattern cutting.

Turnings or no turnings? – all types of pattern

Whether to cut out with seam allowances on patterns or not is a vexed question which tends to provoke fierce argument among dressmakers, and for the more experienced dressmaker it is a question that should be considered early so that a conclusion may be reached. It goes without saying that beginners should always cut from patterns with turnings – there are quite enough pitfalls in cutting out without the complication of having to add your own turnings. It is assumed, however, that if you are reading this book you will have already reached beyond this beginner's stage.

Firstly, the facts. Standard turnings are added to all commercial patterns. They are 1·5cm or $\frac{5}{8}$in for *all* seams. All patterns are originally cut from blocks (unless modelled) *without* turnings so at some stage the pattern has had turnings added. The question is, then, whether it is advisable to *remove* the turnings from commercial patterns before cutting or not, or if you make your own patterns whether or not to *add* the turnings before cutting.

The advantages of having turnings added are to prevent cutting disasters, as it is very easy to make mistakes without them, and also to make the whole job of laying out simpler. It also tends to make for more economical use of fabric and certainly makes the job of calculating quantities much easier and more efficient since trial layouts can be one hundred per cent accurate.

The arguments against having turnings are forceful. First the actual process of adding them to individually drafted patterns is a lengthy business and usually entails the recutting of each pattern piece after all the drafting processes are complete and the final pattern line obtained. Cutting the turnings off bought patterns and adding your own overcomes the problems created by the standard 1·5cm ($\frac{5}{8}$in) turning. For most seams this is far too little as it allows nothing for alterations for fitting, nor for alterations of style,

for example the moving up or down of a yoke line by 2cm ($\frac{1}{2}$in) or so to suit the figure. The amount allowed is also too little for fabrics that fray easily. It does not allow for the construction of certain types of decorative seam, for example the channel, which require extra turnings, and in certain fabrics it is too little to allow the plain or open seam to set well when pressed open. The standard turning can, on the other hand, be too *big* for certain pattern parts, such as the outside edges of collars, and can waste material in cutting.

The usual solution for the worker who sees the advantages of adding her own turnings in different amounts according to the need of the particular edge is to work basically from patterns without, but to avoid cutting errors by writing on each edge the amount of turning to be allowed when cutting, and across the pattern in bold lettering 'no turnings allowed'. When the pattern is pinned on to the material the actual cutting line may be chalked around and checked as a final precaution, before cutting. Pattern lines need careful marking when amounts of turnings differ on various edges.

Alteration of commercial patterns

Information on the techniques of altering patterns for different fittings is very widely available in most elementary dressmaking books and in pattern company literature. It is not necessary to deal here with standard alterations such as lengthening a bodice, adding to width of hip, and so on. A number of more unusual pattern alterations are included in the chapter on fitting, however, in order to demonstrate the difference between altering a garment and a pattern to achieve the same effect. Only one simple method of altering for the purposes of *sizing* is given here, that is an understanding of elementary grading procedures.

Alteration of patterns for *style* reasons are dealt with as these are less well understood by the average dressmaker unless she has taken a full course in pattern cutting. This chapter deals with the addition and removal of flare, adaptation of patterns for sleeveless garments, addition of button stands and openings and the general rules to be observed when combining parts of different patterns into one garment. Covered in later sections of the book as appropriate are details of cutting shaped facings (chapter 12), addition of pleats, shirring, gathers, tucks and amounts for smocking (chapter 10).

The first essential when altering any commercial pattern for style or grading is to remove the turnings (see above). These may be replaced afterwards if desired when the grading or style alteration has been carried out.

Grading

The method of grading the five basic blocks by one size each way is shown in figures 9 and 10 and is self-explanatory. By way of principle, it should be noted that bigger alterations are made to the sides of bodice and skirt than to cb and cf and that lengths of blocks vary also with the widths. It is not the aim of this chapter to deal at great length with the details of grading, which is, after all, a separate skilled job in the pattern-cutting industry, but simple patterns may

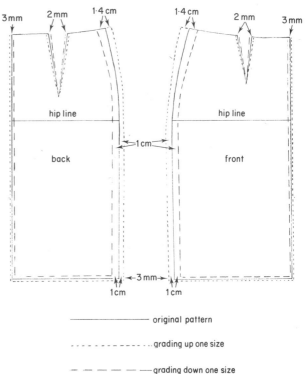

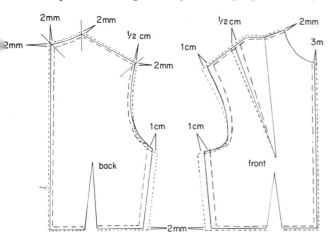

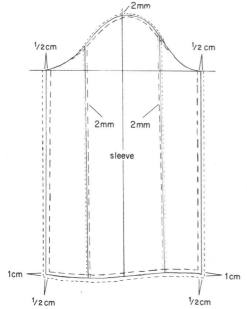

Figure 9   Grading bodice and sleeve patterns

Figure 10   Grading skirt patterns

be graded successfully by the amateur following these principles. Should the pattern have more sections lengthwise, say a panelled skirt or princess line bodice, the grading should be spread throughout the pieces. It is not advisable, without further study of the subject, to grade up or down more than one size, although the principles and methods do not alter.

Addition and removal of flare

Figures 11, 12 and 13 show two methods of adding flare to skirts or removing it. The principles involved are as follows:

(a) the waist measurement must remain unchanged.

(b) the side seams must remain the same (e.g. in figure 11 ac = ab on both front and back.

(c) equal amounts of flare must be added or subtracted on both front and back.

(d) good shapes must be preserved (note blended line at hip of skirt in figure 11, and waist and hemlines in figures 12 and 13).

(e) the altered pattern may then be placed on straight or cross grain according the effect desired.

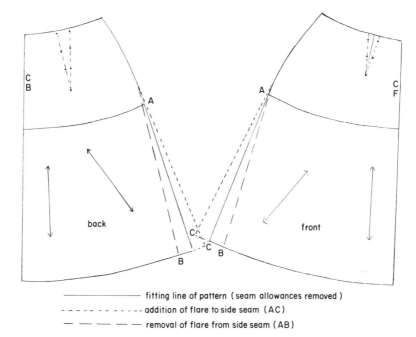

fitting line of pattern (seam allowances removed)

addition of flare to side seam (AC)

removal of flare from side seam (AB)

Figure 11

Figure 11 Flare may be added or subtracted from side seams up to a maximum of 4cm (1½in) at knee level (hem on diagram). To attempt a greater alteration on seams disturbs the balance and hang of the skirt. The new line is blended into the old line just above hip level.

Figure 12 By slashing the pattern piece up the middle and spreading out the side section, any desired amount may be added. To proceed, find the centre point of the waist-line edge and the centre point of the hem edge and fold or rule a straight line between the two. Cut the pattern on this line, cutting up from the hem and leaving just a tiny piece of the line uncut at the waist edge. Pivot the side piece round to add the amount of flare desired at the hem. Pin in a piece of paper to fill the gap left (or stick in with sticky tape). An angle will have formed at the waistline. This must be blended into a good shape. Blend in a good shape at the hem also.

Note. In order to preserve the waistline size it is important that the slash line does not interfere with the dart if there is one. Either the slash line or the dart may be moved a little to prevent this.

Figure 13 This shows exactly the opposite procedure to figure 12. To remove more than the 4cm

(1½in) flare that may be taken off the side seam, slash the pattern and overlap the edges. It is also possible, if preferred, to fold out the extra fullness instead of cutting the pattern, but folding out is more difficult to do accurately. The amount of flare that may be removed is limited by the hip measurement. Care should be taken not to reduce the width of the pattern at the hip line to less than is required to give sufficient ease for movement.

Figures 14 and 15 show flare added to sleeves. The same principles apply, namely:

(a) the armhole edge must not change in length or it will not fit the bodice.

(b) underarm seams must be of equal length and should not change in length.

(c) all unpleasant curves obtained at armhole or hem edges must be blended to a pleasant shape.

(d) flare cannot be added to sleeve underarm seams as this is not the place where it is required and it would spoil the set of the sleeve.

(e) sleeves with flare added may be cut on straight or cross grain according to effect desired.

Figure 14 The alteration of a plain long sleeve (a) to a medieval sleeve (b). First fold the pattern in half and then in quarters to establish the correct line for alteration – it needs to be altered at the back of the arm. Slash up on

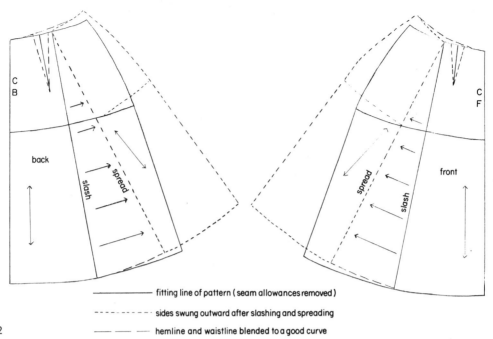

Figure 12

— — — — — fitting line of pattern (seam allowances removed)

- - - - - - - sides swung outward after slashing and spreading

— — — hemline and waistline blended to a good curve

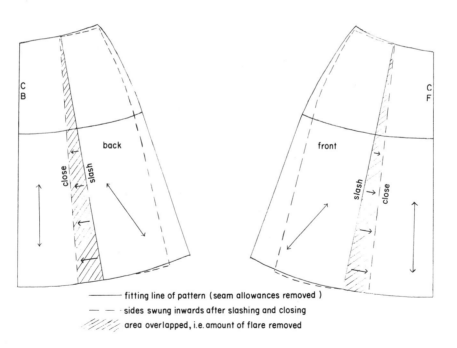

Figure 13

— — — — — fitting line of pattern (seam allowances removed)

— — — sides swung inwards after slashing and closing

///// area overlapped, i.e. amount of flare removed

the back fold and spread the pattern pieces the desired amount, adding in spare paper as with the skirt flare. In the case of this particular style of sleeve a little length should be added on the back line to achieve the draping effect.

Figure 15 The alteration of a plain short sleeve (c) into a cape sleeve (d). Fold the pattern in quarters to establish flare lines. In this case flare needs to be added evenly over the sleeve, so all three fold lines are slashed and spread out. Armhole and hem

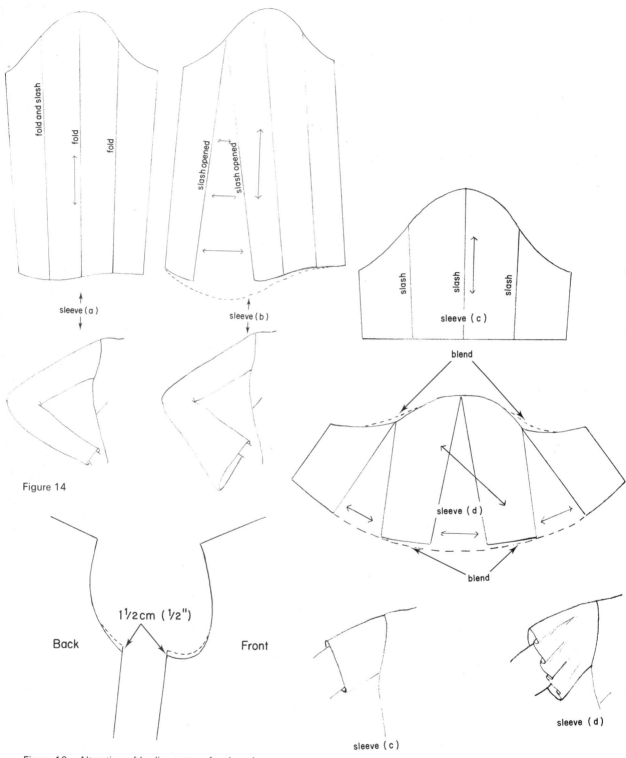

fold and slash

fold

fold

slash opened

slash opened

sleeve (a)

sleeve (b)

Figure 14

slash

slash

slash

sleeve (c)

blend

sleeve (d)

blend

1½ cm (½")

Back

Front

Figure 16   Alteration of bodice pattern for sleeveless garment

sleeve (c)

sleeve (d)

Figure 15

edges require blending into a good shape. This style of sleeve is better cut on the cross, so the grain line should be changed.

Flare may be added to any edge of a garment that hangs loose – collars and peplums are obvious cases in point. The examples illustrated here will have served to illustrate the principles involved, namely that only the edge to be flared may change in *length* – all other pattern edges must retain a constant length so that they may be joined to the other parts of the garment as designed, and that all edges which have changed in *shape* must be blended to graceful shapes, as only graceful shapes make graceful garments.

Adaptation of patterns for sleeveless garments

This is a very simple adaptation, but none the less important (figure 16) as it raises the underneath part of the armhole in sleeveless garments, such as dresses, blouses, when the original pattern intends sleeves. Otherwise there can be a tendency for the bra or slip to show above the armhole. Care must be taken to blend in the new line before the armhole line rises or extra width will be added to the bodice.

Addition of button stand for CF opening

It is important to understand how to calculate how much to add to a pattern for a button stand in cases where the original design was for a garment with a CF zip or fold. Figure 17 (a), (b), (c) and (d) illustrates the calculation. It will also be evident that if buttons other than the size suggested on the pattern are to be used, not only the length of the buttonhole should be changed, but also the width of the button stand. When altering a pattern to make a CF opening remember that it will be necessary to cut a facing. The method for this is given in chapter 12.

Combining patterns

Many dressmakers see the possibilities of combining pieces of different commercial patterns to obtain the

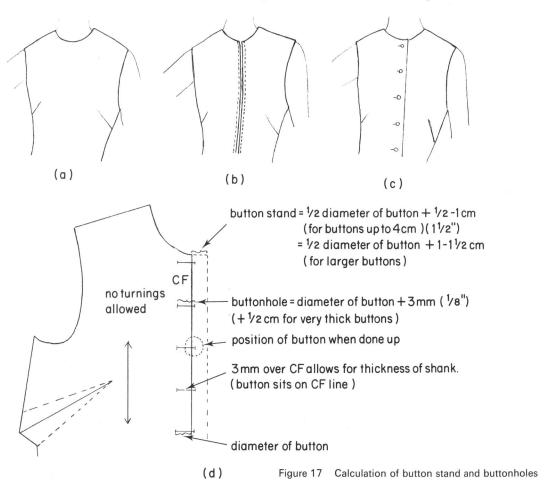

(a)   (b)   (c)

button stand = ½ diameter of button + ½ -1 cm
(for buttons up to 4 cm)(1½")
= ½ diameter of button + 1-1½ cm
(for larger buttons)

CF

no turnings allowed

buttonhole = diameter of button + 3 mm (⅛")
(+ ½ cm for very thick buttons)

position of button when done up

3 mm over CF allows for thickness of shank.
(button sits on CF line)

diameter of button

(d)   Figure 17   Calculation of button stand and buttonholes

style they want. This is indeed a practical way of obtaining a unique style and of using up old patterns without repeating a style previously made. There are however certain principles which must be observed.

(a) The patterns to be combined must be of the same size.

(b) The garments must be of the same type, e.g. both coats or both of the layer which goes on the body immediately after underclothing. This is because extra allowance for ease is made for garments intended to be worn over other garments. This is not always easy to interpret. To decide whether a 'top' is designed to be worn over another garment or on its own, for example, it is best to examine the designer's sketch on the pattern envelope.

(c) All combinations of pattern pieces are possible, e.g. sleeves from one pattern into the bodice of another, bodice and skirt, etc. with the sole exception of collars, which are *not interchangeable*. This is because while skirts, sleeves, bodices, etc. are drafted from a block, collars are drafted from the neckline of the garment they are to fit, and will not therefore fit the neckline of another pattern, unless in very rare circumstances the necklines are *exactly* the same. (This can be ascertained by laying one pattern over the other, matching shoulder seams.)

(d) Seam lines of the different patterns to be fitted together must be checked to see that they fit and altered if they do not. It is important to remember that it is at *seam* lines that patterns fit, not at *cutting* lines. If any alterations are to be made to make seams fit, seam allowances should be removed first, as with any pattern alteration.

(e) In order to unify parts of different patterns used together it is important to standardize on the finish of both parts, e.g. top stitching on both bodice and skirt, or welt seams, etc. on both. Other minor style alterations should be used to make the pattern a whole design, e.g. altering the shape of cuffs to echo the points of a collar, or the shape of the flap of a pocket to echo the shape of a yoke seam.

A special point to watch when using the sleeves of one pattern and the bodice of another is that the armhole lines of the two garments must be the same or the sleeve will not fit. Figure 18 illustrates the three different armhole lines commonly found in designs with set-in sleeves. These vary partly with the purpose of the garment (e.g. the lower, larger armhole (b) is mainly found on very loose fitting casual garments like sportswear) and partly with fashion – there are times when sleeves are nearly always set in on the natural line (a) and times when (c) is more fashionable. The sketch on the pattern envelope must be studied closely to ensure that the two patterns have matching armhole lines. With gathered sleeve heads there is no great problem over matching seam edges, since any amount may be placed in the gathers, but with plain-top set-in sleeves the amount of ease on the sleeve head must be measured and compared with the bodice. A lowered armhole requires a sleevehead about 1·5cm ($\frac{1}{2}$in) bigger and a natural armhole requires a sleeve head 2·5–4cm (1–1$\frac{1}{2}$in) bigger. If this is not correct, the underarm seams of sleeve or bodice or shoulder seams of bodice (or possibly the shape of the armhole or sleevehead) must be adjusted to make it so. A small discrepancy might be left at the pattern stage and adjusted more appropriately at the fitting.

The joining of bodice and skirt from different patterns sometimes gives trouble at the waistline, as it is rare for the side seams and darts to match up and

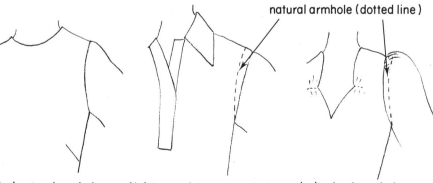

natural armhole (dotted line)

Figure 18   (a) natural armhole   (b) lowered, larger armhole   (c) raised armhole

they must be made to do so. The length of the waist-line edge must also be the same on both pieces. The principle of the adjustment to be made in this case is that the skirt should be adjusted to fit the bodice, as the bodice is the more critical part for good figure fitting and the skirt darts and seams are therefore easier to adjust without distorting the fit of the whole garment.

One such alteration is shown in figure 19, the solid line representing the original patterns. Starting at the CF, measure the distance a–b (from CF of bodice to first dart stitching line) and *ignoring the skirt dart altogether* mark the same distance a–b on the skirt. Follow the same procedure from the side seam d to point c – second dart stitching line. The distance c–b then marked on the skirt is the area to be taken

in by a dart. Note that it is not of the least importance that the skirt dart is a different size from the bodice dart. The dart is simply constructed by dropping a guide line down in between c and b parallel to the CF and using this as the centre line for the new dart.

The same procedure is shown for the joining of the back bodice and skirt.

The diagram shows another possible solution to the dart problem. On the back skirt illustrated it so happens that points f and g when transferred to the skirt from the bodice by the measurement method described above are one and the same point. This back skirt will therefore be cut with no dart at all and will fit the bodice CB and side seam exactly without one. This does not matter as the dress will look perfectly in order like this – the point being stressed here is that *if* both bodice and skirt have darts then they must line up.

Another obvious point where seam matching matters is at the waistline of a dress with panels or princess line seams. The method is the same for this as for the dart – that is, to move skirt seams to match the bodice and not the other way round.

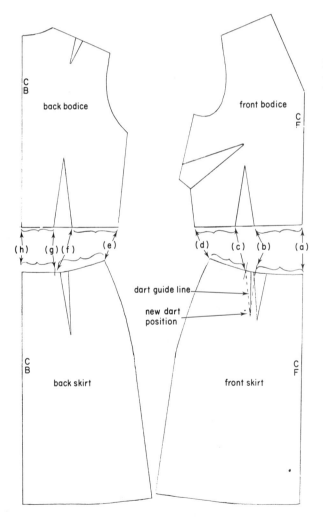

Figure 19   Adjustment of skirt darts to fit bodice

3 Toiles

Toile is an old French word meaning 'cloth' or 'linen', and in dressmaking terminology means one of several closely allied things:

(1) A pattern obtained by modelling mull, calico or muslin on a stand.

(2) A trial of a pattern in any cheap fabric for checking fit or style on an individual figure (the pleated culotte in photo no. 1 was made for this purpose).

(3) A calico test of a personal block for fitting and alteration before use for pattern drafting.

(4) In *haute couture*, a replica of a designer's work, finished as near as possible to the intended garment. This is either sold to the wholesale trade to copy for mass production or used for fitting an individual client. In the latter case it is usually taken apart after fitting and used as the pattern.

Pattern companies use toiles for designers to check whether their intentions have been accurately translated by the cutter. Some small commercial organisations make up commercial patterns into toiles for individual clients, fit them and re-cut the pattern to fit.

The method of making a particular toile and the degree of finish required depends on its purpose. The least finished is the one made to test out a basic block or shell. The quickest method of making this is given:

(a) Cut a piece of calico roughly the right size and rule a line on straight grain down the centre, using ballpoint pen or black pencil and a yard-stick.

(b) Place CB of block to this line, pin and draw round it adding darts, B.M.s and construction lines.

Photo no. 1 Toile for a pleated culotte

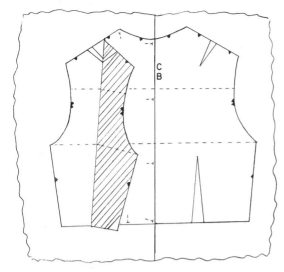

Figure 20   Drawing round the block

A toile of a pattern made for fitting purposes only may be constructed in the same way as it does not need to look neat.

Certain styles should always be made up as toiles first because fitting alterations change the whole shape of the pattern piece. These include raglan or kimono sleeves, shawl collars, cowls, bias cut garments, drapery, trousers and built-up necklines. Garments for very irregular figures for which there have been many major alterations to the pattern should also be tried as toiles. Toiles altered for fitting may be taken apart and used as the pattern for the garment.

Where the purpose of the toile is to see the effect of the style on a figure rather than for fitting, it needs to be made up in every detail by the method intended for the garment to create a realistic effect. For example if a welt or double stitched seam is designed this should be shown on the toile (photo no. 2). The

Photo no. 2   Dress toile

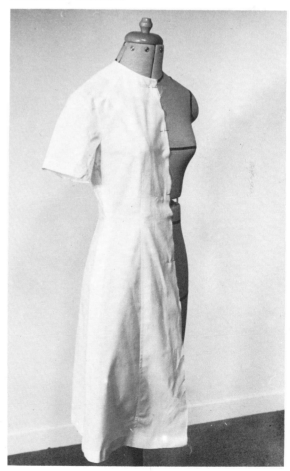

(c) Unpin block, reverse to the other side of the line and repeat the process (figure 20).

(d) Cut out, leaving wide turnings for fitting adjustments.

(e) Repeat for the other pieces. This method is quicker than cutting double and marking later.

(f) Make up the toile with darts and turnings right side out for easy fitting (never do this on an actual garment). Use machine basting or long loose tension machine stitch. The quickest method of joining the seams is to fold one turning under on the seam line, lay this over the seam line of the other edge and topstitch. A toile of a block made by this method should take no more than half an hour from start to finish.

(g) Leave CF seam open for fitting, and snip turnings around armhole and neck before trying on the figure.

(h) Make up the sleeve separately and set in at the fitting (see p. 115), taking care to observe balance marks.

(i) Fit and mark the alterations in a different colour.

(j) Take the toile apart. Use the pieces to alter the drafted block or mark alterations on the shell pattern.

(k) Machine the toile together again on the altered lines, or make a fresh one. Mark in any standard fitting lines desired, such as a standard 'V' or low curved neckline, classic yoke line, etc. and keep for a 'personal' toile. This is the point of reference for future fitting and styling queries.

purpose of such toiles may be to check the position of style lines on the figure, the size and shape of collars, shape and position of pockets, placement of decorative features, and so on, so that the style may be adapted if necessary to suit the wearer. Features such as pockets may be tacked on before or during the fitting.

Any cheap fabric may be used for a toile but the nearer it is to the garment material in weight, texture and handle the better. Fine muslin imitates sheers well and felt is a good leather substitute.

Partial toiles, for example of collar or sleeve only, may be fitted on to a garment on the stand or figure in cases where a complete toile is not considered necessary.

The method of making a toile from a finished garment to use as a pattern is described on pp. 16–17. A toile made in this way can be used as the pattern or a paper pattern made from it.

Further reasons for toile-making are:

(1) To practise and experiment in design. Half scale models not only economize in fabric but are easier to handle, allowing the worker to see more clearly the effect of the whole design.

(2) On the dress stand, the toile may be marked up with lines to represent striped or checked fabric to assess the finished effect.

(3) If made in lining fabric or even calico in some cases, it may be used for mounting the garment.

(4) Where very expensive fabric is to be used for the garment, fitting a toile first allows less turnings to be cut on the garment and a closer lay.

(5) For delicate and fraying fabrics, a toile reduces the amount of handling required in making the garment.

(6) In difficult designs it allows the worker to assess the construction problems she will meet and to practise the chosen methods. Photo no. 2 shows the right hand side of a dress with curved welt seams and a sleeve which is raglan at the front and cut in one with a yoke at the back. The feasibility of the seam was tested and the constructional problems of the inside corners of the sleeve were seen and solved.

4 Equipment for Dressmaking

The Stand

Apart from her sewing machine, the dress form or stand is the most expensive item a dressmaker has to buy and should therefore be chosen with proper consideration. Like the sewing machine, it is an essential. Only elementary dressmaking succeeds entirely without one.

Buying a stand

The best type to buy is the expandable eight-section type which can be adjusted both in circumference and neck-to-waist length. A stand must be well padded to enable pins to be inserted and to give a realistic impression of the figure, and it should be covered for easy pinning, usually in a jersey fabric. The plastic wire mesh type is fitted to the body, but even with its jersey cover is not satisfactory for pinning. It cannot have a layer of wadding under the cover as this would increase its measurements, so it is of little use for most purposes. The cheapest type, made of latex impregnated fibre board, is also adjustable and can with difficulty be made into a padded stand. Directions for doing this are given later.

Whether buying a standard or adjustable model, select one that is well padded and has a tightly fitting cover. All measurements must be correct or less than body measurements. Look for a thin neck, sloping shoulders, bust points at the right height (check by measuring down from front neck and shoulder points). The stand ought to show natural body curves, e.g. over the back shoulder. A non-adjustable stand must not be short in the nape/waist length.

Padding to fit

Use terylene or cotton wadding in thin layers, adding several layers rather than lumps of wadding. Thin out the pieces towards the edges to blend in with the stand. Press the first layer firmly to the jersey covering where it will cling with few pins, and subsequent layers will cling to it. In some areas, for example the waist/hip area, dart the wadding by cutting and overlapping, thinning out both thicknesses to blend in.

To increase the bust cup size cut a circle of wadding about 16–20cm (6½–8in) in diameter, cut a radial slit and fix on the stand in a cone shape, overlapping and thinning the cut edges. One way to check is to try a well-fitting bra over this. Sloping shoulders may be straightened by applying shoulder pads, and narrow ones lengthened by pinning on cardboard supports (figure 21).

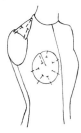

Figure 21   Extending the shoulder and padding the bust

Continually check against body measurements while padding. A final check can be made by observing the fit on the stand of a close fitting garment or the personal toile and comparing this with its fit on the figure. The wadding must be covered with fabric. If it is a temporary alteration, pin it securely to the stand and cover with areas of cotton or synthetic jersey, pinned or tacked into place.

If the stand is always to be used for the same figure a permanent cover should be applied. The simplest of these is made from very stretchy fine jersey such as the wrong side of stretch towelling, sewn into a tube shape. The circumference of the tube should be the same as the waist measurement and it must be able to stretch to fit the widest part. Cut it longer than the stand as it will shorten when stretched to fit over it. It will stretch in a straight line between bust points and must be stitched through to the stand on the centre line between the breasts. Fold out and hem down little darts to fit it around the neck and shoulders. Smooth out all wrinkles before tacking the cover to the stand around its edges.

A more satisfactory permanent cover can be made from mull or calico from a size smaller shell pattern or one drafted to exact body measurements. A princess style is the best as it has no darts or waist seam and is easier to fit. Fit this cover to the body with no ease and adjust until it is exact, if necessary adding horizontal darts from bust points to armhole and CF to fit each breast separately (figure 22). Leaving CB seam open, try it on the stand and pad any obvious gaps with more wadding before overlapping the CB seam and slip stitching it.

To cover a fibre board stand, adjust it to a little less than body measurements and cover with a jersey tube stuck down with glue so that any padding added subsequently will not slip. Make a calico cover to fit the body as above, but before stitching it together mount the pieces on a fairly thick layer of wadding. Fit this over the jersey-covered stand and insert more wadding underneath it wherever it is required.

A useful addition to the stand is a model arm. Make a calico sleeve from a two piece pattern, reduced and fitted to body measurements. Before stitching the seams, mount the pieces on wadding. After stitching together fill out the sleeve form with foam rubber chips, stuffed hard, and complete with ovals of calico at the top and bottom (figure 23).

To complete the preparation of the stand tack on 5mm ($\frac{1}{4}$in) wide tape as shown in figure 24 to define essential fitting lines.

Using the stand

Let it be said quite clearly that using a dress stand is *not* a substitute for fitting garments on the figure. It can help in first fitting stages, but never replaces the figure as it is never exactly the same and the effect of movement cannot be observed nor the feel of the garment ascertained. In exceptional cases where no fitting is possible it is better than nothing. Take a similar garment which fits the wearer well, pad the stand until this garment looks right and fit the new one similarly. While no substitute for figure fitting, the stand is, however, an excellent method of practising fitting for the inexperienced, and if used for early trial fittings much can be learned. Leave one vertical seam open when placing a garment on a stand. Some of the uses of the stand are:

(a) Testing patterns for fit and style and checking pattern alterations.
(b) Modelling (see chapter 2).
(c) Testing the hang and handling qualities of a

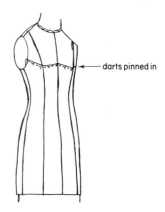

darts pinned in

Figure 22   Princess line stand cover darts pinned in

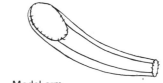

Figure 23   Model arm

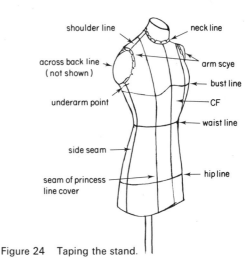

shoulder line   neck line
across back line (not shown)   arm scye
underarm point   bust line
CF
waist line
side seam
seam of princess line cover   hip line

Figure 24   Taping the stand.

fabric to judge the amount of fullness suitable, the effect of drapery and bias cutting, whether or not mounting will be needed and the correct choice of interfacing.

(d) A quick first impression for unusual fabrics, for example, which way to place stripes and checks, the effect of diagonals, planning the cutting of border prints, large patterns and fabrics with lustre or sheen.

(e) As an aid to inspiration in designing and cutting any fabric.

(f) For viewing toiles for line and placement of details like pockets, trims.

(g) For excluding major errors prior to first fitting on the figure.

(h) For testing the cut, stand and fit of collar toiles.

(i) In construction, for setting sleeves (p. 115) and mounting collars.

(j) Levelling hems (some stands have levelling attachments).

(k) Pinning in linings or checking the hang of a garment after tacking in the lining (chapter 21).

(l) Steaming and shaping of tailored collars. Final steam pressing of collars.

(m) Allowing garments to hang before levelling the hem.

(n) A quick general impression of the work at any stage of construction.

manufacturers are quick to flood the market with every kind of gadget varying from the essential to the merely useful and the pure gimmick. It is not possible to dictate what is worth buying since personal opinions differ, but most home dressmakers have far too little equipment and maintain it badly. Many items which would make the task more pleasurable and efficient are inexpensive, an example being an adequate supply of specialist needles for particular jobs. The most expensive items are scissors, but it is very bad economy to buy cheap ones as they can mar the fabric and frustrate the worker. Dressmaking undertaken as an economic necessity without regard for creative pleasure is a missed opportunity. Good and sufficient tools are an investment which can make all the difference in terms of job satisfaction.

Other equipment

In dressmaking, as in every sphere of activity,

Photo no. 3   Cutting board, sidebent shears and electric shears

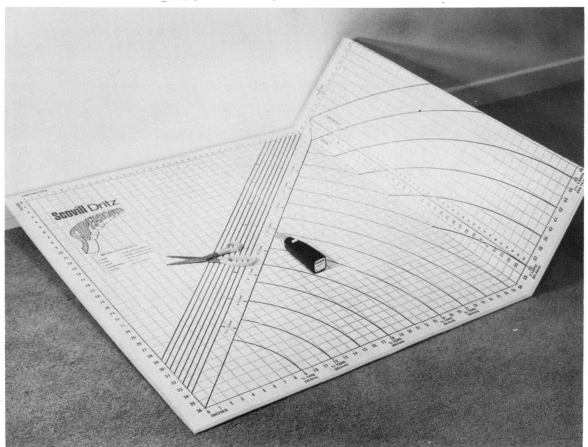

Important items for essential tasks

Cutting out

Cutting board Made of heavy board, folded for storage and opening to about 1m × 2m (3ft × 6ft 6in), surface marked out in centimetres and inches in both directions; some have lines for crosswise cutting, scallops and curves; protects the table, provides good cutting surface, pins may be inserted; keeps grain straight; can be used to straighten and press dampened cloth (photo no. 3).

Shears Scissors longer than about 16cm (6in) with one blade narrow and pointed and one handle large enough for two fingers; side-bent ones are the most convenient (photo no. 3); left handed ones are available; special serrated edge shears for jersey and slippery fabrics (figure 25); battery operated electric shears cut medium weight fabrics quickly and efficiently, but are not essential.

Other scissors required One medium pair for trimming and one small pair for embroidery and fine work.

Photo no. 4   Essential equipment: from top l., clockwise: sliding gauge; tailor's chalk, pencil and block; tracing wheels, smooth and serrated; wax tracing paper; small brass pins (lillikins); point turner; stiletto.

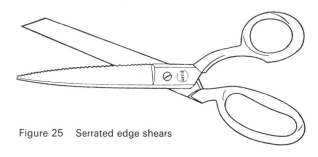

Figure 25   Serrated edge shears

Care Never use for cutting paper; do not drop them, as they become unbalanced; have them professionally sharpened.

Measuring

Essential items include a yard or metre stick for pattern work and hems, a tape measure marked both in centimetres and inches, and sliding gauge for accurate hems, pleats, buttonholes, scallops, etc. (photo no. 4).

Marking

Tailor's chalk (clay type for most fabrics) in pencil form or blocks, sometimes with holder and sharpener, otherwise sharpen with open blade of scissors; wax

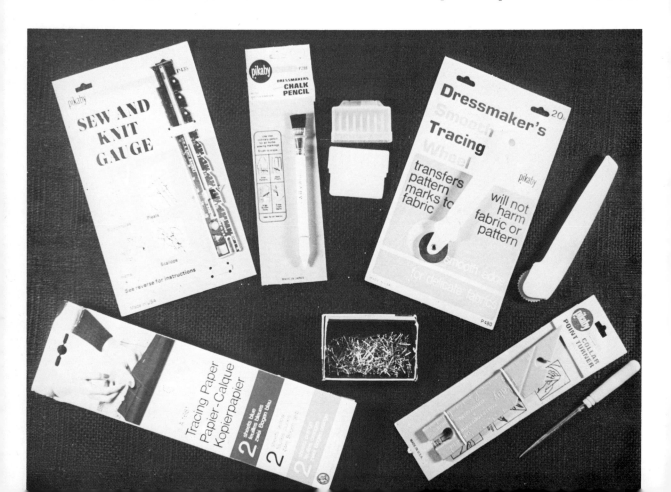

chalk for woollens; tracing wheels for transferring pattern marks – smooth edge for delicate fabrics, serrated edge for normal fabrics, needlepoint only for very thick tweedy fabrics, pattern making and leather work (see p. 168); wax tracing paper – use lightest colour possible to show up, mark on WS only – preferably only on garments to be lined; check first that marks will not show through to RS (photo no. 4).

Sewing

Thimble Steel is best; aluminium may puncture and plastic is bulky. It should fit the middle finger comfortably without falling off when shaken.

Pins Keep three types:

good quality fine 2·5cm (1in) steel pins for general use

finer white brass (lace making or 'silk' pins) for delicate fabrics

lillikins (lills) Very small brass pins for the most delicate work.

Needles Sizes vary from about 1–12, the smaller the number the thicker the needle; for most purposes use the range 7–8 (photo no. 5). All these are needed:

Sharps 7–10 General purpose.

Straws or Milliners 6–9 Long, small eyed needles for tacking, hand gathering, roll hems.

Betweens 7–10 Short needle for tailoring, invisible stitches on heavy fabrics, neat hemming, delicate work, quilting; small sizes for use as pins for fine fabrics.

Crewel All sizes useful: large eyes for embroidery, saddle stitching, etc.

Beading 10–13 Long fine needles for beading.

Calyx-eyed Self threading needles – figure 26 – are a boon to workers with less than perfect sight.

Bodkins for threading elastic, etc.

Ball point 5–10 Essential for sewing knit fabrics without snagging.

Glovers 5–8 Chisel pointed for all leather work.

Miscellaneous items

Point turner For collar corners, etc., plastic, useful shank maker for sewing on buttons included.

Stiletto For eyelet holes (never use punch as this removes a circle of the fabric and leaves a weakness)

Photo no. 5 Sewing needles: top, l. to r., self-threading; bodkins; ball point 5–10; glovers 5–8; bottom, l. to r., sharps; straws; betweens 7–10; crewel; beading 10–13.

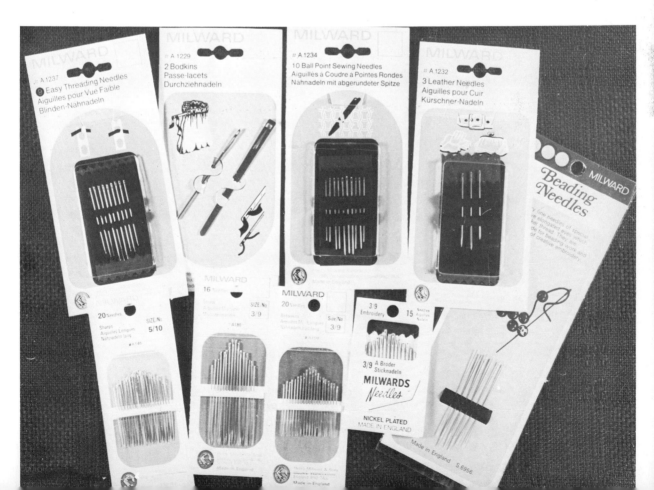

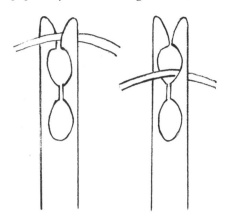

Figure 26   Threading a calyx eyed needle (bottom hole provides spring).

Photo no. 6   Non-essential items. Top row, from left to right: seam ripper, needle threader, pinking shears, tailor tacker. Bottom row, from left to right: magnet, marking set, thread snips.

before oversewing or stapling in metal eye; makes round end of tailor's buttonholes (photo no. 4).

Sellotape   Can take the place of tacking in small areas and with some fabrics such as vinyl (see chapter 24). Always test first to ensure no damage to the fabric.

Beeswax   Rub thread through to strengthen and prevent twisting when sewing on buttons (soft tailoring).

Pressing equipment   See chapter 23.

Useful but not essential items

Magnet

Seam ripper   Rather dangerous for unpicking as it slips easily and cuts fabric, but useful for cutting machine buttonholes.

Needle threader

Pinking shears   For trimming edges of non-fray **fabrics** in garments which are to be lined and dry **cleaned**.

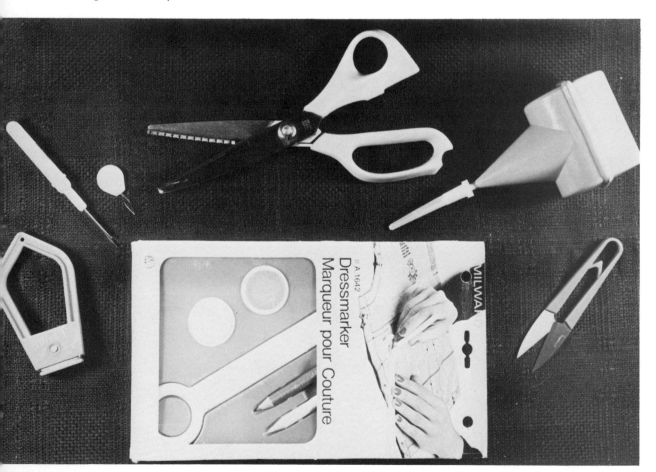

Tailor tacker   For working quantities of tailor tacks on a thick pad of foam rubber.
Thread snips   See photo no. 7.
Marking set   For transferring single pattern marks to both sides of fabric at the same time as an alternative to tailor tacking.

Photo no. 7   Using thread snips. Photograph from J. & P. Coats (UK) Ltd., by Studio Swain, Glasgow

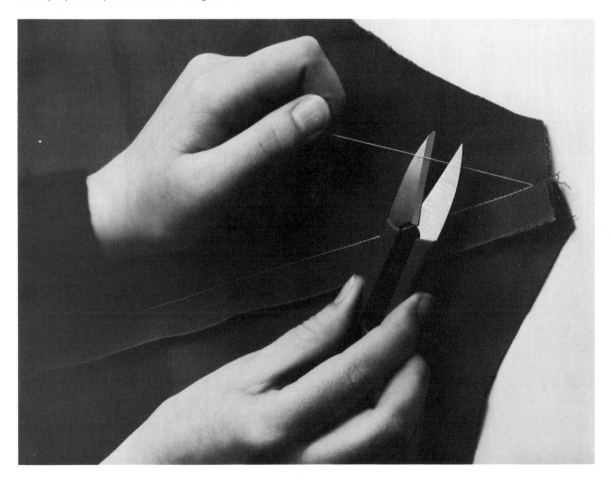

5 The Sewing Machine

The earliest sewing machine, dating from the middle of the eighteenth century, sewed only chain stitch. Machines using two threads appeared about the middle of the nineteenth century, and worked on the same basic principle as do today's machines, that of threads interlocking in the middle of the fabric. It is almost unbelievable that the first swing-needle machine was built in 1882, but about another 50 years elapsed before the Necchi Company finally introduced the first mass-produced domestic swing-needle machine. From then on machines advanced rapidly. 1940 saw the introduction by Tavaro SA of Geneva (the Elna Company) of the first portable free-arm machine, the same firm being responsible for the first domestic machine with automatic and utility stitches in 1952.

Advances since then have for the most part been minor. A self-winding bobbin by Singers, compact lightweight machines such as the Elna Lotus, snap-on interchangeable feet and colour coded simplicity in stitch selection (Necchi and Husqvarna) and machines which are self-oiling (Husqvarna) are examples of modern technology. Probably the most significant recent advance is the 'dual feed' from Pfaff, a method by which the fabric is fed from both below and above it, ensuring that both layers feed at the same rate, a boon when you are matching stripes or checks or working with slippery or pile materials such as velvet. A pneumatic foot control and electronic speed reducer, recently introduced by Elna, make the Air Electronic among the most sophisticated and easily controlled of all modern machines.

Classification of machines

Machines are classified by stitch types into straight-stitch, swing-needle, semi-automatic (sometimes called automatic) and fully or super-automatic. The straight-stitch machine is of little use with modern fabrics since it will not sew knits satisfactorily, and the swing-needle machine likewise has its limitations. Speedy, efficient, pleasurable dressmaking now demands the semi-automatic as a minimum. This type of machine performs other zig-zag based stitches such as the three- or five-step zig-zag and the blind hem. Many also produce from three to 20 decorative stitches based purely on programmed variations in stitch width and user-selected choice of stitch length, the latter control often being used at the extremely short 'satin stitch' length. The Bernina Record is probably the most advanced example of this type.

The fully or super-automatic machine is yet more advanced as the variations are created on a different principle. Programmed stitches are formed not only by different stitch widths and lengths but by the operation of the feed in both forward and reverse motion, creating as it were another dimension to the stitch. The stitches so formed can be of the utility variety for stretch fabrics (see pp. 181–2 and chapter 25, figures 331 (d), (e), (f), (g) and (i)) or ornamental in intricate patterns. This class of machine may be subdivided into two main groups, those with dialled or press button stitch selection, which are easier to operate, or those with removable cams, more complicated to use but providing a wide range of fancy stitches. The variations achieved by the Elna Supermatic, for example, are said to be too many to count. Necchi, Pfaff, Husqvarna and Singer all produce top quality models in the fully automatic range.

What to look for when purchasing a machine

An important feature is the free arm for convenient stitching of areas difficult to reach. There should be a slide-on or lift-up attachment or flap to convert the machine into a flat bed for supporting larger areas of fabric. As far as stitches are concerned, the minimum requirement is the swing needle or preferably the semi-automatic, while the ability to tack, make buttonholes and produce true stretch stitches are the next priorities, coming before a wide range of decorative stitches.

An interesting possibility is available to purchasers of some models of Elna machine. These can be converted into fully automatic machines for about the same cost as the difference between the price of the two models concerned.

Attachments

A wide variety of feet should be available as standards or optional extras. The essential ones, illustrated in photo nos. 9–15, are: a roller or teflon foot for vinyl, leather and bulky fabrics; a piping foot for piping and zips, a buttonhole foot, a blind hem foot, cording/braiding feet for decorative work, and a tucker foot for twin needle or 'air' tucks. Some machines have a useful gathering foot and/or a tailor tacking foot and

Photo no. 10   Piping or zip foot (Elna)

Photo no. 8   Pfaff 'Dual Feed'

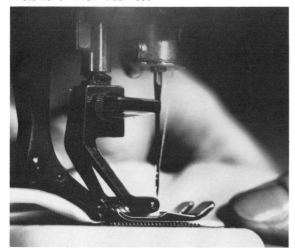

Photo no. 9   Roller foot (Elna)

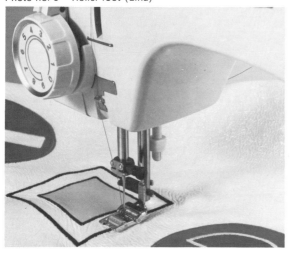

Photo no. 11   Buttonhole foot (Elna)

Photo no. 12   Blind hem foot (Elna)

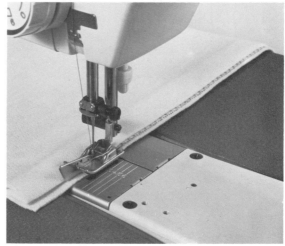

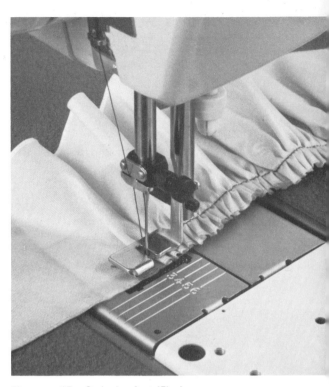

Photo no. 13   Braiding foot (Elna)

Photo no. 15   Gathering foot (Elna)

Photo no. 14   Tucker foot (Elna)

Photo no. 16   Eyelet attachment (Elna)

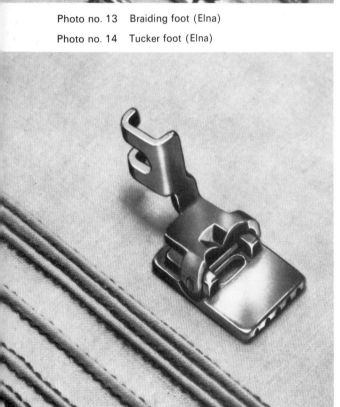

Photo no. 17   Quilting attachment (Elna)

there are a few feet exclusive to certain makes, e.g. the Singer 'Even-feed' foot which has a similar function to the Pfaff 'dual feed'. Where there is a choice, plastic feet are better than metal ones as they afford greater visibility. Felling, binding and ruffling feet are of dubious value in high class dressmaking although useful for household work.

Other useful attachments are those for eyelets (photo no. 16), circular embroidery and quilting (photo no. 17).

Needles

The usual range of sizes of machine needles from fine to heavy is 70, 80, 90, 100 and 110 (continental sizing), the British equivalents being 10, 12, 14, 16 and 18. The size should be selected primarily according to the thread used. Select the thread according to the cloth and the sewing operation, and match the needle to this by checking that the thread fits well into the groove which runs the length of the needle. A good principle is to use the finest needle and thread possible to do the job securely, particularly with modern machines. The most widely used needle sizes for dressmaking ought to be the 70 and 80. The 90 may be used with 40 cotton and larger sizes with topstitching-type threads. Machine manuals often give more detailed suggestions.

Speciality needles include the ball-point which is essential for knit fabrics, the leather point, and those which create decorative effects, such as twin and triple needles and winged needles for hemstitch. With some makes of machine a special needle is required for basting.

Needles should be changed regularly, particularly after sewing synthetics, as these blunt them. It is a bad habit to leave the needle in the machine after completing a job because it is all too easy to forget what size it is and use what is there instead of selecting a needle for the next job purposefully.

Machine controls

Tension   This should not need continual adjusting. Good modern machines have a standard or self-adjusting tension, right for standard procedures on most fabrics if the same thread is used in both needle and bobbin. Most tension faults arise from incorrect threading, unsuitable thread or failure to match thread and needle. If these points are observed it is not necessary to keep testing for tension. When looser tensions are needed, e.g. for knits, both bobbin and needle tensions must be adjusted to preserve the balance (see p. 173). When two different threads are used as in topstitching or embroidery the two tensions may need to be unbalanced. Other operations such as buttonholes, gathering and tacking require irregular tensions. Details will be found in the appropriate sections of this book or machine manuals.

Presser foot pressure   Most machines now have a self-adjusting universal pressure, but where control is left to the user it is important to adjust it when needed, e.g. for bulky fabrics or vinyl. Mention of this is made in chapter 24.

Needle position   Unless there is a reason to the contrary, sew with the needle centrally positioned as this gives maximum control from the foot and feed. A side needle position may prove helpful, however, when sewing zips, edge stitching and parallel rows of topstitching, so that one row serves as a guide for the next. Decorative stitching may be enhanced by varying the needle position, and some automatic processes such as buttonholes and blind hemming require it. Machine manuals should be studied.

Stitch length   Some British machines are graded according to the number of stitches per centimetre or inch, but most foreign machines range 0–4. The stitch length which actually results depends not only on the setting of the control but on the thickness of the fabric. An approximate table is given:

Setting	Sts per centimetre	Sts per inch	Use
1	8–14	20–35	Usually only in combination with stitch width for close zig-zag
2	5–6	13–16	Standard straight stitch for most purposes and fabrics
3	3–4	8–10	Straight-stitch – thick fabrics
4	2–3	5–7	Very bulky fabrics, leather, vinyl, topstitching, gathering

The length may be set at any point between the numbers. Lengths 0–1 are used only with swing

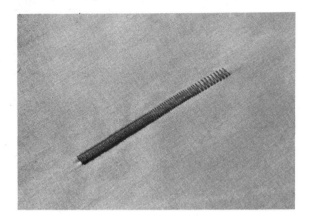

Photo no. 18   Satin stitch variations (Elna)

needle and produce variations in the closeness of satin stitch (photo no. 18). They are used mainly for close overcasting, buttonholes and automatic patterns.

Return the stitch length to O after sewing as a reminder to reselect the appropriate length for the next operation.

Stitch width   The most usual calibration is 0–4, corresponding approximately to the measurement in millimetres.

Mastery of the machine

Speed   Practice until you can sew so slowly that you can stop at a given point with the needle up or down without having to touch the fly wheel. You should be able to make a gentle start without touching the fly wheel and to keep an even steady pace whether machining fast or slow.

Reversing   For perfect finishing off you must be able to reverse stitch so as to make the needle enter the fabric in the same holes as it did on the forward run. Two rows of stitching should not be obvious. A plastic presser foot helps.

Removing the work   Stop with the needle at its highest point and draw the work out backwards to prevent strain on the needle. Cut threads and pull sufficient of the top one through to allow the needle to descend and return without unthreading.

Inserting the work   Lower the needle into the fabric *before* the presser foot so that it will not disturb it. If zig-zagging over an edge, lower the needle into its hole on the right hand swing and move the work to touch it before lowering the presser foot.

Starting   Common problems are knotting of threads and failure of the fabric to move with the feed as it gets pressed down into the hole in the needle plate. Make sure there is sufficient thread at the back of the

machine to allow you to grip the ends and pull them backwards as you start, preventing them knotting and encouraging the fabric to move.

For a smooth start on several layers of bulky fabric make a little wedge of felt or similar fabric folded into three and machined (figure 27 (a)) and insert this under the presser foot behind the fabric before starting to stitch (figure 27 (b)).

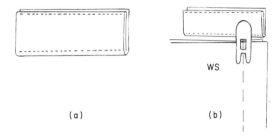

(a)   (b)

Figure 27   Using a wedge for starting on thick fabrics

Guiding the fabric   Develop a sensitive touch to guide fabric smoothly without pulling it or impeding its progress. Use the flat bed plate whenever possible for support. If there is a possibility of the seam stretching or cockling (as with bias seams or knit fabrics) ease a small bump of fabric up in front of the presser foot.

Corners   Sometimes when the needle is left down and presser foot raised for turning corners it is difficult to get the fabric to feed again when restarting. To prevent this, lift the fabric free of the hole and up the needle before lowering the presser foot again and pull it gently back as you restart.

Corners of less than 90° on inside seams (e.g. pointed collars) should have one or two diagonal stitches across them for a sharper effect when turned out (figure 28).

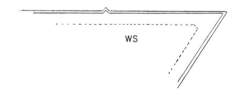

WS

Figure 28   Machining sharp corners

Basting   If your machine will baste (e.g. Necchi, Bernina, Elna, Pfaff) by the use of special discs, needles, feet and/or plates, develop the habit of using this facility. It is a much-neglected aid which can save much tedious work.

Uses of zig-zag

The possibilities of the simple zig-zag are not always appreciated. The following suggestions are worth pondering:

(a) When used for overcasting, vary the width and length according to fabric density, fray, structure, the position of the seam and the use of the garment. Whatever the thickness of threads in construction, use a fine thread (polyester or Sylko 50) and needle for overcasting.

(b) Use for stretch sewing and knit fabrics (chapters 24 and 25).

(c) Whenever unwanted stretch is a problem work a third thread in under the zig-zag stitch, guiding it with the right hand over the presser foot and pulling evenly. The thread may be a regular sewing one or a thicker one, such as crochet cotton. If the seam or edge still looks stretched when completed, pull the thread to restore flatness and fasten off. This technique also makes a method for easing, e.g. when reducing the fullness of the turned hem on a flared skirt (chapter 20, figure 270 (b)).

(d) Attaching elastic. Cut the elastic to fit the body and gather the garment to fit it. Place the elastic on the gathers and zig-zag on without stretching.

(e) Picot edges (see chapter 20, p. 139 and chapter 11, photo no. 34).

(f) Close satin stitch in narrow width for bar tack reinforcements.

(g) Buttons and buttonholes (photo no. 19, left).

(h) Satin stitch worked closely, wide or narrow, with or without cord for a bold decorative finish (see photo no. 19).

(i) Application of lace or braid (photo no. 19)

(j) Simple methods of appliqué (photo no. 19 and chapter 22).

(k) Decorative satin stitch stars (photo no. 19). Work the bars in the order shown in figure 29, leaving the needle down in the centre of the shape before each rotation.

Figure 29   Working a swing needle star

Photo no. 19   Zig-zag stitch (samples worked on an Elna). L. to r., buttons and buttonholes; satin stitch, wide and narrow; lace braid; (below) appliqué; (top) satin stitch stars.

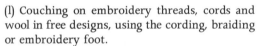

Photo no. 20   Using zig-zag stitch for lingerie (Bernina).
Top, lace insertion; below, hem for jersey fabric;
bottom, shell edge.

Photo no. 21   Lace edge with zig-zag and automatic scalloping (Bernina)

(l) Couching on embroidery threads, cords and wool in free designs, using the cording, braiding or embroidery foot.

(m) Lace insertions for lingerie. Zig-zag as for braid (photo no. 19) and trim away excess (photo no. 20).

(n) Lingerie hem for jersey fabric – use a fine zig-zag at least 1cm from the raw edge and trim closely (photo no. 20).

(o) Lace edge for jersey fabrics. Place the lace at least 1cm in from the edge and sew down with small close zig-zag. Trim away surplus fabric from under lace.

(p) Lace edge for woven fabric. Place the lace at least 1cm from the edge and stitch it on with a straight stitch. Press turning to ws. Work a fine zig-zag over the folded edge to include the straight stitching. Trim away surplus (photo no. 21).

Uses of three or five step zig-zag

(a) Towelling fabrics (see p. 176).
(b) Stretch sewing (chapter 25).

(c) Overcasting edges of thin fabric which would curl under with plain zig-zag.

(d) Attaching elastic (alternative method). Cut the elastic a little less than body measurements, pin at the beginning and end of the work only (some workers do, however, find it easier to proportion the elastic out evenly if pinned at regular intervals) and apply, stretching as you work (photo no. 22). More than one row may be worked.

(e) Decorative work with the twin needle (the maximum width being about 3) (photo no. 23).

(f) Decorative stitching in matched rows (photo no. 24 (b)).

(g) Faggoting (photo no. 24 (c)).

Uses of blind stitch

(a) Machine blind hems (photo no. 12).

(b) Seaming and overcasting in one operation, where no special automatic stitch exists (photo no. 25), not entirely satisfactory as the bulk of the fabric has to be passed under the machine to the right of the presser foot.

Photo no. 22   Attaching elastic on a Pfaff machine

Photo no. 23   Decorative twin needle work (worked on a Bernina)

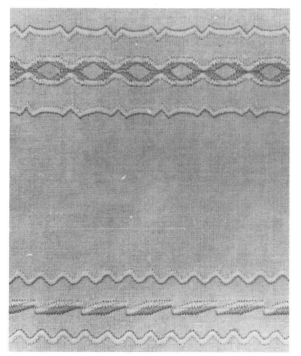

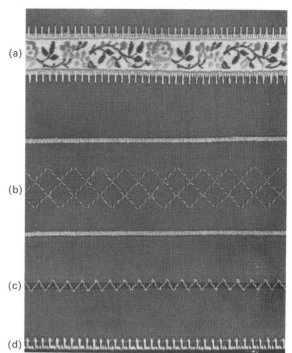

(a)

(b)

(c)

(d)

Photo no. 24   Worked on an Elna Supermatic.

Photo no. 25   Seaming and neatening in one operation (Bernina)

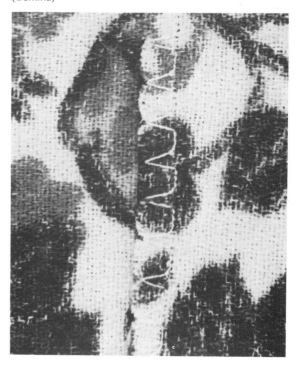

(c) Shell edging, especially on jersey fabrics (phqto no. 20).

(d) Shell tucks (chapter 22, figure 299).

(e) Decorative stitching in pattern work (photo no. 26).

Using the automatic decorative patterns

These may be used in straight lines (photo no. 26), freehand or guided embroidery (photo no. 27), for edges (photo nos. 21 and 24 (d)), with braids (photo no. 24 (a)) or in solid blocks of matching patterns (photo no. 28).

Densely embroidered areas should be supported with iron-on interfacing, on to which the pattern may be drawn and worked from the ws. All the work is firmer and simpler if typing paper is laid under it and torn away afterwards, in which case the stitching is done from the rs.

Photo no. 27   Machine embroidery worked on an Elna Supermatic

Photo no. 26   Pattern stitching on a Bernina Record. Top, blind stitch lacet tape stitched in; centre, inclusion of perle cotton; bottom, patterns match.

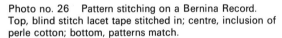

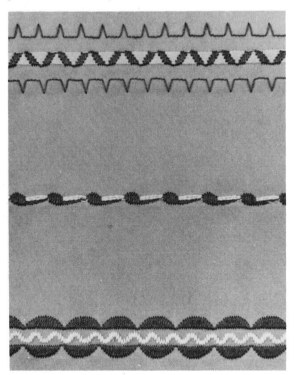

Photo no. 28   Pattern matching to form solid motif (worked on a Bernina Record)

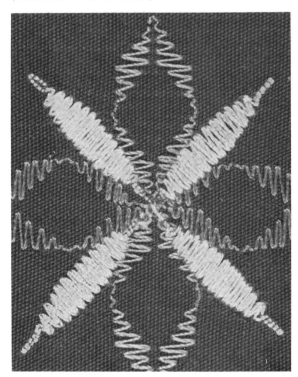

6 Haberdashery

The aim of this section, presented in note form, is to guide the reader in choosing items. The lists are not exhaustive.

Threads (photo no. 29)
The general principles governing the choice of sewing threads for constructional and neatening purposes are to choose the finest possible consistent with strength and to match the thread and fabric fibres as far as possible.
Polyester sewing threads Coats Drima, Gütermann M303, Dewhurst's Star, made of long staple (tow) spun fibres, gauge about 100 which is approximately equal to 50 in cotton threads. All purpose, some recently improved, for hand and machine stitching on majority of fabrics. Ideal for all man-made fibre fabrics and all knitteds whatever their fibre, having about 14 per cent stretch. Threads melt if pressed too hot – test first when using on cotton or linen fabrics – extreme heat is seldom required for these, therefore restrict temperature to within tolerance of thread.

Mercerized cotton Coats Satinised, Dewhurst's Sylko – suitable mainly for woven fabrics of vegetable based yarns, e.g. cotton, rayon, acetates, linen. 50 for fine and medium fabrics, 40 for thick fabrics. Also hand sewing.
Spun silk Gütermann Ideal gauge 100 – best thread for silk or wool. Tacking fine fabrics where standard tacking cotton would mark.
Unmercerized cotton Coats Chain 40 or 50 – tacking or machining. Soft thread with no sheen, black or white only. Mainly household sewing but good for plastic as it does not cut fabric.
Tacking cotton Atlas 40 or 50, Swan 50 – soft unmercerized low twist cotton – breaks easily for removing basting. (Never use left-over machine thread – it is too strong and may mark or damage fabric.)
Buttonhole twist Gütermann M1003, Coats Boldstitch, both gauge 30, Hela Silk Twist (Gütermann) 40 for hand buttonholes, saddle stitching, machine topstitching, buttons, hand worked loops, smocking,

Photo no. 29 Sewing threads

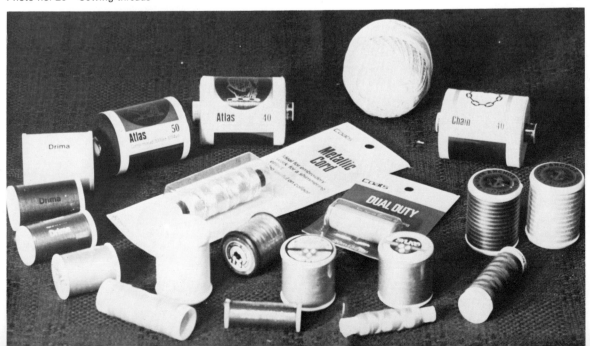

decorative work. Machine needle size 100 (16), ordinary thread in bobbin.

Button threads   Coats cotton-covered polyester corespun glacé, Clarks.

Buttonhole   Gimp 10 in limited range of colours for gimping buttonholes (soft tailoring).

Heavy duty threads   Coats Bear Extra Strong (highly polished glacé cotton thread) for hand or machine, Coats Dual Duty (corespun 84 per cent polyester, 16 per cent cotton) multi-purpose thread for heavy sewing, leather, etc.

Decorative work   Anchor Machine Embroidery 30 (medium) and 50 (fine). Mercerized cotton with high sheen. 50 especially good for machine buttonholes and seam neatening by zig-zag stitch.

Metallic threads   Schurer Lurex — fine flat thread, non-tarnishing, used on top with machine embroidery 30 on bobbin. Size 80 needle, loose tension. Medium weights — (a) English Sewing Co. Lurex — wind on bobbin with machine embroidery 30 on top, work from reverse side (b) Dritz 24 per cent nylon/76 per cent metallic thread on top, needle size 100, same thread or ordinary thread on bobbin. Heavy weight — Coats metallic cord, 67 per cent viscose/33 per cent metallic for couching or winding on bobbin, regular thread on top.

Crochet cord   Coats Mercerized Crochet cord, sizes 10 and 20, for corded buttonholes, easing and gathering (p. 137).

Elastic

Cord and loom for general purposes, widths from about 5mm to 5cm ($\frac{1}{4}$in to 2in), cotton, rayon, nylon and terylene. Select one with appropriate washing/dry cleaning qualities and suitable stretch. Cord is more stretchy than loom.

Round (hat) elastic for fine casings, e.g. in several rows around waistline.

Shirring elastic, usually threaded on machine bobbin or couched on with zig-zagging (see p. 71).

Soft top elastic for skirt and trouser tops in stretch fabrics.

Waist stiffening

There are many types and widths. Waist banding includes:

(a) non-roll, washable, dry cleanable interlining
(b) stretch waistbanding for trousers or skirts in stretch fabric
(c) stiff iron-on interfacing
(d) skirt petersham, boned or unboned, curved or straight, made of rayon or terylene. Curved fits

the waist better and terylene retains stiffness throughout cleaning.

For methods of applying the above, see chapter 17.

For belt making:

(a) belt backing, very stiff, usually iron-on, permanent finish
(b) bonded fibre fabric heavyweight belt interlining.

Tape

Plain or twill weave, cotton, used mainly for reinforcement and staying, widths 6mm ($\frac{1}{4}$in) to 13mm ($\frac{1}{2}$in) — use narrowest practicable. Wider tapes are not used for dressmaking.

Seam binding

Plain weave or twill (Paris or Prussian binding) — straight binding 13mm ($\frac{1}{2}$in) wide for staying (e.g. in turnings at zip openings), supporting pleats, straight hems (method not now commonly used), casings. Also lute ribbon.

Bias binding

Cotton, nylon, 13mm to 5cm ($\frac{1}{2}$in to 2in), many uses, mainly binding, facing, casing.

Cords

(a) Lacing, mostly rayon, in colours for use with eyelets
(b) Piping cord, white cotton, sizes 00 (fine) to 6 (coarse). Finer sizes for piping, coarser for corded belts. Soak in cold water first to shrink, remove ridges by rubbing over table edge, held very taut.

Metal eyelets

Brass or coloured, large or small, with fixing tool. (Make holes with stiletto rather than punch.)

Shoulder pads

Wadding or foam plastic, large or small, round or triangular shape. Covered ones are easy to attach to garment turnings or linings. Keep a selection at hand and choose during fitting.

Horsehair braid

For stiffening hems, black and white, widths 2·5cm to 10cm (1in to 4in).

Other items

Refer to chapters 4 (Equipment), 8 (Interfacing and Interlining), 14 (Fastenings), 22 (Decoration) and 19 (Shaping Techniques).

7 Preparing and Cutting the Fabric

Because they are threaded on to the loom first and must take all the strain of weaving, the warp threads are usually thicker and stronger than the weft. They are more twisted and less resilient because they are pulled tighter in production. Used on the lengthwise direction in garments, they impart stability. They fall stiffly if gathered, which is why strips for gathering should be cut across the fabric and the gathering thread inserted along weft grain. The weft is less stable, stretching a little in most fabrics. To determine the grain of small scraps with no selvedge, pull sharply along both grains. The warp, being more tightly twisted, makes the higher sound.

Correct grain in a garment matters not only for durability but it also dictates the hang (see chapter 9). It must be the same for both sides and creates awkward folds or creases if it is not, being particularly noticeable when the wearer moves. It is possible to have the warp hanging correctly and the weft distorted, so give as much attention to straightness of weft as to the warp when laying patterns.

Fold the fabric lengthwise to see whether or not the straightened weft ends lie together. If they do not the distortion must be corrected before cutting out, particularly if folds or wrinkles appear when the fabric lies folded lengthwise on the table.

Bias cutting

Madame Vionnet introduced bias cutting with great impact in 1929, and it was much used throughout the next decade. Dior revived it in 1947, and the 'sixties and 'seventies have kept the soft fluid look fashionable. Cutting, fitting and construction of bias garments are all highly skilled. In flowing fabrics bias cutting produces cowls and folds, good drape and close, slinky fitting, and in moderately stiff fabrics it makes skirts flare well and garments stand away from the body attractively. Interesting grain effects are produced, including the chevroning of checks and stripes, making becoming designs which flatter the figure. Collars are frequently bias cut for smooth, rounded fitting.

Fabrics to be avoided are very springing or very firm ones, those with diagonal weave or pattern, and checks which are not the same lengthwise as crosswise. As the weight of the fabric is the chief element, time must be taken to experiment with the bias cut on the stand, and modelling is an excellent method of cutting. As little seaming as possible should be the aim. Avoid lengthwise seams joining bias to straight in skirts, as it is difficult to get the seam to hang well.

Since warp and weft hang differently it is better to balance the grain on either side of the garment by having centre seams. A skirt cut as in figure 30 (a) will flare unevenly and the hem drop more at one side, but cut as in figure 30 (b) it will be balanced. For real clinging fit over the hips combined with flare below them, skirts should rest on and hang from the hips, not the waist. Designers achieve this effect by cutting the hip measurement equal or a little *less* than body hip measurement and the waist 4–5cm bigger to ease in. Extra length is required as the garment 'takes up' a little in length.

Figure 30

(a)

(b)

It is sometimes not possible to mount a bias skirt successfully as the two fabrics may not hang equally, and loose linings are a safer bet. Mounting may succeed quite well on other parts of the garment, but test the effect on the stand. Cut bias garments on single fabric and leave large turnings on lengthwise seams for fitting adjustments.

Fabric preparation

Fabric that has been twisted out of true grain during production must be straightened, and can often be corrected by the familiar pulling method, requiring two people for a garment length. If this does not work it must be pinned together along the selvedges and steam pressed into shape, taking care not to press in the fold.

Unless it is guaranteed shrunk by labelling (not by the word of the sales assistant, unfortunately) both unmercerized cotton and wool fabrics must be tested for shrinkage. A measured square of cotton is laundered and a similar piece of woollen fabric steam pressed. It is then remeasured to establish whether or not shrinking is necessary for the entire length.

To shrink, fold the cotton fabric lengthwise, right side inside, and then backwards and forwards into a manageable size for shrinking. Soak in lukewarm water for 15 minutes. Do not wring but allow to dry slowly hanging on an airer, clothes line or broom handle. Press on a padded table, keeping the grain true. This operation destroys the newness of the fabric but unfortunately there is no alternative. Unshrunk cotton fabrics should never be marketed.

Woollens can be shrunk by one of two methods. In either case pin the fabric together as for cottons, and either leave the length overnight rolled in a damp sheet and then steam press lightly, or carry out the whole operation through longer, damper steam pressing with the fabric laid on a table. Continue with light pressure and further moisture until shrinking stops. Hang up to dry as for cottons.

Economy in cutting

Usually alterations of some kind have been made to the pattern, making it impossible to follow the layout given in the primer. In any case it is more economical to play your own layout for this allows you to adjust the amounts left for turnings, which are often insufficient. Provided you follow grain and fold marks accurately, it is simpler and quicker too. Consider the range of possible folds (figure 31), as a middle lengthwise fold is not necessarily best.

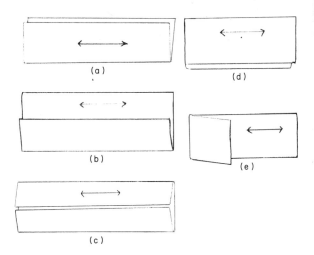

Figure 31   Methods of folding fabric

Sometimes fabric must be cut and two folds used. Lay large pieces first, preferably to the ends of the fabric to leave better shapes for smaller sections. If not cutting facings, bindings, etc. at this stage, plan the leftover pieces so that they will be the right shape when the time comes.

Single layer cutting

This may be necessary for the whole or part of a garment for these reasons:

(1) the pattern pieces may be too wide to cut on the fold

(2) the fabric may have asymmetric stripes or checks

(3) bias cutting

(4) the fabric may have a large pattern requiring strategic placing

(5) asymmetric styles.

Note the importance, in (5), of laying facing patterns the right way up – they reverse the shape of the garment piece. If you make your own patterns, watch this point – facing patterns are frequently cut erroneously like the garment instead of reversed (figure 32). If the fabric also has a right and wrong side this error is disastrous.

The two principles to observe when cutting singly are to duplicate the pattern pieces, clearly marking which way up each is to lie to achieve left or right, and then to cut out on the right side of the fabric.

Common laying-up problems

Some fabrics have centre creases which cannot be removed – never allow these to appear on the garment.

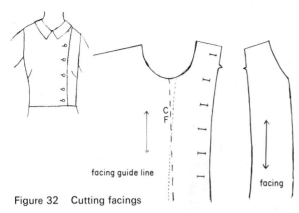

Figure 32 Cutting facings

If the fabric is wide enough refold as in figure 31 (b) or (c). If not choose another pattern with CB and CF seams!

Fabrics with nap, pile, lustre or one-way design including asymmetric stripes or checks need to be laid up one way. Jerseys often come into this category. If unsure, do a lustre check by looping the fabric over the stand so that each end lies a different way up. Stand back and take a long look in a good light. Problems arise when, because of the width of the fabric or pattern piece, fold 31 (d) is required, as this reverses the direction of the top layer. The fabric must be cut across and arranged as in figure 33 to bring right sides together, while maintaining the same direction in both layers.

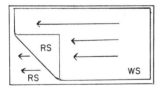

Figure 33 Laying fabric for one-way cutting

Off-grain fabrics which cannot be straightened because they have a permanent finish, such as drip-dry or glazing, or are laminated, must be cut as they lie on the table – off grain. Provided the fabric is flat when cutting, even if the selvedges are not together, the finished garment will not distort because of the permanency of the finish, but the effect may be unsightly if the grain is obvious. There is no solution. Neither is there a solution for fabric printed off-grain, where to straighten would make pattern lines slant or mismatch. The only real answer to such fabric if purchased is to make it up with the pattern correct and the grain wrong, as the pattern will show more than the hang, but a better idea would have been to

have left the fabric in the shop!

Pattern pieces too wide for the fabric may be pieced only if the style is so full that the piecing will not show, and the fabric is patterned or striped in such a way that the join may be invisibly matched. Arrange the pattern so that the piecing falls at a side, not a front or back, seam. To piece, cut out the section and, leaving the pattern pinned on the fabric, move it to the other selvedge, overlapping the selvedges by the amount required to match the pattern. Cut around the piecing but leave the pattern pinned on the main piece until after the piecing seam has been completed. It will always be a selvedge and will not require neatening. Lastly trim up the edges if necessary (figure 34).

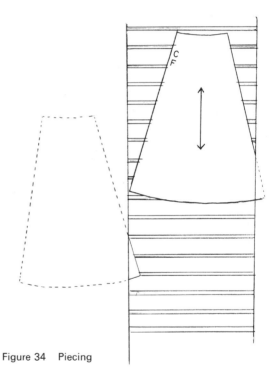

Figure 34 Piecing

Twill fabrics

Unless chevroned, the usual direction for the diagonal lines of twill is from top left to bottom right of garment when viewed from front or back, for all fabrics except cottons (e.g. denim) or Viyella. Twill is not a one-way fabric, but the diagonal changes direction when cut on the wrong side or the weft grain. Although plain fabrics such as gaberdine do not show the twill line too obviously and may therefore be cut in most styles, some dressmakers, including the author, do not care for the obvious conflict caused by certain styles, for example kimono sleeves, straight cut collars and revers, 'V' necks and four-gore skirts (figure 35), all of which are definitely unsuitable for more marked twills such as denim. The best way to deal with this problem is to make a centre seam and chevron the stripes, but this can only be done where

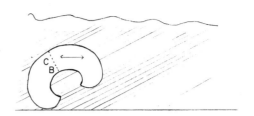

Figure 37   Laying a bias collar on twill fabric

The real problem arises when twill fabric is not reversible or has a one-way pattern. Plain styles with little flare and no vertical seams other than side seams must be chosen. Be mindful also of neckline and collar.

Stripes and checks

Apart from the necessity to match the lines, designs which are symmetrical in both warp and weft present no problem at all in cutting as they are to all intents and purposes the same as plain fabric.

Check which is one-way on the length but balanced across the weft threads is cut as a one-way fabric, and lengthwise bias seams can be chevroned. Check running equally up and down the length, but unbalanced from side to side will not chevron on bias seams unless half the garment is cut one way up and the other half in the opposite direction as in fold (d), figure 31. If this fold is not practicable single cutting is necessary.

Chevrons can be arranged in fabric which is unbalanced in both warp and weft provided (a) there are CB and CF *seams* and (b) the fabric is reversible, and left and right of the garment can be made identical simply by making one side up on the right side of the fabric and the other side on the wrong.

Lack of symmetry in both directions on a non-reversible fabric cannot be overcome. A simple pattern with no vertical seams other than side seams (except straight grain seams) must be chosen. It should have little flare. The garment must be cut as a one-way fabric with the pattern following the same order all the way round the body also. Such fabrics often have a twill weave in addition for which the same conditions apply.

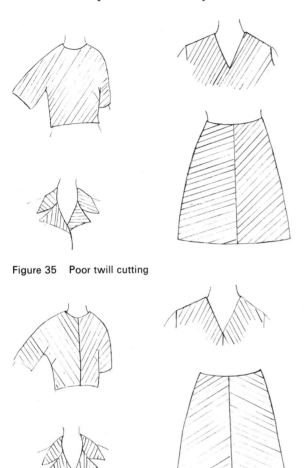

Figure 35   Poor twill cutting

Figure 36   Good twill cutting

the fabric is reversible, so that half the garment can be made up on the right side and half on the wrong side. Figure 36 shows the improved results – note that the collar, along with other pieces, must be cut with a CB seam. No special cutting technique is required – merely reverse one side when making up. All bias seams in twill fabric are better chevroned, although side seams and shoulder seams are acceptable without. Bias collars, unlike straight collars, cut well in twill, provided the CB is on the true cross (figure 37).

One point to ensure in order to chevron bias seams correctly in both directions (figure 38) is that the seam lines of the pattern pieces are at the same degree of slant from the vertical. Places to look at carefully are the side seams of skirts and top arm seams of kimono styles. A correctly cut commercial pattern designed for checks will have the correct angle, but it is a good

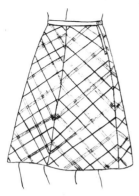

Figure 38   Chevroning checks

point to get right when cutting your own patterns. Skirt flare is easily adjusted to the correct angle and kimono slants ought to be the same front and back for good fit anyway.

Border prints

It is a mistake to think that border printed fabrics are limited to weftwise cutting and that the only place for the border is around the hem. Try putting the border symmetrically down CF or CB or across the skirt above hem level. Borders can be used in bias cutting to make interesting diagonal straight grain seaming. An idea for using the border as an edge is shown in figure 39 and a mitred effect is pictured in photo no. 30. Take time, use your imagination and your dress stand!

Cutting a pattern match

Once the theory of cutting patterns, particularly stripes and checks, to match is understood, the actual practical problems of achieving the match remain.

The usual advice given in text books is to pin the selvedges together matching the pattern and add pins at the centre fold and at intervals across the weft, checking the match through by lifting the fabric to align the pins on both layers. In spite of all this the pieces do not always match when cut, probably because one can never put in sufficient pins and the two layers move a little during cutting.

A foolproof method is to pin slevedges and fold as usual and then pin on the pattern and cut out through the top thickness only, leaving the pieces to lie in position on the cutting table. When all the top layer has been cut, lift the pins already in the work and put them through both thicknesses, matching the

Photo no. 30   Border printed dress (Fabric by K. & H. Fabrics (Leicester) Ltd.) Border transfer print design by Spectrum Papers Ltd. (Photograph by Neville Chadwick Photography, by permission of British Enkalon Ltd.)

Figure 39   Designing for border prints

cut edges of the pattern as you go and adding further pins every few centimetres. The work may not lie flat because of a little grain distortion, but the amount on each garment piece will be slight and most importantly the pattern lines will be absolutely symmetrical and match perfectly when made up. The grain distortion will probably pull itself into correct place on the wearer anyway, as both warp and weft will be straight basically because the stripe or check matches.

Symmetrical printed patterns of all types may be cut similarly.

Matching large repeating patterns

Large patterns require careful placing on the figure and garments must be planned and extra fabric allowed for this. A problem sometimes arises with matching a large, say floral, design to make it con-tinuous across CF or CB. Single cutting is required. Place the pattern piece for one side of the garment on the fabric, and before cutting mark the line of CF or CB on the fabric with trace tacking. To cut the other half of the garment, find a suitable repeat of the

pattern on the other side of the length of fabric, and trace tack the same line to fall in an identical place on this pattern. When placing the other half of the garment pattern apply the CB or CF to this line. The pattern will then continue over the centre line when the garment is constructed (figure 40).

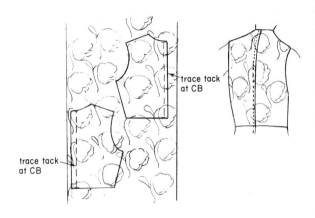

Figure 40   Matching large patterns across CB

8 Interfacing, Interlining and Mounting

Definitions are necessary because confusion exists about the meanings of the terms 'interfacing' and 'interlining' and to a certain extent 'mounting' and 'lining'. Lining is a final process and is dealt with in a later chapter.

Interfacing is a layer of fabric *inserted between garment and facing,* or occasionally one which reinforces other small areas. It is sometimes wrongly called 'interlining' or 'stiffening'. 'Interlining' means something quite different and 'stiffening' implies only one of the many purposes for which it is used.

Interlining is a layer of fabric *inserted between garment and lining,* usually for added warmth, and extends over all or most of the garment.

Mounting, also called 'backing' or in the U.S.A. 'underlining' or 'underlaying', is a layer of fabric cut the same as the garment and attached to the garment pieces before construction, so that the two pieces are made up as one, and in this respect it differs from lining.

Choice of interfacing

Only very soft, flowing garments in fluid fabrics and with no points requiring reinforcing are made entirely without interfacing. The reasons for interfacing are:

(a) adding body and weight, e.g. in collars, front opening edges, hems, across front and back shoulders of jackets
(b) strengthening, e.g. under fastenings, patch pockets, tops of pleats
(c) holding shape, e.g. curved jacket fronts, revers, collars, necklines
(d) holding shape behind areas of ruching or easing, e.g. staying armholes
(e) holding sewn or folded edges crisp and firm, e.g. wherever there are facings or in strips against the folds of pleats

(f) stiffening, e.g. shirt collars, tailored cuffs, waistbands
(g) preventing seam impressions being formed when pressing faced sections
(h) as a means of securing sleeve and skirt hems invisibly.

Because the purposes are so many and the fabrics needing interfacing are infinite, there are an enormous number of types available – strange it is that many dressmakers know of only one or two, and one of these will be the standard bonded fibre type which is by no means best for every purpose! Some idea of the range obtainable in one large department store is given (not all shops stock so many, but maybe this is because it is not demanded?):
(a) *Woven fabrics for medium/heavy fabrics/soft tailoring (dry clean)*
Hair canvas, cotton or wool, with goat hair
Linen canvas
Wool canvas (thick but soft)
Holland or tailor's linen for reinforcements and edges.
(b) *Woven interfacings for medium weight fabrics*
Tarlatan – loose weave, fairly stiff, more for stiffening than strengthening, e.g. bouffant evening skirts
Mull, very stiff, permanent finish, dry clean only
Viscose spun, firm, washable
Haroform, thicker but soft
Rayon tie canvas (nearly sheer), dry clean
Hair canvas, medium weight (as above)
Calico, firm, smooth
Unbleached calico, looser, rougher, cheaper.
(c) *Woven interfacings for lightweight fabrics*
Silk or polyester organza, fine, firm, sheer
Washable cotton organdie, fine, stiff, but edges curl if not secured
Cotton mull, stiff or soft
Cotton lawn
Cotton cambric
Butter muslin, very loose open weave, suitable backing for embroidery, beading, etc

Sanforized cotton, stiff and fine, permanent finish
Victoria lawn, firm, fine, washable
Vanishing muslin, difficult to obtain, support for beading and machine embroidery, removable after working by pressing with warm iron when it turns to a dusty substance.
(d) *For sheers, lace*
Nylon marquisette, in either stiff or soft quality
Nylon net.
(e) *Non-woven bonded fibre* interfacings in heavy, medium, light weights, soft, firm and stretch. Select quality according to manufacturer's recommendations.
(f) *Iron-on* interfacings, woven or non-woven, all weights, including a non-woven for stretch fabrics and knits, a fine knitted nylon for jerseys, transparent for sheers and lace, and fleecy backed canvas.
(g) *Interlinings for warmth*
Domette, wool, fleecy, open, light
Domette, flat, soft brushed cotton
Cotton flannelette or winceyette
Doctor's flannel, red or white, all wool, washable, expensive.
(h) *Waddings for quilting and padding*
Terylene (washable)
Cotton
Lambswool, difficult to obtain, soft, loosely woven fabric with fairly deep nap, but flannelette or domette make adequate substitutes.

The choice of interfacing depends on its purpose and the garment fabric. It should have the same washing/dry cleaning qualities, be of lighter weight and a little stiffer than the garment fabric. It should not be vastly different in handle. Never attempt to alter the hang or character of fabric drastically. Two or more different types may be needed for one garment, e.g. a soft one for a roll collar or revers, a fine firm one for the cuffs and strips of iron-on to reinforce the pockets.

Woven interfacings are more pliable than non-woven and make softer folds. They add weight and bulk, which is sometimes desirable, for example in opening edges and hems, and they follow the grain of the garment, giving a fluid movement. Non-woven interfacings are blended from various proportions of man-made fibres bound by heat and/or chemicals. They produce a stiffer effect, suitable for shirt but not roll collars, and because they do not have the benefit of grain are better for small rather than large areas. On the other hand, they do not add unwanted weight, are economical in cutting and present no fraying/finishing problems. They are being improved year by year and the soft ones have been a helpful addition to the range along with the specialized

stretch and transparent ones which are excellent. Difficulty in obtaining suitable interfacings can be overcome in the U.K. by mail order (see appendix).

Using interfacing

If not guaranteed pre-shrunk, woven interfacing should be shrunk as for wool fabrics. As it so affects the hang and appearance of the garment it should be basted in before fitting. Apply the interfacing to the garment, not to the facing, except for revers, so that the seam turnings will lie behind the interfacing avoiding a ridge or bulge when pressed. Lay the interfacing flat on the table, place the garment piece over and diagonally baste around the edges or down in rows if a large area, avoiding seam allowances if interfacing edges are to be lapped over garment seams in construction.

The processes for attaching interfacing are all based on the principle of avoiding bulk or stitches showing through to the right side. There are three basic seam methods:

(a) For heavy weight fabrics – except for the hem, which is dealt with later, remove all turnings on the interfacing after fitting and catch stitch the edges to the ws garment seam line (figure 41). This is the flattest finish for inside seams (e.g. collars), but is not suitable unless the fabric allows catch stitch to be worked without showing through to the right side.
(b) Keep the interfacing clear when making garment seams and then lap it over them, trimming away unwanted thicknesses. Catch stitch interfacing to itself (figure 42). This gives a

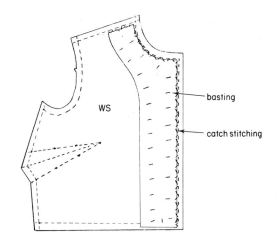

Figure 41   Applying interfacing

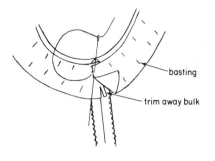

Figure 42   Neck interfacing being lapped over garment shoulder seam

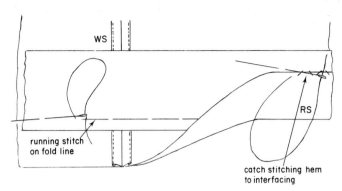

Figure 44   An interfaced hem

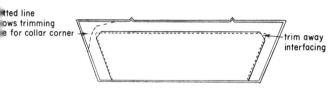

Figure 43   Interfacing a shirt collar

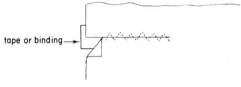

Figure 45   Darts in interfacing

flat seam but is not suitable with a fabric which shows pressing ridges on the right side. Test first.

(c) For medium/fine fabrics stitch the interfacing in with the garment seams and trim away the turnings as far as the stitching before pressing.

Trim away interfacing inside corners as in figure 43.

Avoid doubling interfacing, except for a short distance inside sleeve or jacket hems and all-in-one facings, where it should extend for 1–2cm ($\frac{1}{2}$in) over the fold line and be lightly caught to it with a long running stitch (figure 44) which does not go through to the right side of the fabric. When stitching the hem, catch it to the interfacing only for an invisible finish. (If the garment is not to be lined, the interfacing would have to be cut away shorter than the hem and the hem fixed in the normal manner.)

Darts in interfacing should be cut away down the stitching line, the edges brought together with three-step zig-zag or herringbone, supported by a length of tape underneath (figure 45).

Under buttonholes, thick interfacing may be reduced by cutting away a rectangle and replacing it by catch stitching over the hole a patch of finer interfacing.

Interlining

This is done to add warmth (e.g. domette for a velvet evening cape) or stiffness and weight (e.g. a stiff layer under an evening skirt.) It is possible to mount each fabric piece separately and make the two up together, but this is seldom suitable as it makes bulky seams. Generally the interlining is made up as a separate garment layer with overlapped seams and darts, and fixed to the garment around the edges before the facings are added or, in the case of a skirt, the waistband is mounted.

Mounting

The reasons for mounting include:
(a) adding body, weight or stiffness to a whole garment
(b) backing a transparent fabric
(c) giving stability to a loose weave to preserve the garment shape or prevent the seams from pulling out
(d) reducing the handling of the garment fabric by being the ground for marking out and forming a fitting toile before mounting to the fabric
(e) decorative effect, e.g. contrast under broderie anglaise

(f) preventing wrinkles and creases in the garment when worn

(g) producing a neat, self-bound seam finish (see below)

(h) acting as a 'hanger' for hems and facings, avoiding stitch marks on the garment fabric (see p. 138).

Garments may be lined as well as mounted.

When choosing a mounting fabric, match the garment fibre if possible and consider handle, weight, comfort and cleaning properties. Commonly used are jap silk or silk organza, but many other fabrics are possible, for example another layer of the garment fabric, such as chiffon, if the top layer is embroidered, mull, lawn, taffeta, calico, muslin or tricot for jersey fabrics. The choice will depend on the reason for mounting.

Baste the two fabrics together as for interfacing and sew as one. Darts may present difficulties – fine or slippery fabrics should be stitched together down the centre line of the dart to keep the layers together. If the garment fabric is thick, the mounting fabric will tighten the area either side of the dart. To prevent this, slash both darts down the centre line and ease back the cut edge of the mounting fabric before stitching (figure 46). Press the dart open and neaten the cut edges.

The self-bound seam finish (for straight seams) is made by trimming either the garment or the mounting fabric and folding the other over it to edge stitch. The thinner of the two fabrics should be folded over and the thicker trimmed (figure 47).

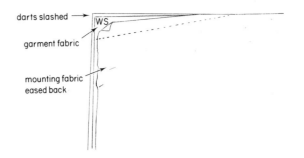

Figure 46   Working a dart on heavy mounted fabric

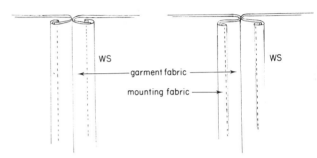

Figure 47   Two versions of self bound seam for mounted fabrics

9 Fitting

As discussed in the introductory chapter to the book, fit is one of the criteria by which we judge the success of a garment. It is also the facet of garment construction most dreaded by amateurs. Observation of a few basic principles will help to take the terror out of fitting.

(a) Patterns drafted individually from a personalized block seldom present problems. Once the block is perfected, most of the difficulties have been eliminated – a powerful reason for learning pattern cutting.

(b) Practice in fitting is best acquired by modelling. A good dress stand, preferably one which can be easily altered for size and shape, a supply of mull or lightweight unbleached calico and the basic instructions given in chapter 2 are required to start. Try the basic pattern with the stand adjusted for several different fittings, then model other simple styles. No amount of studying of theory or consulting friends or teachers will ever teach the learner as quickly or as thoroughly as modelling practice.

(c) If commercial patterns are used, buy the right size. This seems too obvious a comment to make but many dressmakers do not do this. Measure the figure carefully and compare with pattern companies' charts – often the 'Half Size' or 'Women's' pattern is more suitable than the 'Misses', but these other fittings are all too often not purchased. Buy blouse and dress patterns by the bust size, and skirt and trouser patterns according to *hip not waist* measurement, as the hip is more difficult to adjust than the waist. What to do if your size falls between two pattern sizes? Commercial patterns are generous in ease, so as slimmer and younger people usually prefer well-fitting garments, if you are round about size 12 or less it is better to buy a size smaller in these circumstances, but the older and plumper woman will often desire a looser fit and also will present more fitting problems, so for safety in these cases, say size 14 upwards, buy a size larger when in doubt.

Another tip for easy fitting of commercial patterns is making use of shell patterns as described in chapter

2. Alterations made to the basic shell are transferred to other patterns before cutting.

(d) Cut out with plenty of allowance for seams. The usual 1·5cm ($\frac{5}{8}$in) is absolutely useless for fitting purposes. Seams on which more, even as much as 6cm ($2\frac{1}{2}$in) should be allowed are side and shoulder seams, panel and yoke lines, neck and armhole edges, particularly under the arm. CB and CF seams are rarely altered, especially if on straight grain. Crotch seams on trousers also require cutting with extra allowance for fitting. When cutting with larger turnings, remember to mark the original seam line very clearly on all pieces. Failure to cut with sufficient turnings is the most frequent cause of failure to fit properly.

(e) If in doubt about the fitting, make a toile of the garment or of part of the garment first. A little time and money spent in this way can prevent expensive mistakes in fabric.

Commercial patterns

Make as many alterations as you can to the *pattern* before you cut. Points to watch are these:

The bust measurement on commercial patterns assumes a 'B' cup, and unless the pattern is altered, figures with a small bust ('A' cup) will find the garment too loose in the bust area, and possibly tight across the back, while on figures with 'C' or 'D' cup the garment may be tight across the bust and flatten the figure. The method of alteration is shown in figure 48 (a), (b) and (c). 48 (a) shows how to cut the pattern into four, keeping parallel with, or at right angles to, grain line and avoiding the darts. 48 (b), the adaptation for a small cup, shows the pieces overlapped in such a way as to shorten the pattern at CF and over the bust and reduce the width at the bust without affecting shoulder or waist measurement. The side seam is restored to its original length (essential to match the back pattern) by reducing the size of the dart by an amount exactly equal to the overlap (CC = XY). This also gives the smaller bust dart required for the small

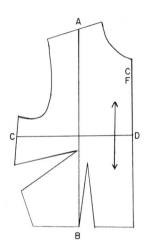

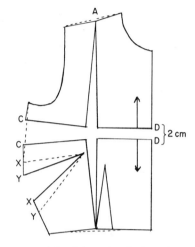

Figure 48 (a)   Cutting the pattern   (b)   Adaptation for small bust cup   (c)   Adaptation for large bust cup

cup bust. 48 (c) shows the four pieces spread on the same principles for the larger cup, and the bust dart made larger to compensate. (cc equals the sum of the two xys.) These alterations take into account the fact that a smaller or larger cup affects the bust measurement in both a horizontal and a vertical direction.

Omitting to adapt the pattern for the small or large bust cup can lead to many complicated fitting problems such as sagging armholes or necklines, tight creases or loose folds in the bust area, i.e. faults in balance, set and grain.

Back width measurement   1 to 2cm (about $\frac{1}{2}$ to $\frac{3}{4}$in) ease is required here. Adjustments are made by folding or spreading the pattern on the vertical line in figure 49. The shoulder seam may need to be adjusted afterwards.

Shoulder length   To alter back shoulder, cut as in figure 50(a) and overlap or spread, blending in smooth shoulder and armhole lines, and leaving the shoulder dart untouched (figure 50 (b) and (c)). A similar alteration is made to the front pattern.

The widest part of the hip   Many dressmakers take this measurement too high. The tape should be slid up and down until the widest part is reached, and the distance down from the waist of the hip measurement should be noted. Compare this with the hip line on

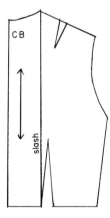

Figure 49   Adjustment line for back bodice width

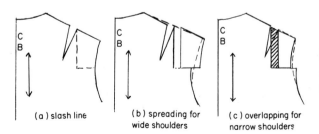

(a) slash line   (b) spreading for   (c) overlapping for
                         wide shoulders   narrow shoulders

Figure 50

the pattern and adjust the length of the waist-hip area by folding or spreading (figure 51 (a) and (b)). Attention to this point at the pattern stage prevents many faults in grain, set and balance about the hip.

Waist measurement should be adjusted evenly at all the darts. Large amounts of alteration can involve side seams as well, but rarely CB or CF. Be careful to keep bodice and skirt darts matched up.

Pattern length alterations are the last to be made. These are not dealt with in detail as all dressmakers are familiar with folding and spreading at the lines marked on commercial patterns (e.g. bodice length between armhole and waist, skirt lengths, sleeve lengths above and below elbow and the alteration line for crotch length in trousers). Where alterations are made, seams must be blended back to a good shape (figure 52).

NOTE   *Style* alterations to a pattern are not made until after sizing alterations are complete.

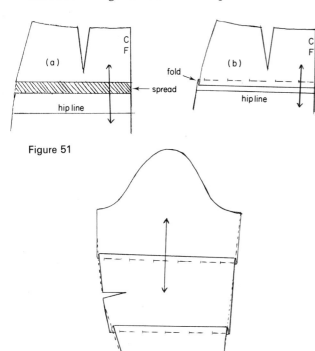

Figure 51

Figure 52   Blending seam lines after pattern alteration

Why is fitting necessary?

With an individually adjusted commercial pattern or one made from a personal block the amount of fitting required should be minimal. Why is it necessary at all? There are several reasons:

(a) possibility of error or miscalculation

(b) the figure may be irregular, i.e. right and left sides not equal

(c) every fabric works up a little differently from every other. A pattern that has worked well with little fitting problem in one fabric may not fit so well in another, e.g. less ease is required generally on thick fabrics

(d) a fitting gives the wearer satisfaction and enables her to make suggestions

(e) the style lines may not suit the wearer even though well-proportioned on the pattern. Examples are moving a yoke line up or down 1 or 2cm (less than an inch) to flatter the bust, or, more commonly, moving panel lines slightly towards the centre or away from it

(f) the amount of ease may be adjusted to suit the wearer's taste, and the garment needs to be seen on a moving and a seated figure as well as standing. This is particularly essential with sports or active clothes.

(g) most important of all, the hang, set and balance of a garment cannot be judged entirely from measurements or from a knowledge of theory, but must be seen with the garment on the figure. A basic knowledge of human anatomy is a help.

Elementary anatomy

Bone structure and the covering of fatty tissue
Figure 53 indicates how the main bones of the skeleton and in particular the spinal column and the pelvis affect body posture, on which the balance of garments depends. The following variations can occur:

(a) round back and hollow chest
(b) erect figure, sometimes with prominent bust
(c) sway back posture with prominent seat
(d) round shoulders and forward leaning neck
(e) individual crotch depth
(f) prominent hips.

The bones of the shoulder area, (clavicle, scapula and the top of the humerus) are responsible for a wide or narrow back measurement, length of shoulder, squareness or slope of shoulder. The balance of garments at the top of the bodice area is entirely dependent on the shape and size of the shoulder.

Figure variations caused by the amount of fatty tissue and muscle present are the ones that go around the body, e.g. waist, top arm, thigh, bust.

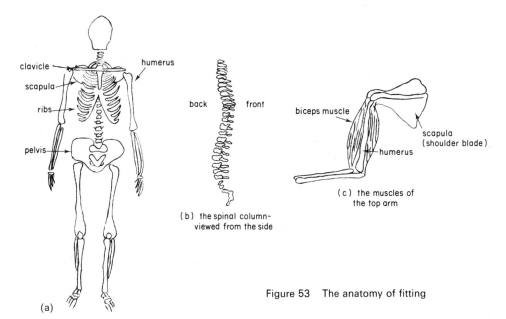

(a)

(b) the spinal column–
viewed from the side

(c) the muscles of
the top arm

Figure 53   The anatomy of fitting

The reduction of fullness in the block

In order to place and move darts and ease correctly it is important to understand how they relate to the figure.

(a) the point of the bust is a specific point of the figure and all darts for bust shaping must point directly towards this point. They may be moved around the bust to any area, but this condition of *direction* must always be fulfilled. The distance between bust points varies with individuals as does the level, and fitting must take this into account.

(b) reduction of fullness in the waist area (usually by seaming or darting) is not essential at any specific point, since the waist is formed by the gap between the rib cage and the pelvis (figure 53 (a)) and darts and seams are placed around the waist as the style and fashion demand.

(c) the fullness of the back shoulder is made necessary by the scapula, but as the scapula is not one specific point but extends across the back for several centimetres, back shoulder darts may point to any part of it and are frequently replaced by easing of the back shoulder seam. Some reduction of fullness is, however, essential. Beginners in pattern cutting sometimes omit this and give insufficient room for movement across the back.

(d) Sleeve head ease is essential over the top arm to accommodate the biceps muscle in movement (figure 53 (c)). This muscle thickens when contracting.

(e) elbow ease is essential in garments with long tight sleeves to allow for bending the elbow.

Fitting faults

The causes of incorrect fit should be established before faults can be adequately corrected. Bad fit shows up in one or more of these ways:

Incorrect grain Unless part of the garment is deliberately cut on a different grain for effect, in a simple garment the warp grain should run perpendicularly at CF, CB and down the top line of the sleeve, i.e. from the shoulder point with the arm in a straight position. The weft grain must be horizontal across the back between shoulder and the lowest point of the armhole, across the front chest, i.e. 6 to 8cm (2½ to 3¼in) above the bust point, across the top arm at the level of the bottom of the armhole, and across the hip line in trousers or skirts (except where the waist shaping has been achieved by transferring the darts into flare at the hem, i.e. where there are no waist darts and a very curved waistline seam), (figure 54).

Incorrect balance shows up by the way the garment hangs on the figure, and depends largely on the shoulders, hips and posture. A garment should hang equally on the figure, back and front and the two sides the same. Poor balance in a skirt shows up as side or centre seams not vertical (figure 55 (a) and (c)) or the fullness hanging unevenly (figure 55 (b)). Alterations are made by raising or lowering the waistline, front or back, until the skirt hangs evenly, not by altering the seams. Poor balance in a bodice refers to the difference in lengths between the front and the back and is due to slumping or over-erect posture, small or prominent bust or shoulder angle.

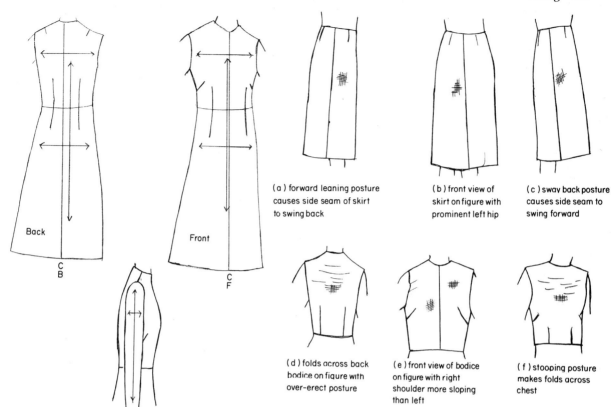

(a) forward leaning posture causes side seam of skirt to swing back

(b) front view of skirt on figure with prominent left hip

(c) sway back posture causes side seam to swing forward

(d) folds across back bodice on figure with over-erect posture

(e) front view of bodice on figure with right shoulder more sloping than left

(f) stooping posture makes folds across chest

Figure 54   Correct grain lines

Figure 55   Incorrect balance and grain

Gaping necklines and armholes and loose folds *across* the body are an indication (figure 55 (d), (e), (f)). In sleeves poor balance shows up as twisting in the top arm area, and may be due to a wrongly shaped armhole or sleeve head but more frequently to incorrect setting in.

Since faults of grain and faults of balance are essentially one and the same, the same alterations apply. The reason for listing them as separate *causes* is that in some garments the poor hang shows up most noticeably, but in others, often simpler styles in fabric with clear grain structure or checked or striped pattern, the bad grain is more noticeable.

Incorrect ease   Ease is very much a matter of personal taste and depends partly on the use of the garment and on fashion, but as a guide the following minimums are given:

across back   1–2cm ($\frac{1}{2}$ to $\frac{3}{4}$in)
across chest   none
bust   5cm (2in), sleeveless garments – 4cm ($1\frac{1}{2}$in), evening/sun dresses with straps or halter necks – 2cm ($\frac{3}{4}$in)
waist   2·5cm (1in)
hips   5cm (2in), (occasionally 2·5cm (1in) when very tight fitting skirts or trousers are in fashion)
top arm   2·5cm (1in)
elbow   1·5cm ($\frac{5}{8}$in)
wrist   1cm ($\frac{1}{2}$in)

Leotards, swimsuits, etc from stretch fabric require nil or minus ease.

Incorrect line   All lines should flatter the figure and be graceful curves. Neck and armhole lines come into this category, together with style lines such as panel seams. The proportions of a garment affect the line also.

Number of fittings

The minimum is two. The first fitting checks the grain, balance, set, ease and line of the main parts of the garment, i.e. bodice and/or skirt, and the proposed positioning of decorative or other features, such as pockets. Extensive alterations at this stage require a check fitting. The second fitting checks sleeves, collar and hem and may also need a check fitting after alterations. If the style is complicated the second fitting may need to be done in two or more stages. A final fit after the garment is complete is a good idea.

Preparation of the garment for first fitting

(i) Cut out and mark thoroughly, including feature positions, CB and CF and seam allowances, at least at the corners and more if in doubt.

(ii) Stay stitch where necessary and baste in all interfacing.

(iii) If the fabric is to be mounted, do this.

(iv) If sure from previous experience of the figure that back shoulder darts and CB seam are in order (these are seldom altered) complete them and insert the CB zip. If unsure, tack only.

(v) Work gathers, smocking, pin tucks, etc.

(vi) Tack up the pleats and remaining darts. Do not stitch.

(vii) Tack all main seams. Do not stitch.

(viii) Tack skirts and trousers, properly eased, on to a grosgrain ribbon or petersham at waist.

(ix) Pin or tack pockets into place.

(x) The line and proportion of the garment are better judged if the hem is roughly tacked.

General procedures for fitting

(i) The wearer must wear correct foundation garments and shoes.

(ii) She should stand still for the first observation, but must also make appropriate movements, e.g. sitting down, at a later stage.

(iii) Fit the garment *right side out*. (If fitted wrong side out, the left of the garment is fitted to the right of the body and vice versa, also a poor impression of the finished garment is received.)

(iv) Alter the right-hand side only transferring marks by trace tacks or tailor tacks to the left hand side later. (Do this by direct measurement or by folding in half down the centre line.) A little fitting may have to be done to the left side in order to judge the total effect. If an irregular figure is obvious at this stage, fit both sides. Otherwise it will show up at the check fitting and may be altered then.

(v) Never do one large alteration if two small ones will have the same effect. This helps to preserve the line and style of the garment.

(vi) Remember, one alteration often causes another: carry these through; e.g. varying the width of the bust dart alters the length of the side seam, and armhole alterations affect the fit of the sleeve.

(vii) Start from the top and work down, since any alterations to the shoulder, for example, will affect the rest of the garment.

(viii) When dealing with loose folds or tight creases establish their cause first. Your knowledge of female anatomy will help here. Loose folds are caused by poor balance or too much ease. Pin them out. Tight creases indicate tightness in the direction of the crease. Let out the dart or seam at the end of the crease. Creases ending at the point of the bust from whatever direction they come indicate tightness at bust point and the need for a larger bust dart. There is only one way to correct these accurately. Pin out the extra 'dart' formed by the crease, mark an identical one in the bodice front pattern, transfer this into the existing bust dart, and recut the front bodice with the larger dart. The examples shown in figures 56, 57 and 58 demonstrate this and underline the need for adequate turnings to be left when cutting out garments.

Two basic methods of alteration

Fitting Method Darts and seams are unpicked where necessary, defects dealt with by arranging the fabric (as in modelling) to eradicate folds, creases, poor grain, etc and repinned. This is suitable only for simple alterations or where the number of fittings that can be arranged is limited and the effect must be seen immediately. It is the more difficult method of the two, is less accurate and involves both wearer and worker in a long session.

Pattern Method Without unpicking, unless to let out, alterations are pinned in, the garment taken apart later, the pattern altered and the garment or part of it recut. A correction fitting is then required unless the alteration was elementary. This is much more accurate, takes less time at the fitting and leaves the pattern ready to cut the lining. For complicated alterations, such as the bust dart difficulties in figures 56, 57 and 58, it is the only way.

First fitting procedure

(i) Observe the general effect of the garment, its hang, proportions and silhouette and make a note of details to be attended to.

(ii) Check CF and CB, then other points of horizontal and vertical grain (figure 54). Eradicate loose folds caused by poor balance.

(iii) Watch the corrected grain lines carefully throughout the rest of the fitting.

(iv) Check on the accuracy of darts, that they do not 'poke' at the ends. If so decide whether it is due to a poor tacking line or whether the dart length needs

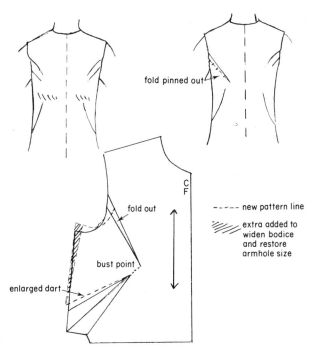

Figure 56 Pattern alteration for crease formed by prominent bust

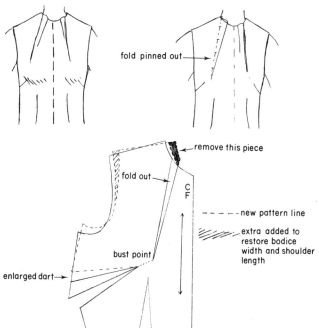

Figure 57 Pattern alteration for crease formed by prominent bust

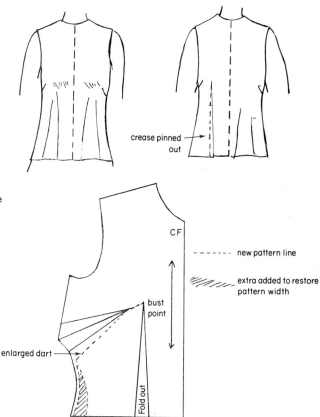

Figure 58 Pattern alteration for crease formed by prominent bust

adjusting. Watch the bust dart length especially. It should end about 4cm (1¾) from the bust point, a little less if it comes from CF. It must point exactly to the bust point.

(v) Check the amount of ease with the wearer standing, sitting, moving, etc.

(vi) Check and adjust styling lines if necessary to flatter the figure.

(vii) Check feature positions, e.g. trimming lines and pockets.

(viii) Check the lines of the garment that will affect the next construction steps, e.g. armhole, neckline, waist. They must be good smooth curves and the right size for ease.

Preparation for second fitting

Tack up the right sleeve and (a) tack into the armhole according to balance marks and knowledge of grain (figure 54) OR (b) place the garment on a dress stand

and pin the sleeve into the armhole, removing from the stand to tack, OR (c) wait until fitting to pin in place on the wearer (p. 115) (only in difficult cases as this is similar to the 'fitting method' of alteration and has disadvantages.)

In most cases the collar should be made up and tacked into place. If strong doubt exists, merely baste interfacing to the top collar and tack this to the neckline so that the collar style, depth and so on may be assessed as well as its set around the neck. Tack up skirt and sleeve hems, or if preferred arrange them at the fitting, but this is more difficult. Flared and pleated skirts should certainly have hems turned and tacked in the flat, not the wearing position.

Second fitting procedure

(i) Recheck all the points covered at the first fitting.

(ii) Check on constructional work done and pressing.

(iii) Check the collar for symmetry and set.

(iv) Check the right sleeve for ease at top, grain, hang all the way down with the arm in lowered position, with elbow bent and with the arm raised upwards and forwards. Make sure the bodice is not unduly pulled with arm movement. If so, the armhole may need to be raised. (See figure 60.)

(v) Check the fit of skirts and trousers on to waistbands or waist finishes, looking particularly at the area immediately below the waist.

(vi) Check sleeve and lower edge hems.

(vii) Take a final survey of the garment for overall impression. In most garments this will be the final fitting.

Some common problems

Figures 59 to 73 show some of the fitting problems commonly met with. Additional points to note are:

Figure 61 The maximum alteration for the skirt shown in figure 55 (c). In mild cases it is sufficient to alter the back of the skirt only.

Figure 63 To judge the amount required as an addition, unpick the shoulder seam at the fitting and allow the bodice to fall into place. The front shoulder will require a similar alteration.

Figure 64 At the fitting unpick the shoulder seams and allow the back to drop, keeping the front shoulder on its original line, until the upward curve at the waist disappears and the grain straightens. Measure the amount dropped at CB neck. Make the alterations in two stages on the pattern. The extra dart added at the neck (which could be left in

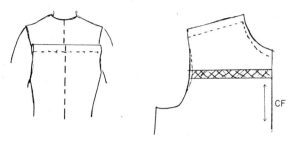

Figure 59   Pattern alteration for long front balance shown in fugure 55 (f)

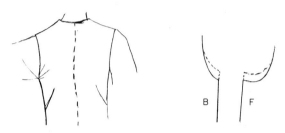

Figure 60   Bodice alteration for armhole cut too low

Figure 61   Pattern alteration for sway back, skirt illustrated figure 55 (c)

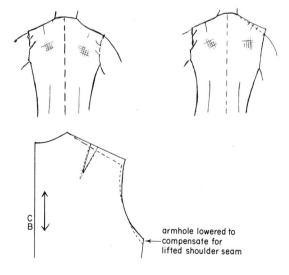

armhole lowered to compensate for lifted shoulder seam

Figure 62   Pattern alteration for sloping shoulders

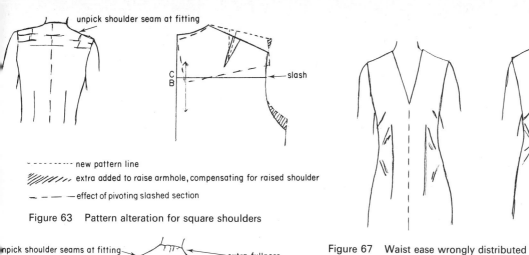

- - - - - - - new pattern line

/////// extra added to raise armhole, compensating for raised shoulder

— — — effect of pivoting slashed section

Figure 63   Pattern alteration for square shoulders

unpick shoulder seams at fitting

extra fullness

— — final shoulder line

waist line rises at CB

fold out

slash

C B

C B

Stage 1

Stage 2

Figure 64   Pattern alteration for round back (prominent shoulder blade)

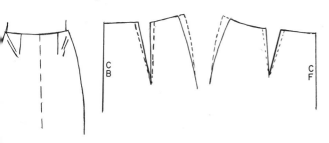

Figure 65   Waist ease wrongly distributed

C B

C F

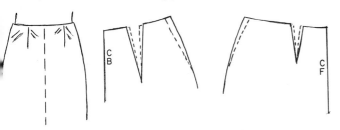

Figure 66   Waist ease wrongly distributed

C B

C F

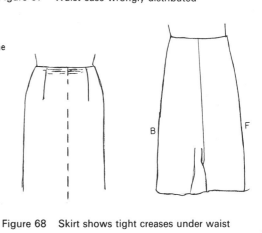

Figure 67   Waist ease wrongly distributed

B   F

Figure 68   Skirt shows tight creases under waist

Figure 69   Side seam out of balance due to faulty stitching

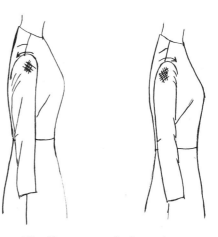

Figure 70   Sleeve set too far forward

Figure 71   Sleeve set too far backward

this position if the style alteration is acceptable) is required to restore the neck to its original size *or less*, which this figure requires. The method of adding this dart to the shoulder dart is shown in stage 2.

Figures 65 to 67 illustrate the waist ease, correct in total but wrongly distributed, causing the familiar creases of a badly setting garment.

Figure 68 is a very common fault caused by reducing the skirt to exact waist measurement before adding the waist finish. The area immediately below the waist, at the back particularly, is too tight for the figure. To avoid this allow 2 to 3cm ($\frac{3}{4}$ to $1\frac{1}{4}$in) ease on the waist when planning darts and seams and *ease* this amount into the waistband.

Figure 69 demonstrates the differences between bad fit because of an error in the pattern and bad fit caused by faulty stitching. The back edge of the side seam has been stretched and is springing back into place. To correct, unpick and re-stitch the seam.

Figures 70 and 71 show sleeves wrongly pitched causing grain faults. Move the sleeves round in the direction of the arrow until the fault disappears.

Figures 72 and 73 show errors in depth of crown of the sleeve.

Fitting trousers

Trousers cause dressmakers concern quite unneces-

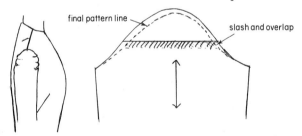

Figure 72   Pattern alteration for too deep sleevehead

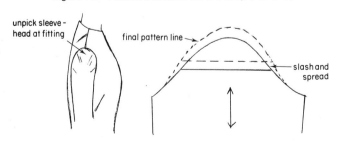

Figure 73   Pattern alteration for too shallow sleevehead

sarily as their fitting is no more complicated than that of other garments. In the waist/hip area fitting is the same as skirts. Balance is as for other garments – trousers must hang equally either side of the leg when viewed from back, front or side, and balance adjustments are made at waist level as in skirts. The only difference in their fitting lies in the crotch area, and this seldom exists if the crotch line on the pattern is adjusted before cutting out. Figure 74 shows how to measure and adjust crotch depth. Allowance for ease must be at least 2·5cm (1in) at the thigh, even when tight-fitting trousers are fashionable. For safety, cut with plenty of seam allowance at crotch, CB, CF and waist.

As in all garments, tight *horizontal* creases indicate a lack of ease round the body and these may occur at thighs, hips, waist, across abdomen or seat. Very little alteration may be done at hip level on the side seams as the hang of trousers is soon spoiled. The side seam may be let out or taken in *all the way down* as much as required, but at the hips only the maximum alteration is 1cm ($\frac{1}{2}$in) each side of the seam, (figure 75). If more is required it must be done at CB or CF and the waist dart adjusted to compensate.

Figure 76 shows the alteration for thigh width. Note that in all these alterations the crotch point (x) must remain static.

Looseness in the crotch is felt more often than seen. There are two main reasons for a loose crotch. The first is because the crotch line on the pattern was too low. If the situation is righted by pinning out a horizontal fold (figure 77 (a)), then this is the reason. The pattern must be altered as shown in figure 74 and the trousers recut. If, however, pinning the fold is not a satisfactory solution the reason is probably too much length in the CF/CB seam (total crotch length) and too great a slope in the seam. Usually the fault exists only in the back, and the pattern alteration is shown in figure 77 (b). The extra width added at CB may be removed at the side seam or darts, whichever fits better.

Too high a crotch line or too short a crotch seam give the tight crotch shown in figure 78 (a). To establish whether this *is* due to too high a crotch line or not, carry out the measuring process shown in figure 74. If the crotch line seems satisfactory, the fault is probably due to a large seat or abdomen, which will be readily seen. In this case carry out the alteration as shown in figure 78 (b) to front or back or both. Compensate for loss of width at the waist by adding on the side seam. The new CB or CF seams give more length and greater angle of slant necessary for a large seat or abdomen.

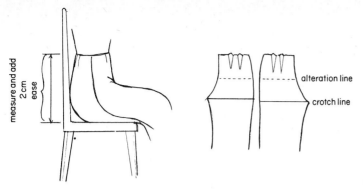

Figure 74 (a)   establishing crotch line for trousers

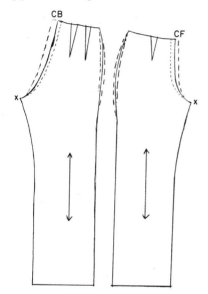

Figure 75   Enlarging or decreasing hip width

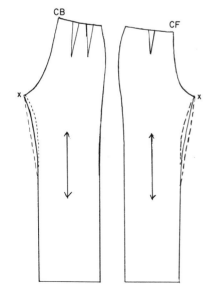

Figure 76   Enlarging or decreasing thigh width

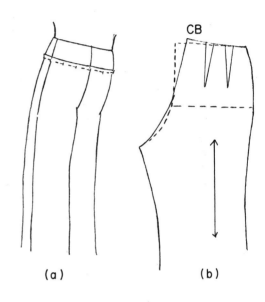

(a)   (b)

Figure 77   Altering a loose crotch

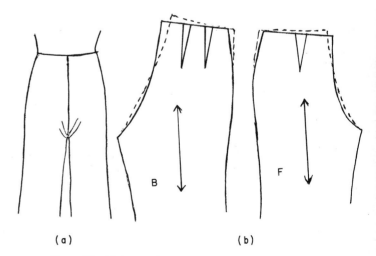

(a)   (b)

Figure 78   Tight crotch

10 The Reduction of Fullness

The fullness required in parts of a garment must be reduced in other areas (a) to give the garment shape, as in darts, (b) to allow for easy movement and close fitting in the same garment, as in pleats, and (c) to add decoration and interest as in shirring and smocking. There are many methods, but not all fabrics lend themselves to all methods and the reduction of the fullness must be one of the prime considerations when linking pattern to fabric.

Making better darts

Darts are for shaping and rarely add to the style or decoration. All fabrics take darts satisfactorily. In some they need special attention with trimming or pressing. Although simple to construct, this basic process can be mishandled. Never stitch a dart, with the possible exception of the back shoulder, until after the first fitting. After tacking and fitting, and before machining, remove the tailor tacks as they can be difficult to remove subsequently, especially at the point end. Check the length of matching pairs of darts and put in crosswise pins at the points to mark them accurately (figure 79). Machine from the wide end to the point, avoiding a 'poke' at the end by curving in the last few stitches along the fold. On firm fabrics finish by reverse machining, but as this tends to stiffen the dart it is better to thread the ends back for a distance on fine or soft fabrics.

It is a mistake to think that all darts must be straight. Darts from waist to hip follow the curve of the body slightly (figure 79 (a)), while front waist darts in a bodice may curve inwards after fitting on a figure with a slim midriff (figure 79 (b)). Even these must be finished with a curve along the fold.

On a bulky fabric a lump may form at the point. The effect of this is minimized if another strip of garment fabric is machined in with the dart and pressed the opposite way to balance the stitching line (figure 80 (a)). Alternatively, bulk may be reduced by trimming the dart and pressing the point open,

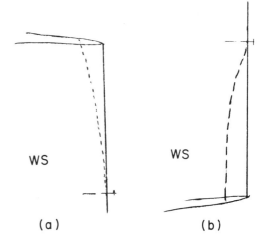

Figure 79   Shaped darts

(figure 80 (b)). Further advice on darts in difficult fabrics and on pressing is in chapters 23 and 24.

Tucks

Tucks which are sewn the full length of the garment section are for decoration only and not reduction of fullness. These are dealt with in chapter 22. Tucks which release their fullness may be stitched on the right or wrong side and are known as 'dart tucks'. Photo no. 31 shows a blouse with dart tucks acting as a yoke and releasing fullness to the bust.

Gathers

Only soft thin fabrics gather well. Attention should be paid to the amount of fabric in a gathered section to prevent it looking either crowded or skimpy. The minimum amount for effect is $1\frac{1}{2}$ times the space to be covered, and fine chiffons need 3 to 4 times. A sample worked in the fabric to be used will help to suggest the right ratio. Patterns may be slashed into sections and spread to add more fabric for gathering as the sleeve in figure 81. Where more width is added

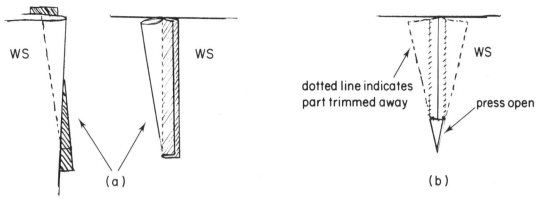

WS WS WS

dotted line indicates
part trimmed away

press open

(a) (b)

Figure 80   Darts in bulky fabric

Photo no. 31   Dart tucks and shirring

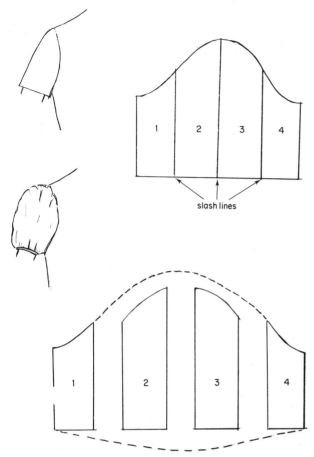

Figure 81   Widening a pattern for gathering

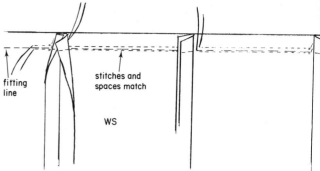

Figure 82   Gathering in sections between seams

a little height needs to be added to create the correct 'puffy' effect.

Gathers may be worked by hand or machine. Machine gathers are quicker and firmer, but hand gathers are accurate and even, giving delicate folds, and are to be preferred whenever time allows. Use silk or synthetic thread for strength and a fine, long needle, to prevent holes showing if the thread is removed. Work the first row marginally under the fitting line and the second row 3mm (about $\frac{1}{8}$in) above it, matching the stitches and spaces exactly. As with machine gathers, the finer the fabric the smaller the stitch. Never gather over a seam, but leave ends and start another section the other side, (figure 82). To set the little pleats evenly, when drawing the gathers hold the two ends together in one hand and ease the fabric along with the other (this method prevents the thread straining and breaking) until it is tightly closed. Small creases will form and will help even the pleats when the gathering is let out again to the

desired length before tying off. Machine gathering, suitable for long lengths such as frills, is worked from the right side with a loosened tension and long stitch. The bobbin thread is pulled up. When the gathers are set into the seam only the lower row, which shows, should be removed.

Shirring

To shirr, work as many rows of machine gathers (preferably not by hand, as shirring needs to be firm and an uneven effect is desirable) as required to fill the area, e.g. sleeve top, yoke or the whole of a bodice of a child's dress. Use the quilting guide for accuracy. Pull up the rows together but tie off separately. A small machined pin tuck on the ws each end secures the work (figure 83). The area should also be stayed on the ws with a lining of fine firm fabric hemmed around the edges and basted row by row through to the shirring with fine stitches which do not show through to the rs (figure 84).

Tucked shirring, a variation for sheer fabrics, is to work each row as a pin tuck either on right or wrong side (test a sample first) and pull up as usual. This gives attractive little ridges.

Another variation is corded shirring. Several rows of fine casings are pulled up with cord or rouleau

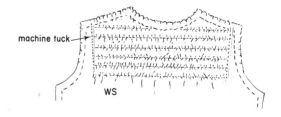

Figure 83   Machine shirring

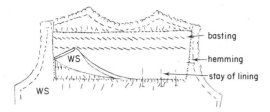

Figure 84   Staying a shirred area

Figure 85   Corded shirring

strips to form a shirred effect, as in the waist of the dress in figure 85.

Shirring with shirring elastic produces a stretch effect (see photo no. 31). Two methods are to hand-wind the bobbin with shirring elastic and use sewing thread in the needle with a loosened tension and long stitch. It is difficult, however, to judge the amount of gather produced in this way and tests must be made with varying lengths and tensions. A better method is to use ordinary thread in both needle and bobbin and work a 2/2 zig-zag on the ws over shirring elastic. (Some machine feet have a hole through which the elastic may be threaded automatically.) The elastic may then be pulled up and fastened to the desired length. See photo no. 32.

Photo no. 32   Shirring (wrong side)

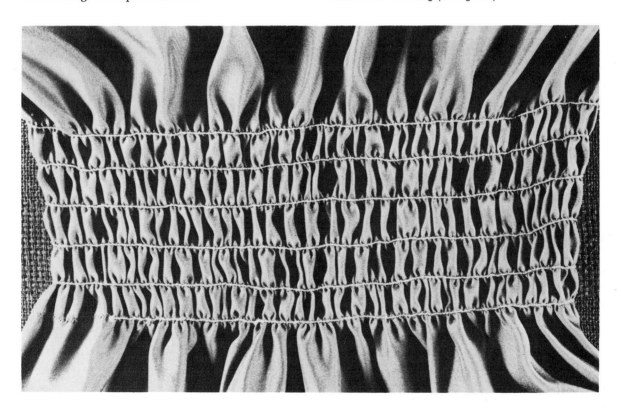

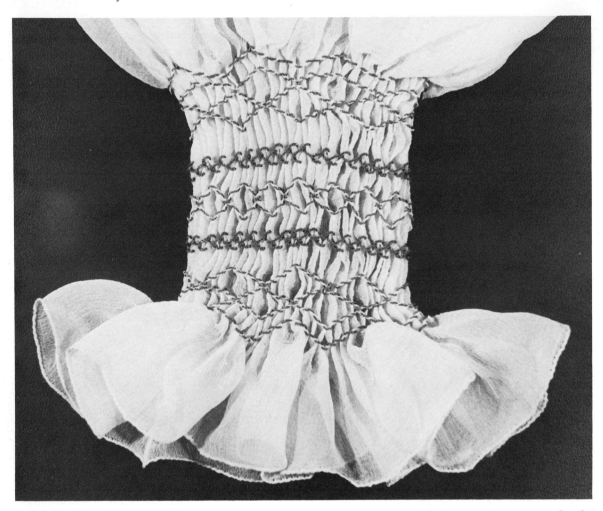

Photo no. 33 Smocked chiffon cuff with hand rolled and whipped hem

Ruching or gauging

These are similar to shirring, except that the gathers fall into deep, even folds. The threads are inserted from the ws, picking up small amounts and leaving long spaces (figure 86). The threads are pulled up and

Figure 86 Inserting threads for ruching or smocking

the area stayed as in figure 84. More commonly, the pleats are embroidered, and this is known as smocking. In this case the gathering threads are withdrawn afterwards and the stay omitted, leaving an elastic effect. A smocked cuff is pictured in photo no. 33. Four times the finished width is the fabric required.

Casings

For the best effect with elastic casings, make the casing no wider than is necessary for the elastic. To case a thickish fabric, use a fine casing or purchased bias binding. When using a hem as a casing, stitch both the hem and the fold, as two rows of machining give a neater effect (figure 87).

Easing

This is often confused with gathering, but is quite

Figure 87   Making a casing from a hem

different. Gathering pulls up tiny folds in the fabric but easing merely crowds the threads of the fabric closer together, and is only really successful where there is a degree of bias. No folds or gathers must be seen in the completed seam. It is often worked at sleeveheads, back shoulder instead of a dart, on princess seams and setting a skirt on to a waistband. Care must be taken to ease the long edge to the short one, not stretch the short one. A thread may be worked in to pull up, but an experienced dressmaker will work the fullness in with her fingers as she pins the seam. If the part to which the ease is being stitched is bias or of stretchy fabric, the seam should be stayed with tape.

Shrinking

Easing on *woollen fabrics only* is subsequently shrunk in. A gathering thread needs to be worked and pulled up. Place the gathered edge over a tailor's cushion and using plenty of moisture, preferably a damp cloth *and* a steam iron, hold the iron over the work then touch very lightly to work steam into the fabric. Continue remoistening in this way until the puffiness disappears. Be careful to press only the edge to be eased as the area beyond it, for example the sleevehead, needs the fullness to be left. Press a few millimetres past the fitting line only. Finally press gently with a dry cloth until dry. Seam to the adjoining edge and stay the seam. Woollen mixtures will not shrink.

Pleats

Pleats need to hang with good straight sharp edges, not sag at the hem, and should show no gape when hanging at rest, that is, when the wearer is standing still the pleat should close right up. There should be no unnecessary bulk in pleated skirts at the hem or the waist. Not all fabrics pleat well. With the exception of woollens, remember that a crease-resisting fabric is also a pleat-resisting fabric. Many modern materials will make only unpressed pleats satisfactorily, and if sharp edges are required, professional pleating is

called for. Top-stitching the fronts or backs of pleats may be successful but is not always suitable to the style.

Adding a pleat to an existing pattern is a simple matter if it is remembered that three times the finished width of the pleat is required. They may be added with effect to parts other than skirts. Figure 88 shows how to alter the pattern for the front jacket (a) to produce the front jacket (b). The two single pleats are cut in one with the lower jacket as straight pleats do not cause a change in grain. Flare pleats are added to the back of jacket (a) in figure 89, to produce jacket (b). Because of the flare the edges are on the bias and separate pieces for pleat and pleat underlay must be cut to preserve the straight grain line.

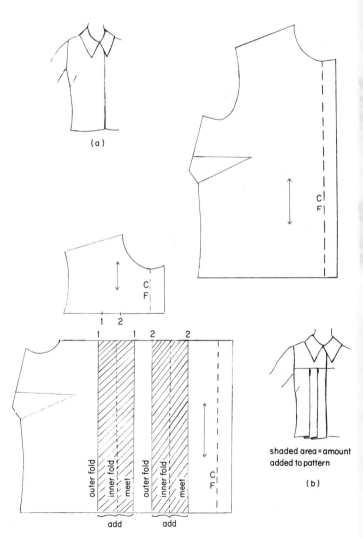

Figure 88   Adding knife pleats to a pattern

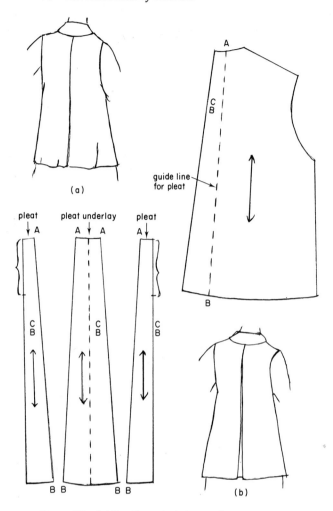

Figure 89   Adding flare pleats to a pattern

After cutting mark all edges clearly in trace tacking using different colours for inner and outer folds if there are many pleats, as the lines can be confusing. Arrange the pleats first, diagonally basting them for their entire length, whether or not they are to be stitched or pressed (figure 90). Rebaste pleats in position for all fittings after the first. Work flat on a table.

Where skirt pleats are stitched part of the way, releasing fullness on or about the hip line, the bulk over the hip to waist section is best removed by trimming away the back portion of the pleat and replacing it with lining (figure 91 (a)) or supporting it with tape (figure 91 (b)). There are two methods of treating the bulk at the hem line. Figure 92 (a) is the better method as it conceals all turnings within the hem, but with very obstinate fabrics which pleat badly the method in figure 92 (b) has to be employed.

Support to prevent pleats sagging and reinforcement to prevent pulling in wear where the machining ends are vital. The methods of support shown in figure 91 can be supplemented by topstitching as in figure 93 if the appearance is liked, and reinforcement is best achieved by applying a small piece of iron-on interfacing or firm lining to the back of a pleat before stitching, and ending the stitching with a slanting line which will absorb the stress of movement (figure 94). Arrowheads and bar tacks are fashionable from time to time for pleat and pocket ends. Bias seams in pleats (figure 89) must be taped to avoid sagging.

Professional pleaters will set pleats in almost any fabric. Possibilities include knife, box, accordion, sunray and crystal pleating (figure 95). You should cut the fabric, stitch some main seams and fix the hem first. Full details of preparation, fabric required, and so on, are obtainable from the firms involved.

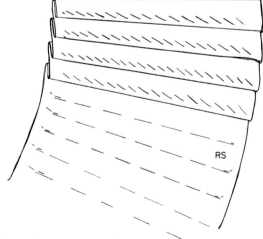

Figure 90   Basting pleats for fitting

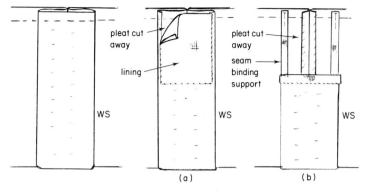

pleat cut away

lining

pleat cut away

seam binding support

WS

WS

WS

(a)

(b)

Figure 91　Supporting trimmed pleats

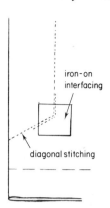

iron-on interfacing

diagonal stitching

Figure 94　Reinforcing a pleat

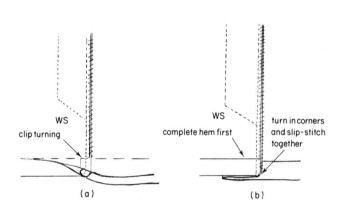

WS

clip turning

WS

complete hem first

turn in corners and slip-stitch together

(a)

(b)

Figure 92　Hems on pleated garments

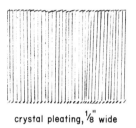

crystal pleating, $\frac{1}{8}$" wide

sunray pleats (semicircular fabric)

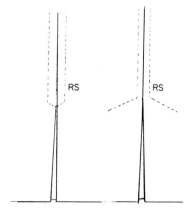

RS

RS

Figure 93　Supporting pleats

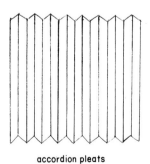

accordion pleats

Figure 95　Examples of commercial pleating

11 Seams and Reinforcements

Seam faults

Seaming is apparently so simple an operation, that it is often taken for granted, and performed with little consideration as to what will make for success or failure. Poor seaming can ruin the appearance of a garment or reduce its life.

The most serious fault is breakage, which arises because the stitching does not have so great a flexibility as the fabric when too large a stitch is used, or the wrong thread, or a straight stitch when a zig-zag or stretch stitch should have been employed. Breakage from these causes does not show up until the garment is being worn, when movement of the body extends the fabric, causing too great a strain on the seam.

Seams may also fail when strained across them. This happens in loosely woven fabrics or slippery materials such as satin and is worse on seams on straight grain and in close fitting garments. Smaller stitches and backing tape or a second row of stitching are called for in this case. Slippage, as this fault is called, is also caused by using too large a needle for the fabric.

The use of a regular instead of a ball-point needle when sewing jersey fabrics may break the threads, and rough throat plates can damage any seam.

Puckering, another common seam fault, can be caused by using the wrong thread, too large a stitch, too tight a tension or too great presser foot pressure. Closely woven and very smooth fabrics show this most of all. Sometimes pucker shows up only a considerable time after the seam is sewn, with the relaxation of the sewing thread, which is why it is wise when testing out a seam to leave it several hours before assessing the result. Pucker caused in this way cannot be removed by pressing.

Cockled seams result from bias fabric being too stretched as it passes under the needle.

Failure to match patterns or grains when preparing a seam gives an unsightly effect.

Faults which occur after the main stitching are failure to deal with turnings properly and to reduce bulk, especially where seams cross or where the interfacing has not been properly cut away at the seam line. Lastly a seam can be spoiled at the pressing stage, either by insufficient pressing or over-pressing, as well as by faulty techniques.

All these faults can be avoided by studying the chapters on machines (chapter 5), threads (chapter 6), interfacing (chapter 8) and pressing (chapter 23).

Criteria of a good seam

What, then, are the qualities of a successful seam?

Firstly one must consider whether the seam is to be merely functional, such as side or shoulder seams, or the edges of collars and facings, or whether it ought to be conspicuous because it forms one of the style lines of the garment. If it can and should be seen, this may be accomplished by the use of different fabrics in the construction of the garment, or by the differences in grain or design of the fabric at the point where the seam joins. A yoke, for example, may simply be cut on the weft grain instead of the warp to have this effect. If, however, these methods are not employed, thought should be given to making the seam conspicuous by employing a decorative seam or finish. Many a garment fails to achieve its full effect because style seams are 'lost' in the fabric instead of being obvious. Often simple topstitching is all that is required, but there are many more interesting methods.

All seams, whether functional or conspicuous, must also have strength and elasticity and a good smooth line. They should be properly neatened and pressed. To achieve these aims, attention must be paid to the correct choice of thread and needle, size of stitch and machine tension and pressure. The smooth line of machining is more easily achieved if not worked too slowly. The type of seam and finish must be chosen according to the fabric and the part of the garment. Many choices are given in this chapter and further advice on particularly difficult fabrics will be found in chapter 24.

Consistency of seam types and finishes within a garment also makes for a professional finish.

When using an unfamiliar fabric it is a good idea to experiment first on a scrap to find the best methods. There is no substitute for experience and experimentation. Perhaps you will even invent a seam of your own!

General techniques

A few general points need to be observed which will add to the success of all types of seam and make for quicker and easier sewing.

Stay stitching This is often advised on pattern primers, but is not always necessary. Its purpose is to prevent stretching on curved and bias edges, such as necklines. The time when stretching is most likely to occur is during fitting, and therefore if more than one detailed fitting seems likely and the fabric is not of the firmest type, stay stitching is advisable, but to be effective must be done immediately after cutting out and marking. The machine stitch should be lengthened and the stitching done just inside the seam allowance as near to the proposed stitching line as possible. Take care how you feed the fabric into the machine, for it is possible to do more harm than good if it is at all stretched as it goes. Generally if stay stitching is not required to support the fabric during fitting it is best omitted and the added strength given to the curved seam by two rows of machine stitching, or by a shortened machine stitch when making the seam. Stay stitching is always essential, however, in areas where the fabric has to be slashed before sewing, for example, inside corners (figure 118) and needs to be done before slashing.

Taping This is done on very loose weave or knitted fabrics on curved seams or horizontal ones, such as the shoulder, where stability is needed. Unlike stay stitching, taping is not done at an early stage, but at the same time as seaming.

Directional stitching Some trade patterns show in which direction the seam should be stitched by pattern markings. The principle is that seams should be stitched with the grain, not against it, to minimize the fraying of the edges, (figure 96). As a rough guide, think of sewing from the wider part of the piece to the narrower, that is from hem to waist of a flared skirt, underarm to waist on a bodice and neck to shoulder (figure 97). Attention to this detail will not affect the set of the seam or the hang of the garment; it will make the job of seam neatening easier.

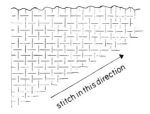

stitch in this direction

Figure 96

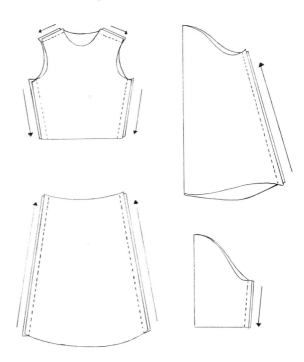

Figure 97   Directional stitching

Preparation of the seam   An experienced dressmaker ought not to be tacking every seam for sewing. Garments must be *properly tacked, not pinned, for fitting*, but the aim in sewing should be to do as much as possible without, as tacking is both monotonous and time consuming. After the first fitting, most seam tacking has to be undone to allow darts, pleats, gathers, etc. to be completed and pressed. The seam should be tacked again if it is likely to present difficulties, for example setting gathers, very curved seams, fabric where the pattern must be finely matched or difficult fabrics such as satin or velvet. Experience tells when a seam may be machined with pins only, and many side, shoulder, panel, sleeve seams, etc. fall into this category if the material handles easily.

The minimum preparation required is to pin the

seam together first at the balance marks, then at the top and bottom, then as few as possible in between. It is important how pins are placed. They should pick up as little material as possible for stability and accuracy and be exactly on the stitching line, at right angles to the raw edge (figure 98). (Pins placed parallel with the edge tend to distort the seam.) If a

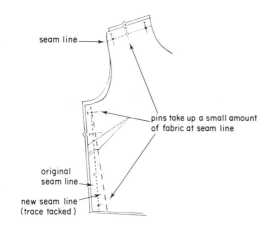

Figure 98

seam alteration has been found necessary at the fitting, the new line will have been marked with trace tacking or tailor tacking and the pins must then take up the fabric exactly where these markings are, (figure 98). If no alteration is necessary fewer pins will be needed as, with turnings cut accurately, the seam guide on the machine will be the means of keeping straight. It is worth while paying attention to really accurate pinning since, with skill, much tiresome tacking can be avoided.

The simple, open or plain seam

This is the most commonly used seam in dressmaking and is for sections of the garment where the seams should be inconspicuous. A great variety of finishes exist, however, and it is important to choose the best one for the fabric, the position and shape of the seam. A good dressmaker takes pride on the appearance of her garments on the inside as well as considering their durability.

Edge stitching or clean finish This is about the quickest and surest finish of all and ought to be the first one considered. It is not suitable, however, for any fabric thicker than the average summer weight cotton print or where two edges must be neatened together (e.g. armholes). Practice is needed to perfect this finish – the turning must be as narrow as

possible (at most 4mm ($\frac{1}{8}$in)) and the machining right on the folded edge, not on the raw edge, or the seam will not lie flat. Ideally it is done *after* the seam has been pressed open with the turning lifted so that the wrong side of it is on top facing the worker, who then uses both hands to guide the fabric under the machine, making the turning as she goes. Until

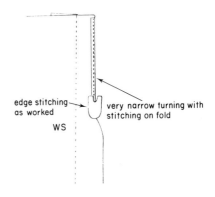

Figure 99

experienced at this, she will need to work at a slow speed and to stop occasionally to re-arrange the fabric, but the aim is to do the operation smoothly and without stopping. The turnings should never be pinned or tacked or the edge will become uneven (figures 99, 100).

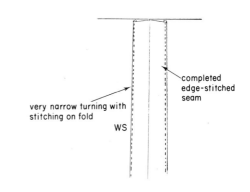

Figure 100

Over-edging or zig-zagging This is the most frequently misused and badly executed seam finish, partly because it is frequently done on unsuitable fabrics, partly because the size and length of the stitch are not always adjusted to the fabric and partly because it is not always done exactly over the raw edge and frayed edges are still left. There are two methods of zig-zagging, the first being to trim the edge before stitching, which is quicker and makes it impossible to cut the stitching threads. It is, however, more difficult to control the edge by this method and unless the fabric is firm it tends to stretch and fray, so for looser fabrics it is better to employ the second method, to zig-zag first and cut away afterwards. Deeper turnings are required for this method and a very steady hand and sharp small scissors to cut accurately right up to the stitches. In order to prevent lumpy turnings, as few stitches (i.e. as long a stitch) as is practicable to prevent fraying should be used, although for unlined garments closer zig-zagging looks better. The stitch width should be as wide as possible but not so wide that the edges turn and become bulky. If they still do this when half the full width available is used, then this is an indication that zig-zagging is not the proper method for that fabric. The looser the fabric the wider and closer the stitch required. It will be seen that every fabric requires special consideration, and there is no form of seam neatening in which it is more vital to work a test piece on scrap material first, (figure 101). Always work *with* and never *against* the grain.

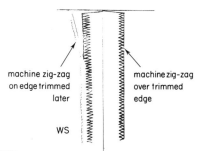

Figure 101

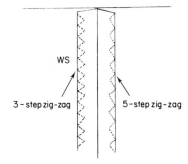

Figure 102

Three- or five-step zig-zagging This is a variation of the last method, suitable for fabrics which fray little, especially jerseys (figure 102).

Straight machine stitch and pinking, overcasting or blanket-stitching (loop stitch). These methods are laborious and never quite so successful as zig-zagging, but are the alternative when no swing-needle machine is available. As with zig-zagging, they are only used when the fabric is too thick to turn under for edge-stitching, (figure 103). It should be noted that to

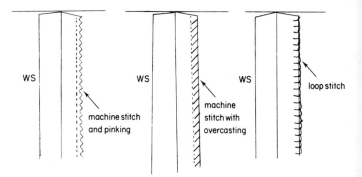

Figure 103

give firmness to the edge there must be a row of plain machining about 4mm ($\frac{1}{8}$in) from the raw edge before the finish is applied. Pinking is suitable only for really non-fray fabrics in garments that are also to be fully lined.

Straight edges only may be bound with straight seam binding (Paris binding). It is very difficult to apply this by folding in half and securing both edges with one row of machining (figure 104) and if she attempts to do this the worker may well end up with one side of the binding not caught in the stitches in various places. A safer method is shown in figure 105, using two rows of stitching.

Curved edges are bound with purchased or made bias binding (figure 106). If you cut your own binding, use

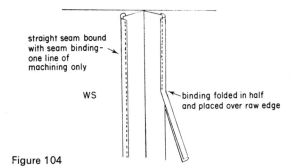

Figure 104

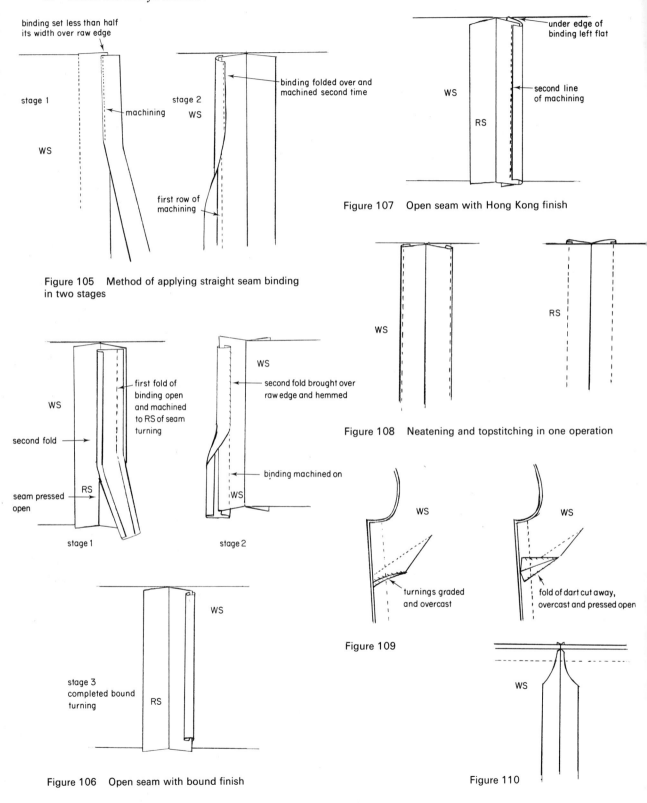

binding set less than half
its width over raw edge

stage 1

WS

machining

stage 2

WS

binding folded over and
machined second time

first row of
machining

Figure 105   Method of applying straight seam binding
in two stages

under edge of
binding left flat

WS

RS

second line
of machining

Figure 107   Open seam with Hong Kong finish

WS

RS

Figure 108   Neatening and topstitching in one operation

first fold of
binding open
and machined
to RS of seam
turning

WS

second fold

seam pressed
open

RS

stage 1

WS

second fold brought over
raw edge and hemmed

binding machined on

WS

stage 2

WS

turnings graded
and overcast

WS

fold of dart cut away,
overcast and pressed open

Figure 109

stage 3
completed bound
turning

RS

WS

WS

Figure 106   Open seam with bound finish

Figure 110

a fine firm fabric, such as jap silk or any kind of light-weight lining fabric. This is the best finish for jackets or unlined garments and gives an expensive looking finish.

Hong Kong finish This is similar to bias binding and is very suitable for thick, fraying fabrics, being slightly less bulky than conventional binding and having two rows of machining. It is shown in figure 107. Instead of turning under the free edge of the binding and hemming to the garment turning, it is left free to lie under the turning while a second row of machining, done from the right side, goes through all thicknesses on top of the first row. The edge of the binding, left raw, cannot fray as it is cut on the cross.

Binding with net This is suitable for very loosely woven bulky fabrics, such as those made from mohair, where wide turnings are used because it frays so badly and the conventional narrow bind would not hold. Strips of dress net or tulle can be cut as wide as required and can either be applied as a bias binding or by the method given for straight binding since the edges of net do not fray and there-fore do not really require enclosing. If a wide net bind is used, several rows of machining through all thickness spaced at, say, 5mm (about $\frac{1}{8}$–$\frac{1}{4}$in) from each other, increase the security of the finish. One drawback of using net is that it can be a little rough and may snag tights or underwear so garments neatened in this way should also be lined.

Simple seams in which the edges are pressed and neatened together may be finished by any of the methods discussed except edge-stitching. Seams which are to be topstitched must be neatened first. Occasionally on very firm fabric no further neatening will be required if the topstitching is not done too near the seam line. A method of topstitching and neatening an open seam all in one is shown in figure 108.

The problem of bulk

Failure to deal with bulk in seams is one of the causes of the 'home-made' look on a finished garment. A possible problem arises

(a) whenever seams cross each other or cross the ends of darts, pleats, etc.

(b) whenever more than two edges are to be joined, e.g. in attaching collars to neck edges, when there will be two collar edges, one neck edge, one facing edge and two edges of inter-facing all in the same seam

(c) whenever seams lie on top of one another, such inside hems or facings

(d) inside angles of 90° or less, such as the points

of collars or the corners at the bottom of a front opening blouse, where the front facing and the hem turn back on each other.

The principle of dealing with all these cases and the many similar ones that arise in dressmaking is to cut away as much surplus material as possible. In corners, removing the excess is known as 'mitring', while trimming the edges of seams so that layers do not lie together is called 'grading' or 'layering'. Several examples of this principle serve to demonstrate how it can be applied in other situations.

Figure 109 shows two methods of reducing the bulk where a horizontal bust dart enters the side seam. Hand overcasting or loopstitch neaten the cut away edges.

Figures 110 and 111 show two methods, one by grading (110) and one by mitring (111), of reducing the bulk where two main seams cross at right angles.

Figure 112 shows the mitring of corners in collars and cuffs.

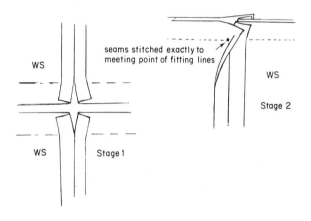

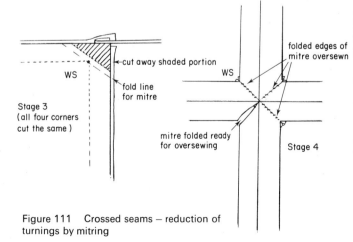

Figure 111   Crossed seams – reduction of turnings by mitring

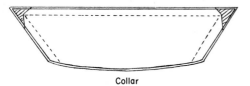

Collar

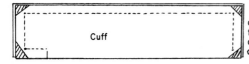

Cuff

Note that where angle at corner is less than a right angle the line on which the mitre is cut is not straight

a straight cut for mitring a right-angled corner

Figure 112

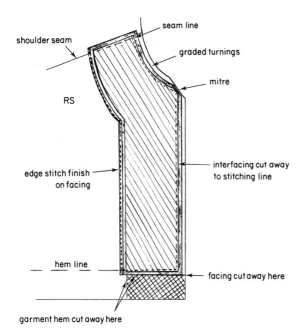

shoulder seam

seam line

graded turnings

mitre

RS

edge stitch finish on facing

interfacing cut away to stitching line

hem line

facing cut away here

garment hem cut away here

Figure 113

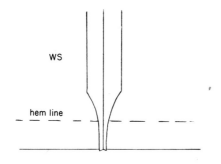

WS

hem line

Figure 114

Figure 113 shows an all-in-one front edge and neck facing, with interfacing, graded at the seam, and mitred at the neck corner, and the facing bulk removed at hem level.

Figure 114 shows the grading of seams inside hems.

Reinforcing the weak points

Seams need reinforcing wherever for any reason turnings have to be cut into. Generally the slashing has been done to enable the turnings to be pressed flat against the garment. Sometimes a row of stay stitching before seaming or a double row of machining on the seam line suffices. If the slash comes at a vital point of the garment where there may be considerable strain, such as at the point of the gusset inserted to give ease to a dolman sleeve, or where slashes have to be made on easily fraying fabrics, more substantial methods of reinforcement must be employed. These include taping, applying small areas of interfacing and strengthening with facings of lining, cotton lawn, organza or other firm, fine fabric. Several examples will serve to illustrate the principles.

The first, figure 115 (a), (b) and (c), shows three ways of strengthening the slash made for the insertion of an underarm gusset. Method (a) is suitable only for very firm fabrics with little fray. Two rows of small-sized machine stitches are worked inside the stitching line before cutting the slash. In method (b) a strip of suitable firm, fine fabric is cut and basted on, then stitched and the opening slashed. The strip in this example is cut on the bias as the stitching line is curved, but in the case of a straight stitching line for a triangular gusset, straight seam binding should be used. Method (c) gives the best reinforcement for weaker fabrics. A small piece of iron-on interfacing is applied to the area before stay stitching and slashing.

The same three methods are suitable for all 'slash-to-dot' situations. Another frequent place for this process is at the internal corner at the shoulder/neck point of the collar cut-in-one or shawl collar, (figure 116).

Sometimes right-angled corners are used in overlaid seams, as in the bodice of the dress, figure 117. In this case the slash required at corner (i) is made after stay stitching just inside the fitting line as usual, (figure 118), then the seam allowances are turned under before topstitching to the other section. Reinforcing fabric is added in one of two ways.

In the first method, after stay stitching, a piece of reinforcing fabric is pinned or tacked on and machine-stitched with a small stitch close to the fitting line. The slash is made through both layers (figure 119). Excess turnings on the reinforcing

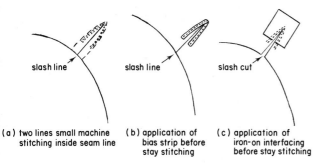

(a) two lines small machine stitching inside seam line

(b) application of bias strip before stay stitching

(c) application of iron-on interfacing before stay stitching

Figure 115

fabric are trimmed (figure 120), before it is turned through to the ws and pressed with the seam well underneath. Turnings are pressed under on the fitting line ready for application as an overlaid seam, (figure 121).

In the second method, stay stitching is done first, then the corner is slashed (figure 118). The reinforcing piece is cut as a right-angled triangle, with the straight grain on the long edge, (figure 122). Place right sides of the garment piece and the reinforcing piece together, with straight cut edge against the slash. Pin and stitch with a small machine stitch from

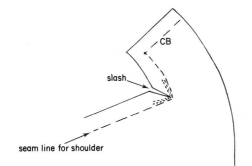

Figure 116   Reinforcing the slash at neck point on shawl collar

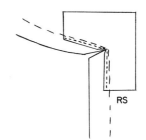

Figure 120

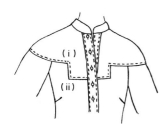

Figure 117

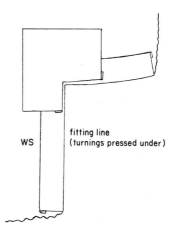

Figure 121   Fitting line (turnings pressed under)

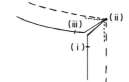

Figure 118

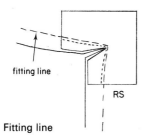

Figure 119   Fitting line

Figure 122

(i) to (ii), the corner of the fitting lines, (figure 123). Leaving the machine needle in the work at the corner, raise the presser foot, open up the slash into a straight line, pin at (iii), lower the presser foot and stitch to (iii), (figure 124). Figure 125 shows this reinforcement when pressed to ws and garment turnings pressed under ready for the top-stitched seam.

Difficult open seams

Three situations make the plain or open seam more difficult. These are (a) when it is curved, (b) has a pattern which requires very accurate matching or (c) is cut on the bias.

The curved seam   The curved seam in figure 126 should have two sets of balance marks, at the beginning and the end of the tightest part of the curve, and is really simple to put together accurately if you remember to pin at the balance marks first, putting the pins in on the seam line at right angles to the raw edge, taking in as little fabric as possible, (figure 127). The rest of the seam can then be pinned at close intervals, remembering that the two pieces of fabric must fit together smoothly *at the seam line*, not at the raw edge. Unless this seam is being prepared for fitting, in which case tacking is necessary, it should be possible to machine it pinned, taking out each pin as the needle reaches it.

Correct pressing of a curved seam depends on correct treatment of the turnings by snipping or notching as appropriate. After stitching press the seam open by using the point of the iron only, pressing very lightly while opening the turnings with the fingertips. This partial pressing simplifies the snipping/notching procedure, (figure 128). The edge with the outside curve requires notching, care being taken to remove *the exact amount of fabric required to allow the turning to lie flat, single thickness*, the small cut edges closing in on one another exactly. *No fabric should be removed* from the inside-curved edge, but snips made, as few as possible to allow the turnings to lie flat. Take care not to snip any deeper than is absolutely necessary – this is a bias edge and can be stretched a certain amount, (figure 129). Since this snipping and notching weakens the seam it is a good idea to strengthen it with a double row of machining, using a smaller than usual stitch.

The pattern-match seam   This is probably easier to do accurately when pinned rather than tacked. As for all pinned seams, pin top, bottom and balance marks first, then place pins at very frequent intervals in between (pp. 77–8). If the fabric is slippery as well as patterned it is possible to machine *over* the pins, provided the stitch is not too small and the

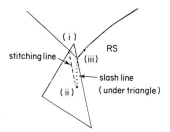

Figure 123

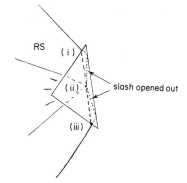

Figure 124   Slash opened out

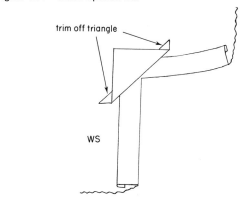

Figure 125   Trim off triangles

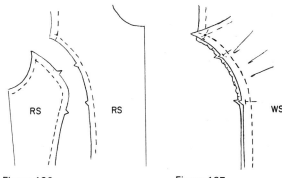

Figure 126   Figure 127

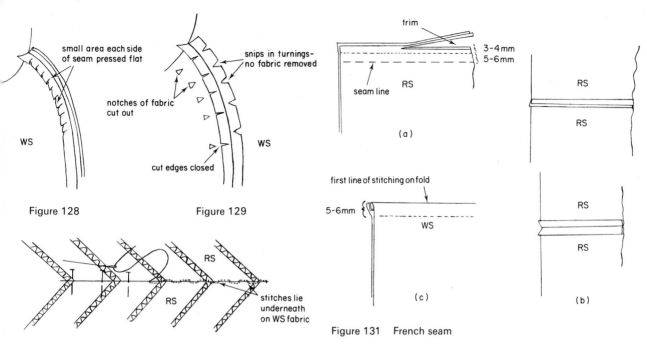

Figure 128

Figure 129

Figure 130   Slip tacking

Figure 131   French seam

machining done slowly and without jerking. If the seam has to be tacked for fitting, you may prefer to slip-tack (figure 130) but to hold a patterned seam securely stitches must be small, accurate and very firmly placed. A tacked seam is safer if pins are added as well. The difficulty when machining matched seams arises because however carefully they are pinned or tacked, the top layer tends to move towards the worker when passing under the presser foot. Gentle manipulating with the fingers while machining slowly helps to avoid this.

The bias seam   If not handled well bias seams stretch and cockle when machined. Preventive measures are to slacken off the presser foot pressure, use a long machine stitch at least for the first row – a second row of smaller stitches may be added if desired – and manipulate the fabric as it passes under the foot pushing it slightly so that a very small 'bump' of fabric enters the foot. This should not be overdone or the seam will not be straight. Regrettably there is no substitute for experience here! Seams which seem likely to cause trouble in wear (e.g. those on the true cross or bias seams on loosely woven fabric) should be taped. Close, firm pinning is required as for the pattern-match seam. Where a bias edge is to be stitched to a straight edge, the bias edge must be on top.

Other inconspicuous seams

Other inconspicuous seams besides the simple or open seam are the French seam, the mock French seam, the lingerie seam, and a seam based on the traditional mantua maker's seam.

The French seam is for use on straight edges or for *gentle* curves (more skill required here) on fine fabrics only. It is self-neatening, an excellent method of dealing with badly fraying fabrics, and particularly suitable for children's wear, lingerie and all garments made from transparent materials. It is a delicate seam and the finished width should not be more than 5–6mm ($\frac{1}{4}$in). The secret of success lies in the pressing. Figure 131 shows the method. Pin or tack the edges, ws together, machining 5–6mm ($\frac{1}{4}$in) inside the seam line. Trim turnings 3–4mm ($\frac{3}{16}$in) from stitching (a). Press the stitches into the seam, as for all seams (chapter 23) then press the turnings open or to one side with the point of the iron, (b). Turn RS together and pin or tack on the stitching line, making a sharp crease at the edge, on the first row of stitches, with the fingers as you go. (On springy fabrics the iron should be used again at this stage.) Machine, remove tacking (c). Press the stitching into the fabric before pressing again to leave the seam lying towards the back of the garment. *Five* separate pressings will have been done.

The mock French seam is sometimes easier to construct accurately on curved edges, although it involves hand sewing and is therefore more time-consuming. Machine the edges RS together, trim the turnings if necessary and turn their edges in upon each other with oversewing or slip-stitch.

The lingerie seam is the alternative to the French seam for delicate garments and fine fabrics. It is not so secure for fraying fabrics, but can be finished much narrower, as little as 2mm ($\frac{1}{8}$in) wide when finished if the fabric is fairly firm. A simple seam is machined, turnings cut away narrowly and zig-zagged together (photo no. 34). Some automatic machines have a stitch which does this seam in one operation.

Photo no. 34   Lingerie seam and picot edge

For attaching frills and flounces to a straight edge, a variation of the *mantua maker's seam* will seam and neaten in one operation. It is suitable for fine fabrics only. Press down, on RS of garment piece, a small turning 2–3mm ($\frac{1}{8}$in) wide. With RS frill and garment together, pin and tack on fitting line. Trim frill turnings to 5mm ($\frac{1}{4}$in) (figure 132 (a)). Bring folded edge down over frill turnings and pin it exactly on the tacked fitting line, (figure 132 (b)). Machine on fitting line through all thickness, removing pins as you go, take out tackings and press turning toward garment.

Conspicuous or decorative seams

Overlaid or lapped seam   This is a simple seam to make and shows the machine stitching on the right side. It is commonly used on yokes and for centre front button bands. The seam allowance on the top piece is turned under and pressed before applying

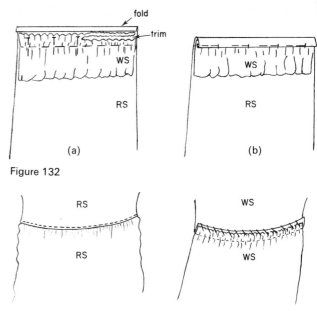

Figure 132

Figure 133   overlaid seam

it to the under piece, and when done on straight lines is a suitable seam for stitching without tacking. It is not suitable for heavy fabrics as both edges must be neatened together and frequently the lower edge is gathered, (figure 133). If desired a second row of topstitching may be added to give a mock double-stitched seam effect.

Where the top portion is curved it must be notched to remove the excess turning or clipped to allow the turning to spread as required. The process is the same as in the treatment of turnings in curved simple seams (figure 129), the actual fold line having been lightly pressed under with the point of the iron first. Inside corners must be reinforced and snipped (page 83) and overlapping turnings trimmed by mitring, (figure 117, corner (ii)).

The overlaid seam is frequently decorated by the insertion of lace, ric-rac or other trimming between the two layers, (photo no. 54).

Tucked seam   This is a variation of the overlaid seam, where the stitching is done further away from the folded edge to give a tuck or flap of fabric. Five to 10mm ($\frac{1}{4}$–$\frac{3}{8}$in) is the most usual distance, although it is entirely a matter of personal taste. The principles of preparing the top portion are the same as the overlaid seam, except that if the top has deep curves or sharp corners it will require to be faced with a shaped facing of garment material (if thin) or lining fabric (if thicker) before being applied to the under portion. For this reason tucked seams are usually reserved for straight or nearly straight lines. The top portion requires extra seam allowance to allow for tuck and turnings (figure 134).

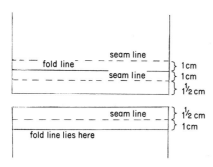

Figure 134   Cutting the allowances for a 1cm tucked seam

The welt seam   This is a very effective top-stitched seam used to best effect on tailored garments and in thicker materials to give it the necessary padded look, and appears at its best on self-coloured fabrics. To heighten the effect it may be stitched with button-hole thread. Figure 135 (a) shows the first line of machining, as for a plain seam, with one layer being trimmed away 1–2mm ($\frac{1}{8}$in) shorter than the finished width of the welt. The longer edge should be neatened as appropriate for thick fabrics. This edge is then pressed over the short edge, covering it. To prevent an unsightly 'pull' on the completed seam, it should be tacked firmly down before machining, (figure 135 (b)). Possible variations on the welt seam are to pad the seam further by pulling through stands of knitting wool or to add another row of topstitching close to the seam line, making it a 'double welt' seam, (figure 136). The long turning of the welt seam is usually turned away from the sleeve at an armhole, upwards on yoke lines, towards the front on a shoulder or side seam and towards the centre back or front on panels.

The double-stitched seam is often used on sports or casual garments, where it lies flat and has a tailored look. Fine or medium-weight materials are suitable. It is worked entirely on the right side. Figure 137 (a) shows the first stitching, trimming and pressing of the two edges, and (b) the finished seam. The seam is often marred by bad pressing at the intermediate stage and care must be taken to get both right and wrong sides pressed flat before adding the second stitching line.

The flat-felled seam is worked the same as the double stitched seam, but from the wrong side and shows only one line of topstitching on the right side. It is

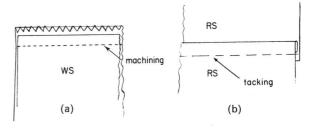

Figure 135

Figure 136   Double welt seam

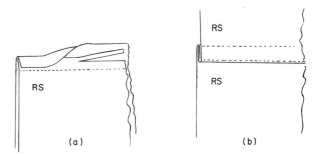

Figure 137   Double stitched seam

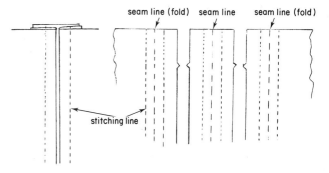

Figure 138   Cutting a straight channel seam

used for casual shirts, skirts and trousers. Both these seams are especially useful for garments that must be frequently laundered as the pressing of the seams is simple and the turnings, being completely enclosed, cannot fray with wear or washing.

Piped and corded seams are variations of the plain seam and are dealt with under decorative processes (chapter 22).

Channel seams have been one of fashion's favourites for many years, and constantly recur in the fashion cycle. They must be carefully planned as extra turnings are required and sufficient extra fabric is required for the strip, (figure 138). A curved channel seam, like a curved tucked seam, requires a shaped facing for the edges of the main pieces, and a shaped piece for the strip. This can use more fabric than one would at first think and must be planned for. Figure 139 illustrates how to cut the facing patterns for the two front panels of the blouse and figure 140 shows the seam line of the centre front panel traced off and the appropriate widths for the strip and its turnings added.

Figure 141   Grading the seam

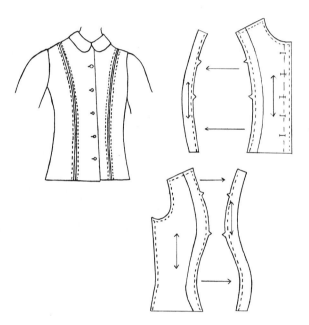

Figure 139   Cutting facings for a curved channel seam

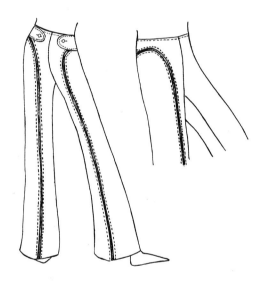

Figure 142   Channel seams on a pair of trousers

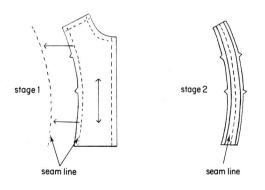

Figure 140   Cutting the strip for a curved channel seam

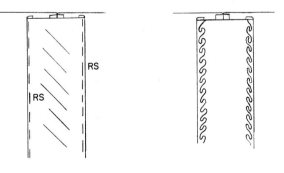

Figure 143   Preparation of the strap seam

Figure 144   Decorative strap seam

After cutting the strip, the seam line must be carefully trace-tacked. The panel sections are faced, care being taken to grade turnings and snip or notch as required and to press correctly (see chapter 23). The faced sections are applied to the seam line on the strip, pinned at right angles to it, tacked and machined. The turnings of the strip and facing might have to be graded before neatening (figure 141) as the seam tends to be thick and somewhat stiff. Figure 142 and photo nos. 35 and 36 show a design for a pair of trousers and the right and wrong sides of the completed channel seam.

The strap seam is stitched on the right side and the turnings trimmed and pressed open. There is no need to neaten them as the strap is applied over the top. The strap may be cut from a contrasting fabric or the same fabric on the regular or cross grain. It is basted on top of the seam (figure 143) and the edges turned under and tacked down before topstitching into place. The topstitching may be done on the edge or further in to give a tucked effect. Variations include topstitching with a decorative machine stitch (figure 144) or the use of woven braid for the strap.

Decorative seams are also discussed in chapter 22.

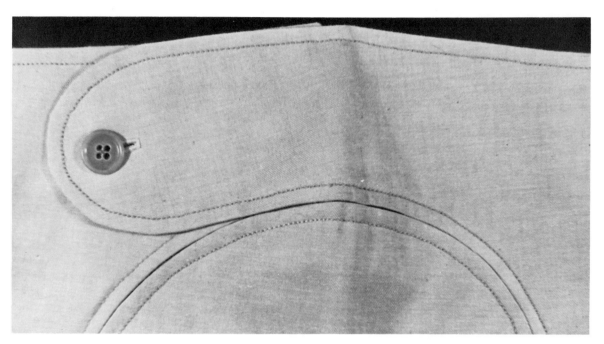

Photo no. 35

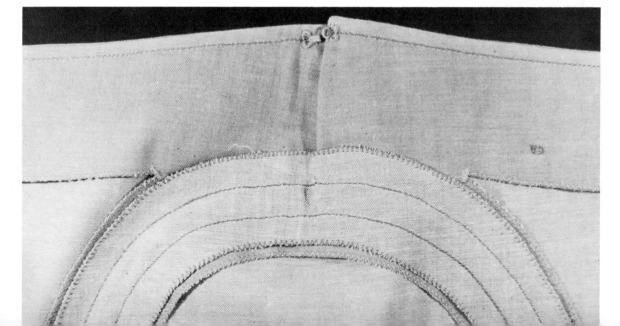

Photo no. 36

12   Facings and Bindings

The purposes of facings are to neaten edges invisibly, give support and body to the garment, and create an even, firm line at the edge. Decorative facings also perform all these functions, except, of course, that they are not invisible, adding to the style of the garment.

A good facing lies flat to the garment and keeps the garment flat to the wearer. It shows no sign of bulk (if the garment fabric is bulky the facing may be of another fabric complementary to it). The fold edge is smooth and does not roll to the RS nor show the edge seam. Facing seams match garment seams and are of even depth all the way round. The free edge must be secured sufficiently to keep it in position but without stitches showing or the imprint of it pressed through to the right side.

Facings are of three types, extended, shaped and bias.

Extended facings are only found where the edge is on straight grain and occur principally at the CF and CB or on wrap edges. Their advantage is the lack of bulk through having no joining seam. Hems are really extended facings.

Shaped facings are cut to the same shape as the garment and are about 6cm (2½in) wide. A pattern is required to cut them and to hold firm they must be cut on the same grain as the garment.

Bias facings are less common but have many advantages. They consist of a straight strip of fabric no wider than 2·5cm (1in) cut on the true cross, and sometimes therefore require less fabric than shaped facings. They are flatter, having only one joining seam and no outside edge to neaten. They are flexible and should be moulded into the required shape by steam pressing before mounting. It is simpler to ease a slightly loose edge into them than into a shaped facing, and for this reason they are a good choice for wide necklines. They cannot, however, be used in all circumstances, as they will only mould to gentle curves such as wide necklines and sleeve hems – they do not fit armscyes well.

At this point it is essential to banish any doubt which may remain over the difference between a facing and a binding. A facing lies flat when in position and can be seen from one side only. A binding doubles over an edge to both sides. This is why the hem finish illustrated in chapter 20, figure 274 is correctly called a 'faced hem', not a 'bound hem'. Students sometimes get confused over this.

Cutting a pattern for a shaped facing

There are two reasons why it is essential to know how to cut shaped facings. Firstly if you are altering the style, say making a garment sleeveless, collarless or skirt on a facing instead of a waistband, there will be no facing pattern for you to use. Secondly, if you have made fitting alterations affecting faced edges, for example at the shoulder seams, your facing pattern will no longer fit the garment. This is why, when in doubt, it is better not to cut facings until after first fitting.

Figure 145 shows the principles involved where there are darts. Remove the pattern seam allowances, draw in the facing line 6cm (2½in) from the edge, parallel to the edge, trace off to another piece of paper, fold out the darts (there are no darts in facings), pin to another piece of paper, blend the lines smoothly and reverse the pattern.

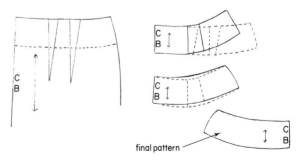

final pattern

Figure 145   Cutting a shaped facing pattern

Figure 146 illustrates the principles where seams enter the facing edge. Follow the principles above, finally fitting the panel seams together on the facing, in order to cut it with no unnecessary seams.

Where a pattern is altered to include wrap opening for buttons and buttonholes at the CF, the method of calculating the stand is given on page 23. Remember that the facing is cut the width of the stand *plus* the standard 6cm on the non-stand side of the CF (figure 147).

If you need to cut new facing patterns because you have altered the garment fitting, remember to alter the garment pattern to show the alteration and cut a new facing pattern as in the method above by tracing off on the altered pattern.

General method for applying shaped facings

(1) Complete (i.e. trim, clip, notch, grade, press) all contributory seams.

(2) Join facing seams, making facing a little smaller than garment by stitching inside seam lines 2–5mm, the bigger amount for thicker fabrics and longer edges, e.g. waist finish. This is essential to allow facing to lie smoothly. Do not neaten facing seams, but trim to about 5mm and press open.

(3) Neaten outside edge according to fabric (probably the same as your open seams). Press.

(4) Matching seams and balance marks first, pin at right angles to edge. Unless there are complications with easing, stay tape, etc. machine in on pins.

(5) Trim edges to about 5mm ($\frac{1}{8}$in), interfacing to stitching, grade turnings on thick fabric, notch or clip curves according to the principles for curved seams, mitre crossing seams. Press stitches into the work without giving direction (figure 148).

(6) Turn facing to WS and understitch by machine if possible, catching turnings in with facing (figure 149). If the shape does not allow of machine understitching all the way, it can be completed by hand, working from the facing side.

(7) If the fabric is springy, tack the facing firmly in position around the fold before pressing. To remove basting marks, see page 159. While still warm mould with the fingers into position throughout facing depth.

(8) Attach outside edges very loosely to seams only, or to underlining. On some fabrics it is possible to work small *loose* running stitches

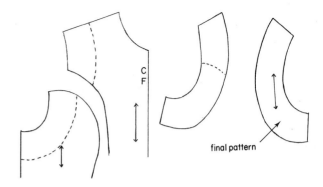

Figure 146 Cutting a shaped facing pattern

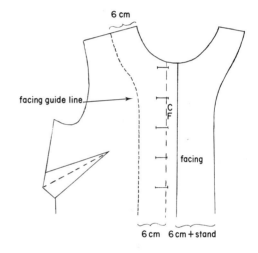

Figure 147 Cutting an extended facing for pattern with button stand

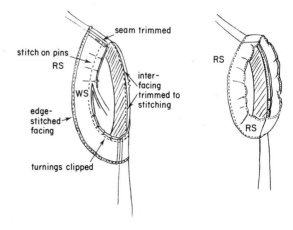

Figure 148 Applying a shaped facing

Figure 149 Hand or machine understitching

from the RS of the garment through the seam to catch the facing. Experiment to find if this is necessary or possible in a particular case.

Special procedures

(1) When applying bias strip facings, pin to garment edge and check the fit of the *outside* edge, if on a curve. To get a smooth fit, stretch the *fitting* edge on a convex curve and ease on a concave curve. Use the iron to help the moulding.

(2) Where ease on the edge must be firmly controlled and stay stitching or stay tape has been used on the garment, it is helpful to stay stitch the facing also before applying.

(3) Where another layer is sandwiched between garment and facing, do not stitch on pins. Attach the layer, e.g. a frill or collar, to the garment by machining with the layer on top. Then pin and tack the facing over the layer, turn work to WS and stitch over the same machining line again. This ensures a good line.

(4) Facings for revers are the exception to the rule about trimming the facing smaller. In revers the garment part is the under layer and this should be the smaller edge over the area which is turned back.

(5) When machining 'V' shaped slits, machine on facing and reinforce (page 83) before cutting the slit (figure 150). A common example is in faced CF neck openings.

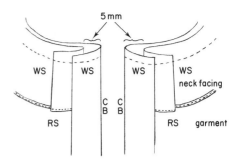

Figure 151   Applying CB neck facing for zip fastener opening (semi-concealed)

(7) Facings of intricate shape, e.g. for scalloped edges, are not cut to shape until after stitching. The best shape for scallops is the top one-third of a circle, flattened a little (figure 152 (a)). Measure the length of the edge to be scalloped, calculate the width of each scallop and using the curve of the facing pattern for a guide, mark out the scallops on tissue paper. Tack this to the tacked facing/garment edge, stitch through the lines and tear away the tissue. Cut the scallops and notch the curves to make them fit exactly into the scallop when turned (figure 152 (b)). Grade turnings before pressing facing to WS and finishing as usual.

(8) If unsure whether or not an already cut shaped facing will fit, pin the pieces, unjoined, to RS garment. Fold back turnings on top of garment seams and slip tack together (figure

Photo no. 37   Neck facing at CB zip opening, wrong side

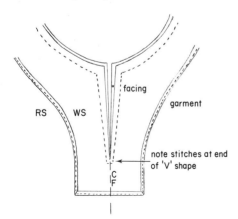

Figure 150   Faced slit opening

(6) An unusual method of dealing with the neck facing when inserting a CB zip is shown in photo no. 37. Figure 151 shows how to work this. The zip tapes are inserted under the facing fold and hemmed into place.

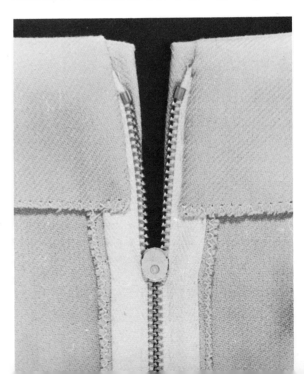

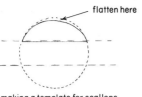

flatten here

(a) making a template for scallops

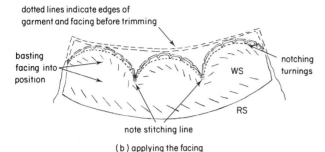

dotted lines indicate edges of
garment and facing before trimming

basting
facing into
position

notching
turnings

WS

RS

note stitching line

(b) applying the facing

Figure 152   Making a faced scalloped edge

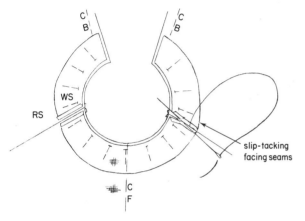

C
B

C
B

WS

RS

slip-tacking
facing seams

C
F

Figure 153   Checking the fit of a neck facing

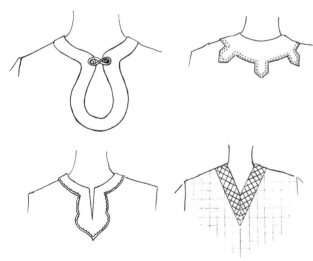

WS

Figure 154   Decorative neck facings

153). If necessary trim fitting edge to match
garment, and then outside edge of facing to
make it an even depth. Proceed as usual.

Decorative facings

Facings may be made decorative by attaching them
to the right side of the garment instead of the wrong
side. The outside edge may be topstitched into
position, slip-stitched by hand just underneath the
fold, or attached by hand or machine embroidery
stitch. The facings may be cut on a different grain for
effect, particularly with stripes or checks, be of a
contrasting fabric, embroidered or have a fancy
outside shape. The possibilities are endless and
some suggestions are sketched in figure 154. The
garment seams must be inverted under the facing for
a neat finish on the WS. Stitch them WS together from
the edge to within a few millimetres of the outside
edge of the facing, snip right through all turnings
and complete the seam RS together in the orthodox
manner (figure 155).

The bias strip facing can be made decorative by
stitching it on as an all-in-one facing and piping. It
needs to be cut wider than the 2·5cm (1in). Figure 156
shows how to fold and stitch it. The loose edge is then
turned to the WS as a normal facing.

WS

RS

Figure 155   Inverting shoulder seams for a right side
facing

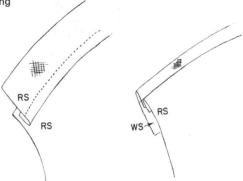

RS

RS

RS

RS

WS

Figure 156   All-in-one bias facing and piping
(measurements as desired)

Binding

A good binding is judged by its firm finish, smooth
and wrinkle-free on both edges. The joins are inconspicuous and on warp grain. No hemming shows on

the RS as it is done into the machine stitches or just above them. It must be cut very straight and on the true cross to prevent twisting, and the smooth set of it needs to be checked as each stage is worked, especially the hemming. This operation should not be attempted without careful pinning.

It is assumed that the reader knows the steps for joining crossway strips and applying a simple binding. The method for curves is the opposite to that for bias facings, that is, bindings are applied eased to convex curves and stretched to concave ones. All garment turnings are removed first.

Corners are a little more difficult and will be explained. The measurements given in the example may of course be adjusted for different widths. The outside corner (figure 157 (a)) has been bound 2cm ($\frac{3}{4}$in) wide with turnings of 0·5cm. Before starting trace out on paper the shape of the corner and the binding so that the difference in measurement between *a-b-c* and *d-e-f* may be measured. Cut binding on the true cross to the measurements:

Width = twice finished width plus 2 turnings
$$(2 + 2 + \tfrac{1}{2} + \tfrac{1}{2} = 5\text{cm})$$
Length = *a-b-c*, plus a little for safety.

Crease or trace tack the turnings on the binding. Measure along the centre of the binding the distance *a-b* and fold it back RS together. Machine or back stitch the corner shape an accurate 90°, ending at the turning each end. (If the binding was cut accurately the stitching will be along straight grains) (see figure 157 (b)). Trim off the corners and press the little turnings open as far as possible (figure 157 (c)). Place the binding to the edge RS together, matching the corner at *e* and pin (figure 157 (d)). Machine from *d* to *e* with the binding uppermost, leave the needle

down, raise the presser foot and pivot the corner, folding the binding corner out of the way, and complete machining to *f*. The binding is then turned on the centre line, folded to WS and hemmed in the usual way.

The method for an inside fold is similar (figure 158 (a)). Calculate the width of the bind as before and the length *d-e-f* plus a little. To make the corner, fold back level with point *e* and machine a corner of 90°. Trim and clip exactly as figure 158 (b). Press the little seams open. Apply the binding as for the outside corner, matching and pivoting at *e*. The inward corner of the garment edge should not be clipped. Complete as usual.

French binding (double binding)

In order to give the necessary stability to a sheer fabric, a double bind is sometimes used. Six thicknesses of binding result, so only very fine fabrics have this finish. It gives a firm solid appearance. Cut the binding six times the finished width, fold in half lengthwise to begin with and proceed as in figure 159.

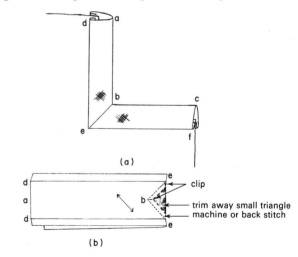

(a)

(b)

Figure 158　Binding an inside corner

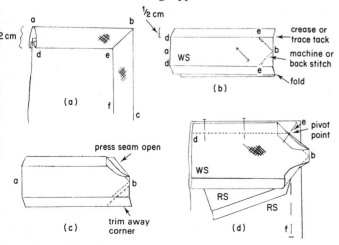

Figure 157　Binding an outside corner

Figure 159　Double or french binding

13　Openings

Certain principles govern the design, cutting and construction of garment openings. An understanding of these gives the dressmaker the opportunity to substitute one opening for another, if she wishes to add her own variety to a commercial pattern or to change the style. She is enabled to design for herself a small part of the garment or to construct the designer's style in the way best suited to the fabric. These principles are outlined below, the term 'opening' being used to mean either an overlap or meeting of two edges, such as would be fastened by buttons or buttonholes or a zip, or the cutting of a slit, such as in a long sleeve opening.

(1) Direction of overlap, if any, for ladies' fashions is right over left at either CF or CB (although the other way around is possible at CB), front over back for side and shoulder, front over back for sleeves.
(2) The opening must be long enough to pass over the appropriate part of the body without strain.
(3) The position of sleeve openings is traditionally on the back line, i.e. one quarter of the way across measuring from the back underarm seam (figure 160).
(4) In overlap openings to be fastened with buttons and buttonholes or other fastenings,

reinforce both sides with interfacing. Tape edges before inserting zips in bias seams or stretchy fabrics. (In firm fabrics the zip tape itself is enough.)
(5) In openings of the cut slit type, reinforce the bottom of the slit adequately, by one or more of the methods illustrated in figure 115 for 'slash-to-dot' seams.
(6) Openings should be as flat as possible – choose one with few layers for medium or heavy fabrics. Be especially careful not to create bulges or pucker at the base of openings. An unusual opening is best tried out first on a scrap of the garment fabric.
(7) All openings should be functional and should also fall into one of two classes – decorative or inconspicuous. If the opening is not a style feature of the garment, e.g. CB zip, sleeve opening, skirt placket, the aim is to make it as inconspicuous as possible by choosing the best method, If it is part of the style, e.g. some front neck or sleeve openings, aim to make it conspicuous and fitting in with the style, and possibly decorative. Often a decorative opening made instead of the purely functional one suggested in the pattern is all that is needed to give the garment its essential touch of individuality.

Slit openings

Basic slit openings include the faced, continuous strip, bound, wrap and facing, tailored shirt sleeve and shirt neck openings, the last two being the only true decorative ones, although the bound is usually chosen for its appearance because it matches a bound edge on another part of the garment.

The faced opening is shown in figure 150 and is suitable for all fabrics. The two edges meet when completed.

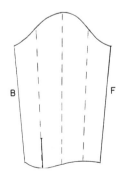

Figure 160　Position of sleeve opening

The continuous strip opening is firm and overlaps when finished. The strip firms the opening as it is cut on straight grain, but is most suitable for fine fabrics as there are many layers. The method of applying the strip to the cut (reinforced) slit is shown in figure 161 (a). Apply the strip without tacking first for better control. Machine from (i) to (ii), arriving exactly at the point, leave the needle down, raise the presser foot, pivot the work around and then lower the foot and machine to (iii). Finish the raw edge of the strip as for a binding. Press the strip to give a wrap which may be secured in position by machining as shown in figure 161 (b).

The bound opening is worked exactly as for the continuous strip, except that the binding is narrow and cut on the cross, making it suitable for delicate garments in sheer fraying fabrics.

The wrap and facing opening is suitable for all fabrics as it is less bulky than the continuous strip. It is worked as for a faced opening with the width of the facing greater on the underlay side than the overlap (figure 162 (a)). Before pressing, the facing is folded as in figure 162 (b) and may be stitched invisibly through the seam and/or across the pleat at the end with springy fabrics. The finished opening is shown in photo nos. 38 and 39.

The shirt sleeve opening for tailored, top-stitched styles is not bulky, but cannot be fastened in its length. Figure 163 illustrates the method:

(a) Make the pattern for the strip by drawing (solid lines) the finished trim, adding the underlay (shaded portion) which should be about 1cm ($\frac{1}{2}$in) narrower than the outside of the strip and level in length with the lower horizontal top-stitching line. Add 5mm ($\frac{1}{4}$in) turnings (dotted line).

(b) If wished, mark out the finished opening on the sleeve with trace tacking, but this is not really essential. The diagram shows the position of the slit in relation to the finished strip. Cut the slit at this stage, noting uneven measurements of the horizontal cut at the top.

(c) Turn to the ws and machine a double 5mm ($\frac{1}{4}$in) hem on the right side of the slit. Baste down turnings on long side and pointed end of the strip. Machine the underlay of the strip (5mm ($\frac{1}{4}$in) turnings) to the left of the slit, rs of strip to ws of sleeve.

(d) Turn strip through to the rs and press turnings as shown.

(e) Top stitch fold of strip as far as the lower topstitching line only.

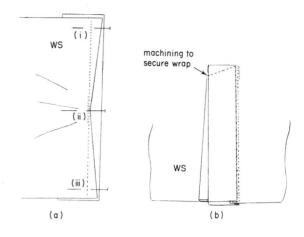

(a)   (b)

Figure 161   Continuous strip opening

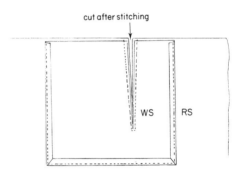

(a) applying the facing piece

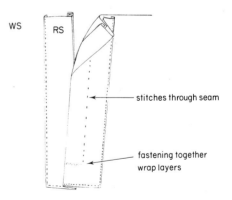

stitches through seam

fastening together
wrap layers

(b) folding and securing the wrap

Figure 162   Wrap and facing opening

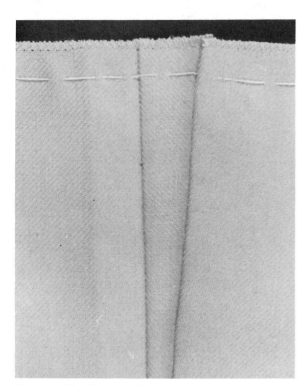

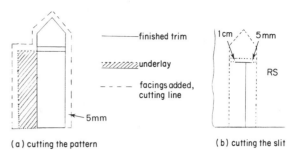

(a) cutting the pattern   (b) cutting the slit

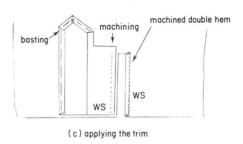

(c) applying the trim

Photo no. 38   Wrap and facing opening RS

Photo no. 39   Wrap and facing opening WS

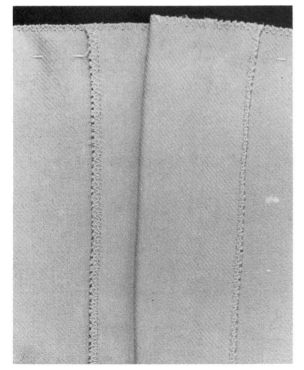

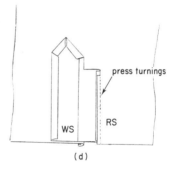

(d)

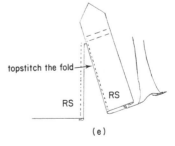

(e)

Figure 163   Shirt sleeve opening

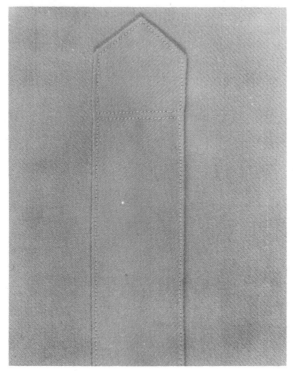

Photo no. 40   shirt sleeve opening RS

Photo no. 41   shirt sleeve opening WS

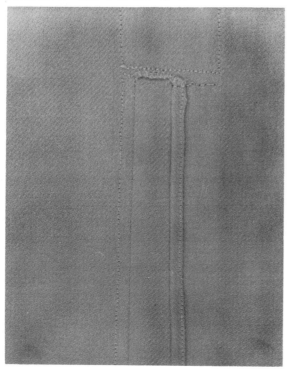

(f) Close the strip into position and topstitch all the other lines shown through all thicknesses. The RS of the opening is shown complete in photo no. 40.

(g) On WS complete by oversewing the remaining raw edge at the top of the slit, taking the stitches through to the underlayer of the strip for strength. See photo no. 41.

The tailored shirt neck opening   Figure 164 shows the finished opening mounted with a shirt collar right to the ends. This, or other collar style, is mounted by the appropriate method and instructions for doing this are not given here.

Figure 164   Tailored shirt neck opening

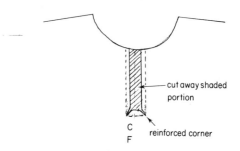

Figure 165   Cutting the opening

Figure 165 Mark out the opening on the garment neck (dotted line), re-inforce the corners with machine stitching and cut away the shaded portion. Snip corners.

Figure 166 Make the pattern for the opening. Take the basic shirt pattern cut to CF and re-move turnings. Pin this to paper, draw round, adding the strip (shaded portion) the same measurements as marked out on the garment. Fold the paper back on the line marked 'fold' and trace all markings through, extending the vertical lines down for a few cms. Draw out the cutting lines for the combined strip and facing as shown. Cut out. Reverse and re-cut in fresh paper, marking in the lines required. Cut from double fabric.

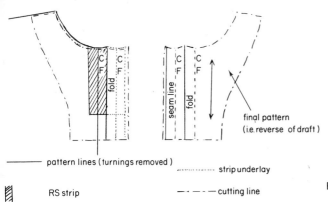

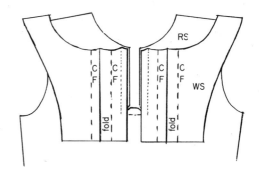

——— pattern lines (turnings removed)

·············· strip underlay

▨ RS strip

— · — — —cutting line

Figure 167 Stitching the facings to the slit

Figure 166 Cutting the combined strip/facing

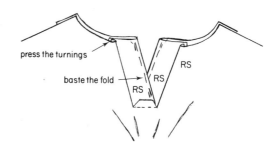

Figure 167 Stitch the facings to the sides of the garment slit, RS together.

Figure 168 Press the seam turnings as shown, fold the strips and arrange them roughly in position. Baste along the folds of the strips.

Figure 169 Arrange the right side strip over the left and tuck in the small flap at the base of the garment slit. Lift up the garment below the opening as shown to baste the lower layers of the facing together and machine the base of the opening through all layers of facings. This completes the right side of the opening.

Figure 170 On the WS, neaten all raw edges, grading turnings if necessary on bulky fabric.

Figure 168 Folding the facings into position

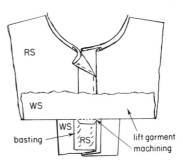

There are other methods of constructing this opening, but this is the least bulky, having the fewest layers of fabric at the lower end. Add a collar in the usual fashion for a faced neckline.

Figure 169 Completing the base

Front fastening openings

Several variations of the basic buttonhole opening are given, but many more can be devised to give variety.

The band opening for reversible fabric only is simply cut as figure 171 (a). Note that right and left sides are cut the same but folded differently. The interfacing is applied to the insides of the hems as shown. Buttonholes in band openings must be vertical to keep them central and should have two square ends if hand sewn.

Band openings for fabric with a right and wrong

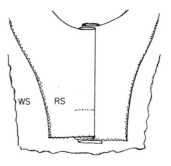

Figure 170 Completing the wrong side

side are more complicated. A separate band must be cut and applied as shown in figure 171 (b) for the right hand side with an all-in-one facing for the left hand side.

Alternatively the 'box pleat' opening makes a flat even opening provided it is cut as given here. (The method given in some books results in uneven layers.) For ease in calculation a band of 3cm is given, but this is adjustable, provided the proportions remain the same. Cut as in figure 172 (a); fold and topstitch as in figure 172 (b) so that the folded edge of the left-hand side exactly meets the fold of the tuck on the ws of the right-hand side, evening out the bulk. In photo no. 42 the trace tacking is the CF of the left hand side, i.e. the button line. This opening must be buttoned up and does not make satisfactory revers.

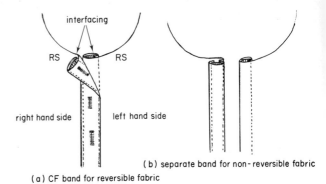

(a) CF band for reversible fabric

(b) separate band for non-reversible fabric

Figure 171   CF band openings

Photo no. 42   RS **box pleat** CF **opening**

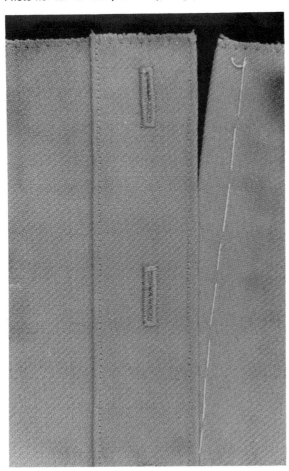

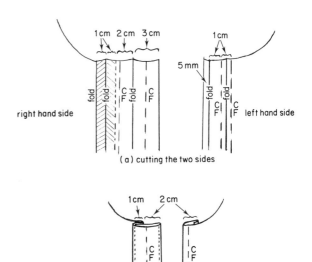

(a) cutting the two sides

(b) folding and stitching

Figure 172   Box pleat CF opening

The edge-to-edge opening for use with frog fastenings or fancy clips illustrated in figure 173 (a) is simply cut as in figure 173 (b) and stitched as in figure 173 (c). It includes an underlap and should be interfaced in a suitable way.

The centre front extension opening is illustrated in figures 174–8. Photo no. 43 shows the completed opening with optional bar tack at base and CF trace tack.

Figure 174 Cut both sides the same, reinforce and slash the inside corners (i) and slash the lower turning at (ii) on the right hand side

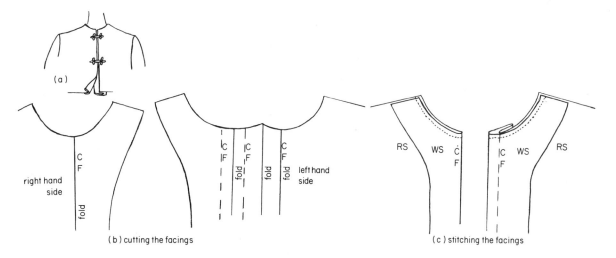

(a)

right hand
side

C
F

fold

(b) cutting the facings

C
F

C
F

C
F

fold

fold

fold

left hand
side

RS   WS   C
F

WS   RS

C
F

(c) stitching the facings

Figure 173   Edge to edge opening with underlap

Photo no. 43   Completed extension opening

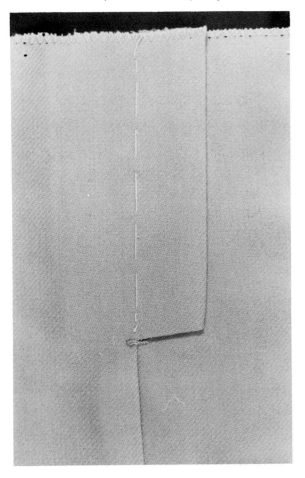

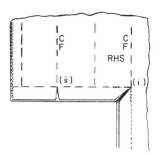

Figure 174   Extension opening: cutting, reinforcing,
slashing, seaming, neatening

Figure 175   Baste

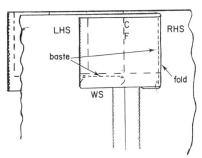

only. Neaten the raw edge of the facing
and join the CF seam below the opening.
Figure 175 Press open the seam and neaten. Fold the
left hand side extension back upon itself
and baste as shown.

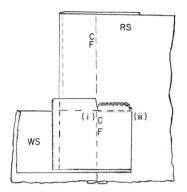

Figure 176

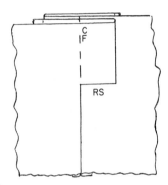

Figure 177

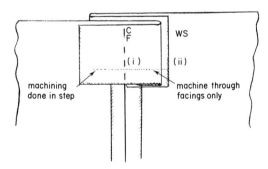

Figure 178

Figure 176 Turn the work to the RS, fold the right extension under on itself. Fold it down towards you and machine through all thicknesses from (i) to (iii). Trim and neaten through all thicknesses.

Figure 177 Fold the opening back up into position and press. The right side of the work is now complete.

Figure 178 Complete the ws by machining through the three thicknesses of facings from (i) to (ii) by raising them up to work. Do not stitch through to RS garment. Neaten all raw edges.

This is the flattest method of constructing the extension opening, making it suitable for all fabrics.

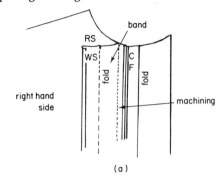

Figure 179   Fly fastening with added band

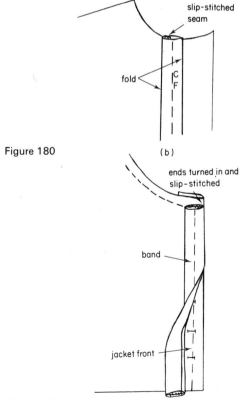

Figure 180

Figure 181

Fly openings

There are a number of ways of cutting and constructing these, all of which are adaptable from a regular front opening pattern.

The jacket shown in photo no. 65 has a simple band added to make the fly. The band was cut twice the finished width plus turnings and machined RS down to the jacket front as shown in figure 179 before the facing was fixed. Figure 180 shows how the band was pressed, the edges turned in on one another and slip-stitched together by hand, the seam coming well underneath on the fly. The raw edges at top and bottom of the fly band were folded in on to each other and slip-stitched (figure 181), the jacket facing being fixed in the normal way afterwards.

A simple band fly suitable for a skirt is shown in figure 182. The band is cut to include the facing. The left side is of course cut in the normal way with an all-in-one facing. All layers enter the waistband together at the top.

A CF fly opening with zip fastening is shown in figure 183. This is simply cut, because the right front, fly and facing are cut in one piece with the pattern adaptation shown in figure 184. The opening is folded and stitched as in figure 185. Turn and press the facing and top stitch through all thicknesses. The left hand side has an all-in-one facing, folding back exactly on the CF.

The type of fly seen in photo no. 44 looks like a regular opening, having no topstitching. It is suitable for a CF opening, being fastened with buttons and buttonholes, and a press stud could be added at the neck. At the lower end (waist or empire seam) all the layers would join together in the seam. Figure 186 shows how to adapt a regular shirt waist pattern for this opening, the shaded area being the addition for the fly. The facing is shown cut separately, but may in fact be cut all-in-one. The stitching is shown in figure 187. When stitched and turned, simply tuck the fly back into position between garment and facing.

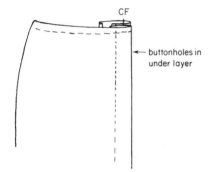

Figure 182   Fly fastening for a skirt

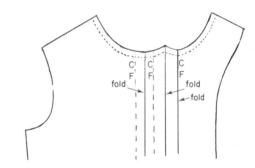

Figure 184   Cutting the right hand side

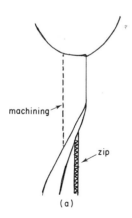

Figure 183   Fly opening with zip

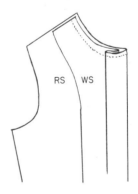

Figure 185   Stitching the right hand side

Photo no. 44   Completed centre fly opening

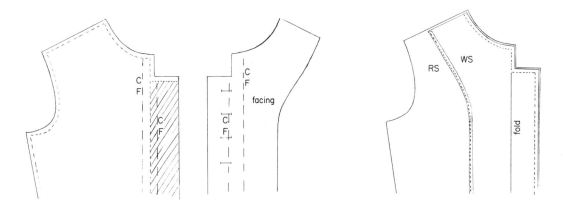

Figure 186   Centre fly opening with no top stitching
(button fastening):

Figure 187   Stitching the fly and facing

Slits and vents

Slits and vents are simple to construct but it is extremely important that they should be well-strengthened to prevent tearing, and well-supported to prevent sagging. Some examples illustrate this point.

Side seam slits   The most satisfactory way to support side seam slits in skirts is to cut the seam with the extra width all the way up as this does away with the need for topstitching at the top of the slit. The seam should be reinforced at this point by inserting a small piece of interfacing as for the top of a pleat or by a bar tack or arrowhead worked on the RS afterwards. The folds of the slit should have a strip of tailor's linen or tape inside. Note figure 188 showing the skirt hem turned before the slit is completed.

sitting, usually to the CB of a skirt, when tight skirts are in fashion. It is better than a kick or inverted pleat as it tends to hang straighter and more closed when the wearer is standing still and does not constantly have to be pressed to keep it sharp. Construct a normal slit seam as described above, then fold a piece of fabric double, WS together, neaten the edges (fold for the hem) and apply as in figure 190, stitching either through turnings only or topstitching through all thicknesses as desired. Add a bar tack or arrowhead if liked.

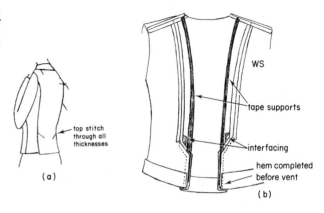

Figure 189   Jacket vents

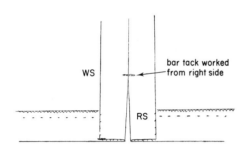

Figure 188   Side seam slit for skirt

Jacket vents (figure 189) should be reinforced as above and are usually supported by diagonal topstitching through all thicknesses (a). If this is not desired, the only solution is to tape the vent into position at the jacket shoulder or neckline (b). It is not a good idea to cut the extra width on the seam all the way up as in a skirt slit, as the bulk shows through in a one-sided way on a jacket vent. Again the hem will be fixed before the vent is completed.

The Dior pleat, invented by the designer whose name it bears, is a method of adding ease for walking and

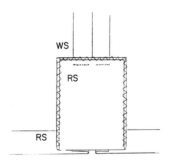

Figure 190   Dior pleat

14 Fastenings

Zip fasteners

To give sufficient strength without overweighting a garment it is important to choose the right type and weight of zip for the particular purpose. It must be long enough to avoid strain on the zip. Clothing zips are made in several weights, the strongest for jeans and trousers, and the lightest for lingerie and knitwear. Avoid the type with a spiral closure, as these are not strong. Zip teeth are made from metal, polyester or nylon and the tapes from cotton or polyester. Choose mainly according to weight of zip, but bear in mind also that the nylon or polyester ones are flexible and most suitable for knitwear and garments which do not require ironing. Do not use them if a hot iron is required for the garment fabric. Special zips include the concealed or invisible type for places where the zip should not show at all, and the open-end, which also comes in several weights, for jackets. Aero Zipps will manufacture 'specials' on a one-off basis for customers' individual requirements.

Photo no. 45   Zip – semi-concealed setting
Photo no. 46   Concealed setting zip

Basic settings

It is assumed that the three basic zip settings (concealed, semi-concealed and visible) are already mastered by the reader. A few refinements in technique are none the less valuable.

(1) Prepare the opening well first by neatening the raw edge and pressing the turnings to the ws to give a firm fold, as it is not possible to press them so well after the zip is inserted. On stretchy or bias fabrics, tape this fold.

(2) Machine in the zip without tacking if possible as the fingers then have full control of the process. The semi-concealed setting in striped fabric in photo no. 45 was worked entirely without tacking, by stitching both sides from the bottom up, while manipulating the zip and the fabric. The concealed setting in photo no. 46 was also worked without tacking. The back view of this zip is shown in photo no. 47. It has a shield to prevent lingerie catching.

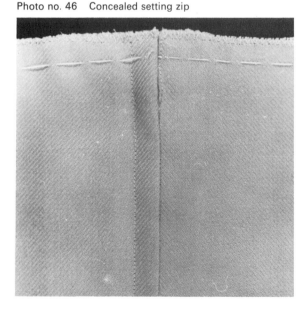

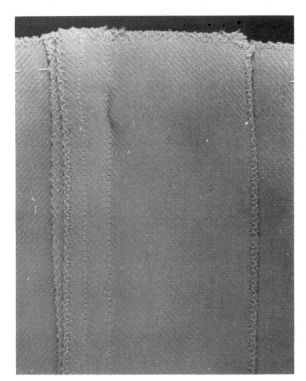

Photo no. 47 Concealed setting zip

Photo no. 48 Hand sewn zip

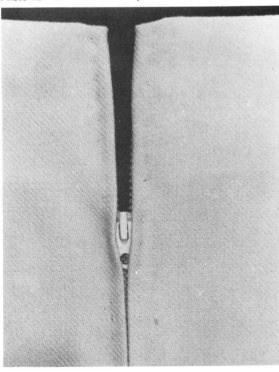

(3) If, because of the springy or slippery nature of the fabric, it is not possible to work without tacking, experiment with sticky tape instead. If it does not mark the fabric when peeled away it provides a better temporary fixing than basting, as it is flatter. Do not machine over the tape.

(4) Unless machine stitching is particularly desired for appearance or extra strength, semi-concealed and concealed zips in fashion garments are better sewn in by hand. No tacking is necessary as the work can be held firmly in the hand while being stitched. Work from the bottom up with the zip closed. The stitch is stab-stitch or pickstitch, illustrated in figure 291. Photo no. 48 shows a hand-sewn semi-concealed setting, the stitches of which are almost invisible as the fabric is of medium thickness and slightly textured. (This is the right side view of photo no. 37.) A buttonholed bar is worked at the bottom for strength, but this is a matter of personal taste. Hand-sewing is also called for on fabrics with large contrasting coloured patterns, when the sewing thread should match the predominant colour, or for absolute invisibility, several different colours are used in the zip length, according to the pattern of the fabric.

(5) If a machined setting is required on a difficult fabric a good method is to prepare the opening and machine the turnings back (both sides for the semi-concealed, overlapping side only for the concealed) before inserting the zip, to give the appearance of the finished opening. The zip is then stab-stitched invisibly by working over the machine stitches again, or it may be machined in exactly on top of the first row. In the concealed setting the zip will first have to be machined in on the underlay side as usual – no tacking necessary – before restitching the overlapping side.

(6) Confusion sometimes arises over the position of the zip in the concealed setting, as one edge must overlap the other. Figures 191–5 clarify the procedure. (For the purposes of clarity the optional reinforcing tape, shield and bar tack are omitted.)

Figure 191 Press or tack down the overlapping edge in the usual way, but on the underlay side trace tack the seam line but do not press back.

Figure 192 On ws, snip the underlay turning as shown to 3mm ($\frac{1}{8}$in) from the seam line. Neaten the raw edges of the slit.

Figure 193 Make the underlay fold from the end of the slit up the length of the opening 3mm ($\frac{1}{8}$in) from the seam line. Press or tack.

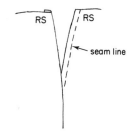

Figure 191　Zip fastener, concealed setting

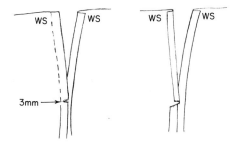

Figure 192　　　　　Figure 193

Figure 194 Holding the overlapping side clear and keeping the zip closed, machine the underlay fold from bottom to top as closely as possible to the zip teeth.

Figure 195 Without tacking, machine the bottom line and up the overlapping side, holding the folded edge to meet the seam line exactly on the other side.

(7) A visible setting may be made more decorative, possibly for a front neck opening, by the addition of braid, the whole topstitched into position (figure 196).

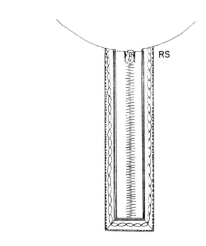

Figure 196　Decorative visible zip fastener

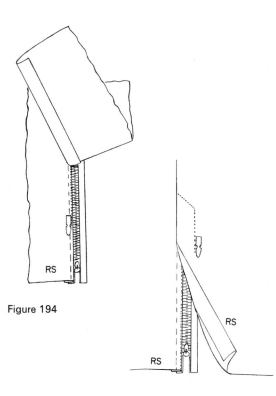

Figure 194

Figure 195

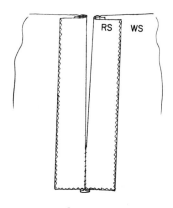

Figure 197　Preparing a buttonhole opening for a zip fastener without a seam

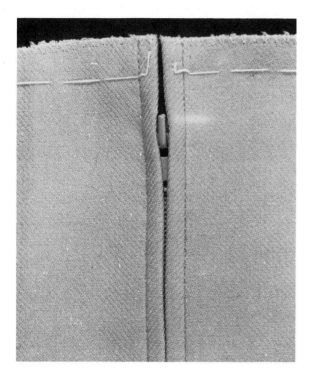

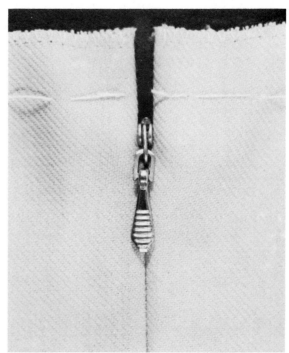

Photo no. 49   Bound buttonhole type zip opening

Photo no. 50   Invisible zip

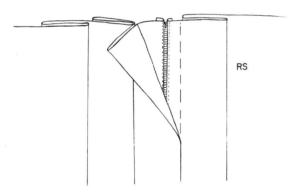

Figure 198   Position of seam and zip opening among continuous knife pleats

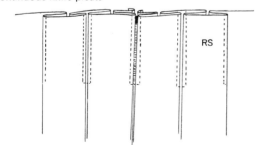

Figure 199   Seam and zip opening among continuous box pleats

Special settings

Without a seam   Where a zip must be set without a seam an opening must be constructed. The most usual is the faced opening, but a bound buttonhole opening (photo no. 49) is more decorative. The facing is applied, cut and turned exactly as for a bound buttonhole (figure 197), and the zip stab or machine-stitched into place from the RS through the seams so that the stitching is inconspicuous.

Zips behind pleats must be placed so as not to disturb the regularity of the pleating. In some cases the pleat is folded over the zip after it is done up. Note that not all such zips are inserted in seams. Two suggestions for arranging zip openings in pleats are sketched in figures 198 and 199.

Inserting concealed ('invisible') zips   These may be inserted by means of the zip or piping foot, but are much simpler with the special inexpensive plastic foot, adaptable to all modern machines by means of a variety of shanks supplied with it. Full instructions are not given here since they are supplied with the foot and are not difficult to follow. It is of interest to note, however, that the fastener gives an opening 2·5cm (1in) less than its length and is inserted *before* the seam is completed, calling for great accuracy in the marking out of the seam lines. The zip does not show at all (photo no. 50) and is therefore obtainable in a very limited colour range. It is an excellent closure for places where zips must be inconspicuous, especially for garments in patterned fabric, where the opening becomes virtually invisible.

Buttons and buttonholes

Types of buttonholes in common use are the hand-worked, machine-worked, tailor's worked, bound and piped, all of which may have a cord or gimp inserted to strengthen them or emphasize them for style purposes. Button loops may be worked by hand or made from cord or round or flat rouleau. It is not proposed to explain them all in detail since the reader will be familiar and experienced with most, but additional advice is given for improving technique and simplifying methods. The piped buttonhole alone will be dealt with in detail since it is not commonly known and used and ought to be.

Positioning and marking

The position of buttonholes on a front opening is shown in figure 17. To mark them equally, trace tack on straight grain two vertical lines for the ends of the buttonholes and divide across with equidistant horizontal lines (figure 200). An alternative method for worked or machined buttonholes is to leave the marking until the garment is nearing completion and then do it with strips of sticky tape, providing this does not mark the fabric. This is quick and straight, but care must be taken not to place the tape so that it will get sewn in with the stitching.

For button loops, no stand at all is added to the right side of the garment but a small stand (1–2cm, ½in) is required on the left, (figure 201). If loops have spaces between they should be marked out on the garment, but if they are continuous the best method is to form them on paper (see later) having marked this instead.

Buttons are stitched on the CF line for either buttonholes or loops.

Working a tailor's buttonhole

Hand worked buttonholes will be familiar to the reader, but possibly not the variation needed to make a tailor's buttonhole. A very small hole is cut at the round end to accommodate the button shank or, on some fabrics, it may be simply formed without cutting by working a stiletto up and down. The entire buttonhole should be worked with waxed thread with the insertion of a gimp, and at the end

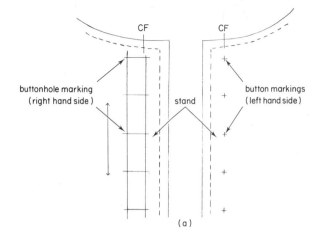

Figure 200   Marking buttonholes and buttons

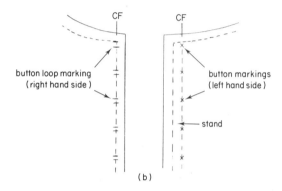

Figure 201   Marking button loops

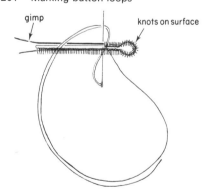

Figure 202   Tailor's buttonhole

Figure 203   Cutting a machined buttonhole

with the hole the knots of the stitches are formed on the surface rather than the edge (figure 202).

Machine buttonholes

A machine buttonhole is worked according to the directions given with each individual machine and usually these include directions for cording also. Machine buttonholes must be stabilized by a piece of firm fine interfacing e.g. organdie, and are improved if they are worked with a slightly loosened upper tension and a very fine thread, say Machine Embroidery 50. It is often better to work round twice with a fairly open stitch than once with a very closed one. An excellent finish can be obtained by working a hand buttonhole over a fairly open machine one. This is especially good for fraying and loose weave fabrics. If a thicker buttonhole is required a buttonhole thread may be wound on the bobbin and the buttonhole worked from the wrong side, but tests have to be made to ascertain the correct stitch length and tension for the fabric. Another version of the machine buttonhole is to replace the zig-zag stitch by the overlock (figure 331 (e)) or the elastic blind hem, (figure 331 (c)) for stretch or knitted fabrics, particularly coarse ones.

When cutting machine buttonholes with the 'unpicker' type of cutter, a pin placed across the ends prevents mishaps (figure 203).

Piped buttonholes

These look like bound buttonholes, but are rather easier to make on all but fraying fabrics and particularly simple to cord, although they are a little more bulky. The steps are shown in figures 204–209.

Figure 204 Mark out each buttonhole (abcd).

Figure 205 Cut piping on true bias or straight grain in one long piece, length sufficient to make for each buttonhole twice its length plus 6cm (2½in), width 3–4cm (1¼–1½in). Insert cord if required and machine the strips, the distance between the machining and the fold being half the total width of the marked buttonhole. Cut piping into pieces, each the length of the buttonhole plus 3cm (1¼in).

Figure 206 Apply one strip to the right side of the garment with the machining on the piping exactly over the trace tacking, and machine very accurately from a to b, tying off the ends or sewing them in on the ws. Do not reverse stitch as this will harden the line. Then apply a second strip c–d.

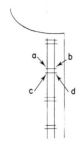

Figure 204   Marking a piped buttonhole:

Figure 205   Making corded piping

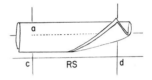

Figure 206   Machining first strip

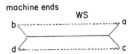

Figure 207   Cutting the buttonhole slit

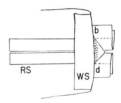

Figure 208   Stitching the ends

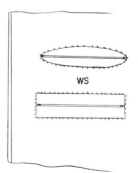

Figure 209   Finishing the facing – two methods

Figure 207 From ws cut the buttonhole slit through the garment (and interfacing) only.

Figure 208 Turn the piping through. Stitch the buttonhole ends at the base of the small triangle through to the piping, back and forth two or three times. If corded, the cord may be cut away level with the end of the buttonhole to reduce bulk. (Unpick the machining on the piping to do this.)

Figure 209 Complete as for a bound buttonhole, trimming and grading the turnings of the piping first. Choose either the curved or rectangular finish for the facing according to appearance, thickness of fabric, and personal taste.

Button loops

If these are to be continuous or very nearly so, accuracy is especially important. Mark out the positions on a strip of typing paper (figure 210). Loops look best if the height a–b is about equivalent to the width c–d. The width may be more but not less than the height if the loops are to sit well. Make a long rouleau strip (flat or round) and turn, pressing the seam slightly to one side, or take a length of cord for the loops. Cut into equal pieces by measuring the length required from the paper.

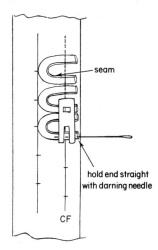

Figure 211   Forming the loops on paper

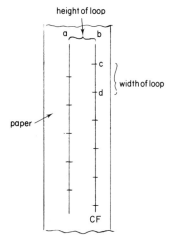

Figure 210   Marking out on paper

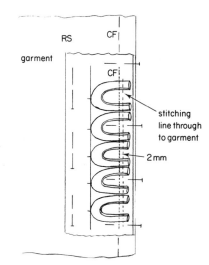

Figure 212   Stitching loops to garment

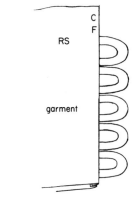

Figure 213   Facing completed

Figure 211 shows how to stitch the loops to the paper (note the position of the loop seam). This is much more easily done without tacking by stitching the first end, stopping with the needle down, lifting the foot to arrange the loop to fit the space marked, and stitching over the second end. Keep the ends at right angles to the marked CF line by adjusting with the point of a darning needle as they pass under the machine foot.

Place the paper with the loops attached over the RS garment, matching CFs, pin and stitch about 2mm in from the CF line, (figure 212). Tear away the paper. Finally, baste on the facing, turn the work to the WS and restitch on CF line (i.e. exactly over the machining which fixed the loops to the paper.) Trim, grade, turn and press (figure 213).

This method is quick as it avoids much tedious basting and is firm for closely trimmed edges, having three lines of machining.

Other fastenings

Press studs – silver, black or transparent. Use as small a size as possible and attach with buttonhole stitch (figure 214 (a)) for strength and flatness. Transparent ones are used where they must sometimes be left open and would show. An alternative, if the garment fabric is fine, is to cover the metal ones. Cut a circle of fabric a little more than twice the diameter of the stud and run a gathering thread round the edge. Place the stud in the middle, draw up and fasten off on the side which will be attached to the garment (figure 214 (b)). Ease the ball gently through the fabric and work it into the socket.

Hooks and eyes Eyes are of two types, bars for overlapping edges and loops for meeting ones (figure 215). Sew on with buttonhole stitch, with straight-over stitching to stabilize. For high-class work, substitute the metal bar with a button-holed one and/or cover the hook with interlacing stitches as shown in figure 216.

Eyelet holes and lacing Make eyelet holes by pushing a stiletto through from the RS. Do not cut fabric away. Overcast the edges tightly to make them firm or place in a metal eyelet with a special tool.

Touch-and-close fastening – known as 'Velcro' – was invented by a Swiss who was fascinated by plant burrs. It is not very suitable for dressmaking as it is bulky, and adjustable fastenings are seldom required except in maternity wear.

Frog fastenings Can be made out of rouleau or cord in a whole range of designs. The design is best drawn out on transparent paper (not tissue) and the rouleau pinned on. By turning the paper over it is easy to see where to oversew the cord together. Tear away the paper before attaching the frog to the garment.

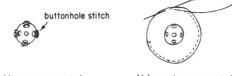

(a) stitching on a press stud   (b) covering a press stud

Figure 214   Using press studs

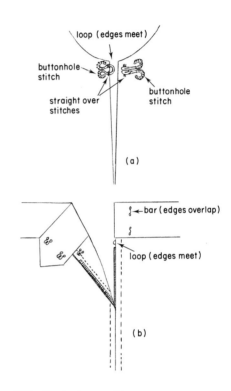

Figure 215   Hooks, bars and loops

Figure 216   Covering a hook with thread

15 Sleeves

The cap sleeve

Since it is merely an extension of the bodice, the cap sleeve is the easiest of all the sleeves to construct, neither is it difficult to adapt a bodice pattern to cut it. The adaptation is given in figure 217.

(1) Mark points A and B 1cm above back and front shoulder points. This gives the necessary ease for movement. Join these points to neck point and extend lines for 8cm (3in) to C and D.

(2) Drop 1cm from C and D to E and F. Join A–E and extend for about 10cm (4in). Repeat with B–F–extend.

(3) Drop underarm points 1cm to G and H.

(4) Using a set square construct lines from G and H to meet the new shoulder lines drawn in (2) at right angles. This forms the basic cap sleeve and is labelled no. 3.

Higher and lower adaptations are shown as numbers 1, 2 and 4, and are spaced for convenience at 4cm (1½in) intervals, but any variation in length may be used. Note that for a smooth line at the shoulder seam the hem should meet the shoulder line at right angles and lines 1 and 2 have been curved round a

little at the top for this reason. Sleeve no 4 is curved at the underarm to give a smoother line. Shoulder seams should be measured to see that back and front fit. It is simple to make small adjustments if necessary.

There are no problems with ease, fitting or bulk, so this style is suitable for all fabrics and looks well in casual clothes. The hem requires a facing.

The set-in sleeve

Most of the problems which arise in setting in a plain sleeve are due to the sleeve head and armhole not being properly prepared and checked first. Frequently an error is made when long sleeve patterns are shortened for use as short sleeves, because after cutting off the length, the sleeve may be too wide at the hem. Attempts to remedy the situation by taking in the side seams leave the sleeve unbalanced and hanging badly. Figure 218 shows the correct way to narrow a sleeve evenly. The pattern must be folded into quarters, cut on the fold lines and overlapped at the hem, keeping the sleevehead the same size. Note that not only does the sleeve narrow, but the shape of the sleevehead and hem alter, which is vital for the correct hang of the sleeve. The principle is the same as that shown in figure 15, for widening sleeve hems.

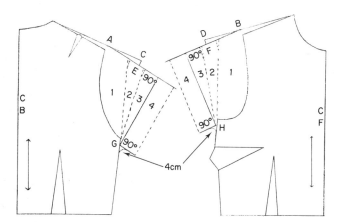

Figure 217   Adapting a bodice to add a cap sleeve

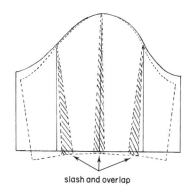

slash and overlap

Figure 218   Narrowing a short sleeve

The armhole should be checked at the end of the first fitting. It should be easy enough for comfort and movement, but too loose an armhole prevents a snug fitting sleeve. If the wearer has a stooping posture or prominent shoulder blades the armhole may gape at the back, while a prominent bust may cause a similar problem at the front. An easing thread will draw in these areas quite satisfactorily up to 1cm ($\frac{1}{2}$in) fullness. Figure 219 (a) shows the areas (a–b and c–d) to ease. The seam needs taping over the area eased when setting the sleeve. More than 1cm fullness requires recutting the bodice (chapter 9). In soft tailoring these areas are usually eased and taped for all figures. The lowest point of the armhole should be 1–2cm (up to $\frac{3}{4}$in) below armpit. Finally measure the armhole accurately round the fitting line, not the raw edge. This is difficult to do with a conventional tape measure, so it is easier to use a length of 5mm ($\frac{1}{4}$in) tape, checking the tape against a measure afterwards. Precise measurement is crucial to success. Write the measurement down.

Before making up the sleeve, check the sleevehead measurement at the fitting line in the same way. The difference between the two is the amount to be eased in. In a firm fabric such as a cotton print, the sleevehead should be 2·5cm (1in) longer than the armhole. In pliable fabrics such as jerseys, woollens, and so on 4–5cm (1$\frac{1}{2}$–2in) is better. By some means sleevehead or armhole or both must be adjusted to this ratio, and it is hopeless to proceed unless it is correct. Remember that commercial patterns are not necessarily correct for the particular fabric you may be using, and that any alteration done to the bodice will have affected the armhole.

A well-fitting sleeve is correctly balanced, free of wrinkles or creases at the top, has correct grain (figure 54), does not slip off the shoulder too far for comfort or style and shows no gathers or pleats at

the shoulder round the armhole seam. It is important to understand where the ease comes on the sleeve-head. The arrows in figure 219 (b) show the areas of bias grain which may be eased. It is possible if in real trouble to ease a little in the underarm sections, but any attempt to ease the sleeve over the straight grain area at the shoulder will result in crinkles.

If it is deemed desirable to pin in the sleeve at the second fitting, figure 220 shows where to place the pins. The first pin matches the underarm seams (not shown), the second establishes correct vertical grain at the shoulder and two further pins establish correct horizontal grain at front and back. Further

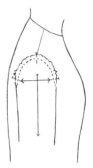

Figure 220

pins may then be placed as desired. An alternative method is to place the bodice on a dress stand. Fit the sleeve with the four basic pins, checking the hang; mark the pin positions on bodice and sleeve with thread marks, remove from the stand and tack the sleeve in for fitting, matching the marks. Figure 221 shows how to place the pins when working off the stand or body. Put in the four basic pins in the same order, then add the rest, as few as possible, more in the areas of ease. Note that the pin takes up very little fabric and is exactly on the fitting line. Worked in the hands in this way, there is no need to work a

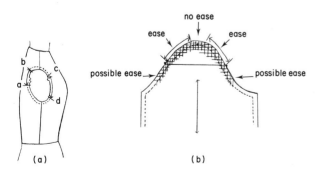

(a)

no ease

ease   ease

possible ease   possible ease

(b)

Figure 219

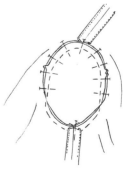

Figure 221

gathering thread in the sleevehead for easing first. A quicker and better result is obtained by manipulating the ease with the fingers and pins. Tack in the sleeve and fit. With experience, if there are no fitting problems, a good dressmaker will be able to machine in the second sleeve on pins alone, especially with pliable fabric.

After machining, turnings above the balance marks are usually trimmed to no less than 1cm ($\frac{3}{8}$in) and provide a little padding at the shoulder, while underarm turnings are trimmed closer for comfort. A very little clipping is necessary before pressing, but it should be the minimum to allow the seam to set well.

The shirt sleeve

Figure 222 shows the casual shirt sleeve with lowered crown and extra width to give an easy fitting. Flat-felled or double stitched seams are often used in this style of garment, in which case the sleeve is set into the armhole *before* side or sleeve seams are constructed. These are then done in one continuous operation.

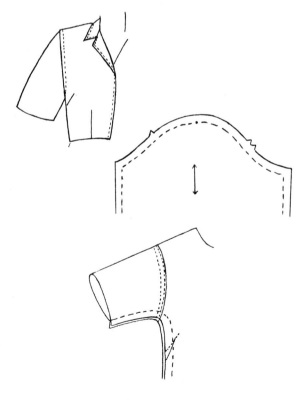

Figure 222   The shirt sleeve

The raglan sleeve

Some pattern primers suggest setting in raglan sleeves by the shirt sleeve method as above, but this is not a good idea as the underarm section sets badly in a raglan. It is better to use the set-in method, i.e. make up the sleeve and the bodice separately and then set the completed sleeve in. Raglan sleeves set a particular problem with ease, as there is generally a considerable amount of ease in the sleeve section, and it is not therefore advisable to attempt them in stiff or closely woven fabrics. Woollen fabrics are the best as shrinking may be used. Jerseys of all fibres are acceptable, but woven synthetics or cottons do not make successful raglan styles.

The fitting of raglan and kimono sleeves

The main fitting problem encountered with these styles is overcoming the effects of sloping or square shoulders. Unfortunately the changes required if the unsightly creases or folds are noticed for the first time at a fitting are so drastic that it is almost impossible to correct them. However in the case of the kimono, bad fitting is not so unacceptable as in the standard set-in sleeve as it is a loose fitting style anyway and by its very nature some folds and creases are always present. Faults are more serious in the raglan but are slightly easier to correct provided ample turnings have been left at the top of the sleeve. The point being made here is that the dressmaker must survey the shoulder area carefully before cutting out these styles. Sloping or square shoulders are easy to pick out and can easily be accounted for in the pattern. Figure 223 shows how to adapt a raglan sleeve pattern and figures 224 and 225 the kimono. Note that in all alterations, both the length and angle of the shoulder seam change. Both styles are better suited to figures with squarish shoulders and erect posture, as they can have a drooping effect. The close-fitting kimono in figure 226 (b) is suitable for most people.

The kimono sleeve

The hang and fit of the kimono are not easy to understand without a little knowledge of how the patterns are cut. Figure 226 shows four styles based on the kimono, and figures 227–231 show how the patterns are arrived at. It will be noted that there is considerable variation in ease, fullness and movement. In each case, ease has been added over the shoulder (point A) and this must not be fitted out again.

The kimono in figure 226 (a) gives an easy fit with

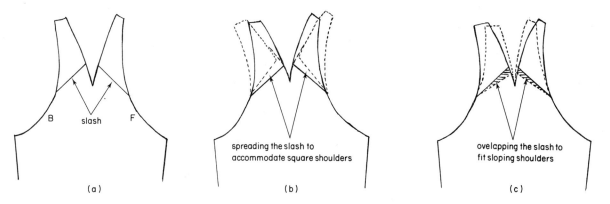

Figure 223   Pattern alterations to raglan sleeves

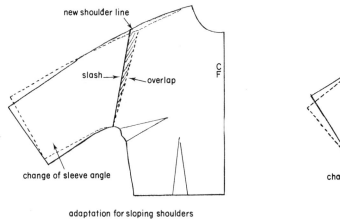

Figure 224   Adaptation for sloping shoulders

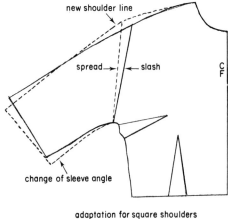

Figure 225   Adaptation for square shoulders

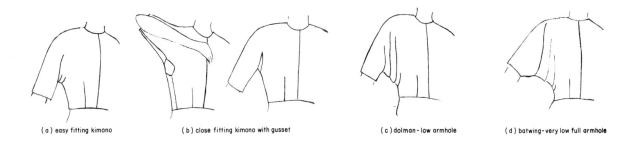

Figure 226   Kimono variations

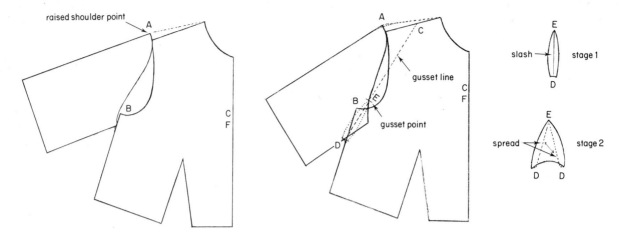

Figure 227   Easy fitting kimono pattern for 226 (a)

Figure 228   Close fitting kimono pattern for 226 (b)

Figure 229 Cutting a melon gusset

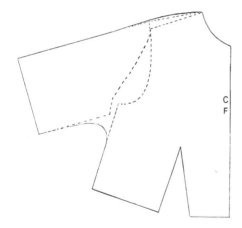

Figure 230   Cutting a dolman pattern for 226 (c)

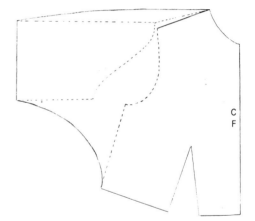

Figure 231   Cutting a batwing pattern for 226 (d)

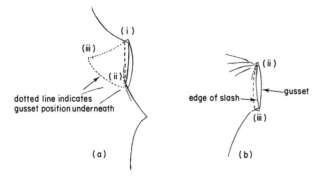

Figure 232   Inserting a gusset

plenty of movement as the shoulder/top arm seam is nearly straight and very little length is lost on the side/underarm seam. It will hang in folds under the arm, and therefore lightweight pliable fabric is required. The sleeve in figure 226 (b) is a close fit, obtained from the angled shoulder/top arm seam. Notice that the underarm and side seam would be far too short, allowing no movement of the arm unless a gusset were inserted. Most commercial patterns are cut as in (a) but if the closer fit is preferred it is simple to alter the angle of the sleeve seams, and the guide-line as to whether or not a gusset is required is to measure the bodice side seam section (i.e. waist to underarm). If this is 4cm ($1\frac{1}{2}$in) or more shorter than your normal side seam (waist to point B on a normal pattern) you will need a gusset.

To construct the gusset line find the point C midway along shoulder, join C–D. E is 8–12cm (3–4in) up this line. This is the line which will be slashed for the gusset. To cut the gusset, the melon-shaped one in figure 229 is the one favoured by couturiers as it is more subtle and less visible than the usual triangle. Trace off the gusset line and dotted line in figure 228 on to tracing paper and cut out (stage 1). Stage 2 is to slash D–E and spread the pieces, curving the bottom line. Cut this shape out in paper for your pattern, add turnings, and cut your gusset on the cross for maximum stretch.

The dolman sleeve in figure 226 (c) is easily obtained by combining standard pattern pieces (figure 230). It hangs low under the arm, has little movement allowance for arm raising and is not suitable for a gusset as it is full under the arm and the gusset would look ugly. This is only suitable for very pliable fabrics and for evening wear or occasions where movement is not required. Figure 226 (d) is a batwing, often cut as a long sleeve. The lower end of the sleeve curves right into the waist (figure 231) a dramatic style for evening wear only in fine, stretchy fabrics. It is simple to cut and make.

Inserting the gusset   The slash on the garment must be reinforced before cutting (figure 115). The simplest way to stitch is to pin at (i) and (ii) (figure 232 (a)), machine from (i) to (ii), leave the needle down, raise the presser foot, pivot the work, pin at (iii) and machine to (iii) (figure 232 (b)). Press the turnings towards the garment.

16 Collars and Cuffs

Collars

Because it is so near the viewer's eye level and frames the wearer's face, the collar is usually the part of a garment that is seen first, and more than any other single detail can make or mar a garment. The criteria of a good collar are:

(a) smooth set without wrinkles, particularly where the roll or fold falls
(b) symmetry, especially with pointed collars
(c) the height of the stand must suit the wearer's neck (for example deep polo collars are for women with long slender necks)
(d) the outside edge must not curl up nor the seam show.

Success with collar making and setting depends on four factors:

(1) the fit of the garment neckline
(2) the cut of the collar
(3) the making up of the collar, including the correct type of interfacing
(4) the mounting of the collar on the garment.

Factors (1) and (2) are closely inter-related because, as discussed in chapter 2, a collar is cut to fit a specific neckline, and any alteration in length or curve of a neckline requires an alteration in the collar that is cut to fit it. When any doubt exists it is always wise to make a partial toile for a collar and fit this first so that the collar pattern may be altered if necessary. The neck facings similarly are better not cut until after the first garment fitting. One must remember to allow for them in the original layout, of course. Altering a collar at a fitting is often impossible because collars cannot be cut with generous turnings – to do so would hamper the fitting.

The fit of the garment neckline

Whether high or low, the neckline should fit closely and firmly to the body. The curve must be a smooth one. In the case of a high neckline it should fit well up at the back and snugly into the pit of the neck at the front. It may be eased in a little and taped, or be stay-stitched. A little clipping of the turnings at the fitting stage may help in determining the finished effect, but mounting the collar is easier when this is kept to a minimum.

The cut of the collar

It is easier to understand collar fitting if the relationship between the shape of the collar and the amount of stand it has is understood. Figures 233–5 are not intended as a complete guide to collar cutting as this is outside the scope of this book (details may be found in a good pattern cutting book) but illustrate the principles involved so that they may be applied to collar alteration and fitting. Bodice patterns, turnings removed, are placed together at neck point, overlapped at the shoulder for 4cm (1½in) to simulate the removal of the normal amount of ease around the shoulder, required for the bodice but not for the collar. A collar cut from the lines A–B–C–D would echo the bodice exactly, but would fit so flat that the seam joining it to the neck would show, (figure 233). If the outside edge C–D were *shortened* it would rest on the dotted line E–F, thus pushing the collar up the neckline to give a stand equal in height to C–E and D–F. This is the collar shown in figure 234, cut by darting out the original pattern. Notice that the length of the neck edge is unchanged as it still has to fit the same bodice, but it has straightened. The collar in figure 235 has an even higher stand by deeper darting and is nearly straight. Its total outside length would rest on the line G–H, producing the stand.

It is recommended that simple collars of this sort should be cut in calico and pinned on the dress stand to prove the point. It will be seen that alterations in the neckline of the garment would affect the cut of the collar and that to raise or lower the stand the collar must be cut a different shape. This is why it is

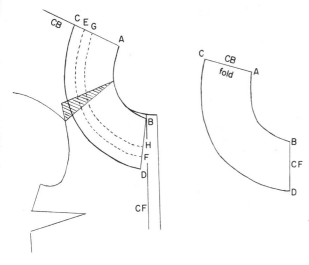

Figure 233

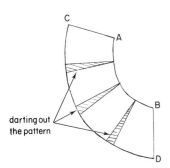

Figure 234 Shaping collars

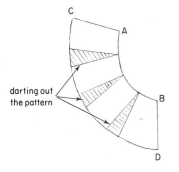

Figure 235 Shaping collars

essential to alter the pattern as such alterations may not be done at a fitting. A calico toile for fitting is the best safeguard.

Following the principle that the straighter a collar the higher it stands, a straight shirt collar can be cut by direct measurement from the neck edge (figure 236). While this can be worn closed as shown

or open as revers, the latter tends to be loose, and an additional stand to make the neck curve the other way can be added to any shirt collar pattern to make an open necked garment fit more closely (figure 237).

Cut the straight bias roll collar, such as the polo collar in figure 238, four times the width of the finished

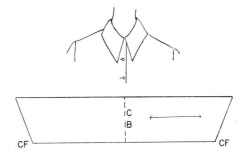

Figure 236 Straight shirt collar

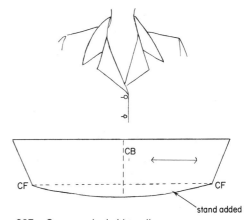

Figure 237 Open-necked shirt collar

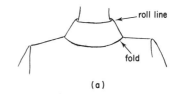

(a)

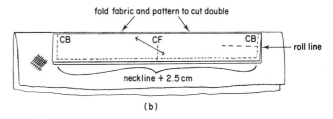

(b)

Figure 238 Cutting out a bias roll collar

collar (double thickness and folded over), and 2·5cm (1in) *longer* than the neckline. When setting on, ease the extra length over shoulders and front neck, which will allow the fold to be longer in relation to it and thus fall to cover the neck seam. The fold may be stretched with the iron to increase this length. These collars often suffer from 'twist' when setting on. This is avoided if they are cut ready folded on the bias (figure 238 (b)) and kept on that fold throughout construction.

Making up the collar

All collars except the soft bias roll require interfacing. Rarely do they need to be stiff – a possible exception is the mandarin – but sufficient body is required to give a gently curving roll. The interfacing chosen should be light in weight and pliable. Iron-on is not suitable for collars. To avoid bulk, which is one of the problems with the enclosed seam, interfacing must be well trimmed and the seam graded and trimmed closely.

On any collar with a stand the top collar must be larger than the under collar. This is partly because the seam must be pressed underneath the collar edge and also because the top collar forms the outside curve and the undercollar the inside, so the top collar has further to go. Failure to account for this during making up results in collars which curl up showing the seam. Except for soft tailoring where a separate pattern is usually given for top and under collars, the under pattern being smaller and cut on the bias, both parts are cut from the same pattern. To achieve the required difference in size, trim away some of the turnings of the under collar (experience will teach how much, but according to the thickness of the fabric, reduce its length by about 3–8mm ($\frac{1}{8}$–$\frac{1}{4}$in)) and ease the upper collar to it when joining the two. After stitching, trimming, etc. press the seam underneath and understitch as far as possible in the shape. Press from the outside to the neck edge. Holding the collar curved in the position it will be when attached, work about two rows of diagonal basting to hold the curved shape. The two edges will probably not fall together at the neck because of the longer outside curve. This is not important. They may be trimmed evenly, but no attempt should be made to pull them together or the curve will be lost. Figure 239 shows the making of a Peter Pan collar but all stand collars are made by the same principles.

Mounting the collar

This will not be dealt with in any great detail as the methods are well-known and will be within the

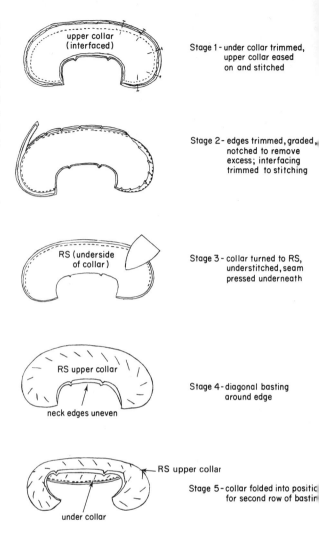

Stage 1 - under collar trimmed, upper collar eased on and stitched

Stage 2 - edges trimmed, graded, notched to remove excess; interfacing trimmed to stitching

Stage 3 - collar turned to RS, understitched, seam pressed underneath

Stage 4 - diagonal basting around edge

Stage 5 - collar folded into positio for second row of bastin

Figure 239   Making up a Peter Pan collar

experience of the average dressmaker. The success of the collar is determined mainly on the first three factors. The three basic methods are to face the collar on with binding for curved collars; to apply by the 'band' method for straight collars, i.e. machining the underside of the collar to the right side of the garment and then turning in the edge of the top collar and hemming over the seam; and thirdly to 'sandwich' the collar between neck and facings for either type.

Two useful tips for mounting are worth noting:

(a) A collar applied by the 'band' method to an open-necked garment should be applied first to the wrong side and then hemmed on the right side (figure 240).

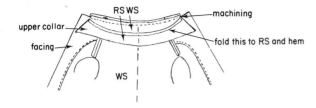

Figure 240 Mounting a shirt collar on open-neck style

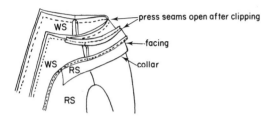

Figure 241 Mounting a straight collar with facings in thick fabric

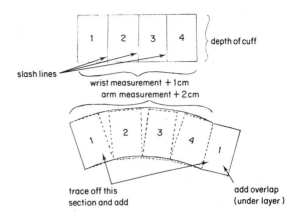

Figure 242 Shaped cuff for long sleeves

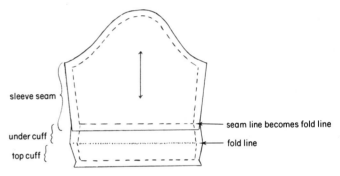

Figure 243 Adding all-in-one cuff to short sleeve pattern

(b) The bulk at the neck seam caused by having several layers of very thick fabric together can be avoided by stitching the undercollar to the garment, the upper collar to the facing and pressing the seams open (figure 241). The two seams are finally linked by small running stitches worked between the turnings.

Cuffs

These cause few problems. A few suggestions may, however, be helpful.

(1) Length of cuff. Straight cuffs for bishop-type sleeves are often too long on commercial patterns. Reduce so that *when done up* they measure wrist plus 1–1½cm ($\frac{3}{8}$–$\frac{5}{8}$in).

(2) Cuffs deeper than 5cm (2in) must be shaped for a smooth fit. Figure 242 shows how to cut patterns for these. Measurements required are wrist plus 1cm ($\frac{3}{8}$in) and arm measurement plus 2cm ($\frac{3}{4}$in) at the point where the cuff is to end. Draw a rectangle wrist plus 1cm ($\frac{3}{8}$in) by the required depth. Slash evenly three times and spread until the arm measurement plus 2cm ($\frac{3}{4}$in) is reached. Add the required amount for overlap. Blend the curves.

(3) Figure 243 shows how to add to a short sleeve pattern an all-in-one turn-back cuff.

(4) Note that the advantage of cutting an all-in-

one cuff is that there is no joining seam to cause bulk, but that the disadvantage is that it can only be cut the same size as the sleeve circumference. On thick fabrics a turn-back cuff fits better if it is 5mm–1cm ($\frac{1}{4}$–$\frac{3}{8}$in) longer because it forms an extra circular layer on the sleeve.

(5) The usual dressmaker method of facing on a cuff with bias binding is shown in figure 244, but the factory method of stitching the cuff on the wrong side of the sleeve, neatening the edges together before turning the cuff up is a short cut worth remembering for cuffs that go all round the sleeve without a break (figure 245).

(6) Two attractive alternatives for bishop sleeves are the circular cuff (figure 246), the circumference of the inner circle being the same as the length of the band cuff, and the sleeve ruffle (photo no. 51) formed by cutting the sleeve 8cm (3in) longer than required, making a deep hem to include a casing, threading fine elastic through. A decorative bias strip is added to cover the casing. This buttons to form a fastening. This is not a true cuff but a sleeve finish.

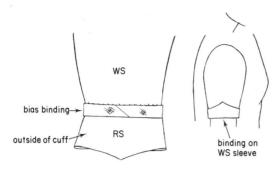

bias binding →

outside of cuff →

WS

RS

binding on
WS sleeve

Figure 244   Separate cuffs:

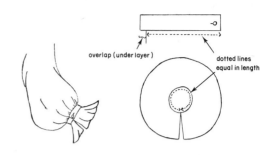

overlap (under layer)

dotted lines
equal in length

Figure 246   Circular cuff on sleeve band

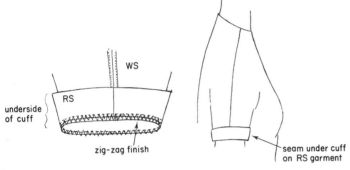

underside
of cuff

RS

WS

zig-zag finish

seam under cuff
on RS garment

Figure 245   Factory method of attaching separate cuff

Photo no. 51   Georgette blouse with sleeve ruffle and decorative tucking

17 Waist Finishes

The setting of skirt and trouser waistlines is a regular process to which the reader will be so well-accustomed that the basic method is not given here. A few techniques covering specific difficulties will be helpful, however, including the correct preparation and fitting of the garment, the cutting of the band (if any), the choice and application of interfacing, the fitting of the skirt to the band or facing, and the avoidance of bulk.

Preparation of the skirt

This is the same whether a fabric waistband or inside petersham is used. For fitting refer to chapter 9. The top of the skirt should be about 2–3cm (1in) bigger than the wearer's waist measurement, but more is required for figures with a prominent seat or abdomen or a disproportionately small waist, whilst very flared skirts need only 1–1½cm (½in) ease as they rapidly get wider below the waist. Horizontal creases below the waist, particularly at the back, are an indication that more ease is required (p. 65). Finish the seams and darts and grade all turnings as they enter the fitting line to reduce bulk. Establish the fitting line by tying a piece of string over the garment at a fitting and marking its position with pins. The fitting line is about 5mm (¼in) below this, but its curve will vary from figure to figure.

Cutting the band

Bands up to 5cm (2in) in width may be cut straight provided the figure is not disproportionately narrow at the waist. For very slim waists or bands over 5cm a curved band is required.

Curved waistbands need to be cut as band and separate facing and joined along the top, but straight bands are better cut with a fold at the top to eliminate an unnecessary seam and bulk. Warp grain should run around the body for stability.

Interfacing

This needs to be sufficiently stiff to prevent buckling, particularly on narrow waistbands. Special waist-bandings are recommended rather than a strip of regular woven interfacing as they are simpler to apply. The iron-on type is very satisfactory, applied to the waistband before setting it on the skirt. Note its position in relation to the fold line and seamlines in figure 247 (a). The sew-in type is applied after the waistband is stitched to the skirt. Note the best method is as in figure 247 (b) as this brings the stiffening next to the RS of the waistband and prevents the impression of turnings when pressing. Petersham is not so commonly used now as other waistbandings are stiffer and flatter, but if it is chosen it should not be boned. Check that the chosen stiffening corresponds with the laundering/cleaning qualities of the garment.

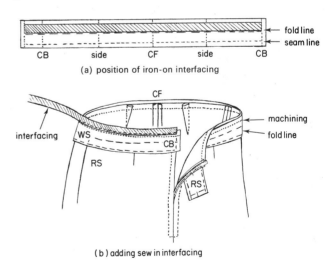

(a) position of iron-on interfacing

(b) adding sew in interfacing

Figure 247   Interfacing a waistband

Fitting and distribution of ease

The ease left on top of the skirt must be evenly distributed to front and back of the side seams as shown in figure 248. If a larger amount of ease than

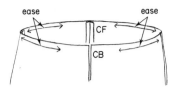

Figure 248   Areas of ease (normal figure)

normal has been left because of the prominent seat or abdomen, some must also be distributed over these areas. Mark the waistband with tailor tacks, chalk or pins at side seams, CF and CB, and fit the skirt to these marks, distributing the ease correctly by pinning first at the marked places and then in between. Place pins at right angles to the edge to control the ease. If a fitting is indicated replace by tacking, but if not the band may be machined over pins with the pins and skirt part uppermost and band underneath.

Avoiding bulk

The standard method of finishing the underside of a band – turning under the raw edge and hemming – is suitable only for fine or medium fabrics but is too bulky for thick ones, particularly where a very stiff interfacing is used. For such cases, cut the band on a selvedge if possible, allowing no turning on the underside, so that the selvedge may be caught down at or just above the machine stitches.

An alternative where no selvedge is available is to cut with a turning, neaten the raw edge appropriately and catch the underside down to the skirt turnings without turning under as in figure 249. Snip the turning at intervals.

Bulk may also be reduced by cutting a waistband with a seam instead of a fold along the top, making the underside of lining fabric.

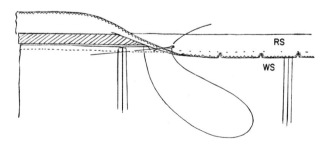

Figure 249   Attaching the underside of a waistband

Stiff waistband

A problem arises when using very stiff interfacing as the ends of the band, especially the overlap, can be difficult to turn through when stitched RS together, and the process can even impair the stiffness of the interfacing. In this case it is better to press or tack the turnings to the WS, mitring where necessary, fold the band and slip stitch the folded edges together by hand (figure 250).

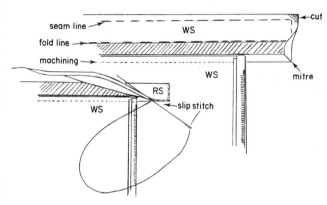

Figure 250   Finishing a stiffly interfaced band

Tailored waistband

A possible variation to the standard band is the tailored band. In this the RS of the band is applied to the WS of the garment and stitched, and the band folded over to the RS and topstitched all the way round.

Finishing a skirt top without a band (setting on a petersham)

The common problems with this finish are creasing and rolling. The creasing can be avoided by interfacing the top few centimetres of the skirt with a suitable fabric, and the rolling is prevented by the correct choice and application of the petersham. Fit and mark the skirt as for a waistband, allowing adequate ease.

Petersham   Boned petersham is good for prevention of rolling, curved petersham fits particularly well, and other types can be obtained with rubber strips on the back to prevent the blouse from coming untucked. Terylene petersham is preferable to cotton or rayon as it is stiffer, finer and does not lose its stiffness with washing or cleaning.

Shaping   Straight petersham must be shaped into a curve in order to fit snugly without rolling. It may be cut longer than required and darted evenly through-

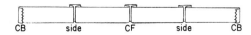

Figure 251   Pleated petersham

out its length or pleated as shown in figure 251 at
sides and centres before applying. For some figures it
is advisable to pleat curved petersham as well. Cut
with seam allowances at each end and turn and
neaten the ends with zig-zag.

Application   Petersham will roll if applied to the RS
of the skirt waist turning instead of the WS. It should
therefore be applied to the eased skirt waist as in
figure 252 (a) on the WS just above the seam line and
machined along the edge. Turn the work to the RS
and cover the raw edge with Paris binding machined
as shown in figure 252 (b). Fold petersham to WS on
the fitting line.

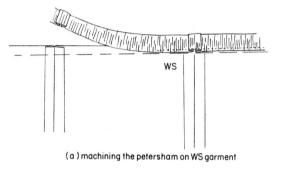

(a) machining the petersham on WS garment

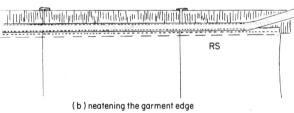

(b) neatening the garment edge

Figure 252   Setting on a petersham band

A flat closure under the zip is achieved if the ends
of the petersham do not coincide exactly with the
edges of the opening. Figure 253 illustrates this.

Stretch finish

Stretch petersham or soft top elastic is simple to
apply as shown in figure 254 where the appearance
of the three- or five-step siz-zag is acceptable on the
right side. If the garment is so stretchy as to be made

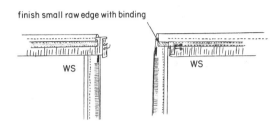

finish small raw edge with binding

Figure 253   Hook and eye closure for petersham band

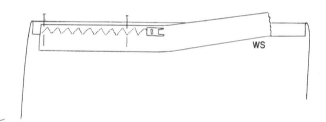

Figure 254   Setting elastic on stretch fabric waist

without an opening, cut the elastic to a little less
than waist measurement and join into a circle first.
Pin the elastic to the garment matching centres and
sides and machine with elastic on top, stretching as
you work, as in photo no. 22.

18 Pockets

A pocket is first and foremost a functional feature and whatever its type or position it must be usable. Ornamental pocket flaps, welts and so on unrelated to real pockets are a form of artificiality and in bad taste. That is not to say that pockets should not be decorative or a style feature of the garment. In fact all, with the exception of the pocket hidden in a seam, should be designed with their appearance as well as their function in mind. To be functional a pocket should be of a suitable size with an opening big enough to get the hand in without straining the fabric, in the right place and at the right angle. The bag of the pocket should be deep enough to hold the contents safely, particularly in the case of the pocket in a seam.

The pocket style must be chosen with the total effect of the garment in mind, pocket flaps being rounded or pointed to match the collar, for example. Patch pockets offer much scope for design originality. Welts, flaps and patches must match the garment grain and pattern, unless designed to feature the interesting use of checks, stripes and contrast fabrics.

The position of the pocket is determined not only by its use but also in order to flatter the figure. Patch pockets, particularly, are unbecoming if badly placed or unbalanced.

The two problems to overcome in the construction and application of pockets are to minimize the bulk and to add sufficient support and reinforcement. Bulk is minimized by careful grading and notching of turnings and by replacing one or both layers of garment fabric with lining. To stabilize their shape, all patch pockets, welts and flaps need interfacing and all pocket openings must be reinforced underneath before the slit is cut or the patch pocket stitched on. Strips of a suitable interfacing fabric are applied by catch stitch for this purpose, or iron-on interfacing is very suitable in small areas. If the slit is to be cut on bias grain reinforce with a strip cut on straight grain to prevent the opening stretching.

Seam pocket

The aim is to produce a flat inconspicuous pocket. If the fabric is bulky or loosely woven the bag should be made of lining or other suitable fine, firmly woven fabric.

Cut the garment as in figure 255 (a) with seam extensions which hide the seam inside the garment. Interface as in (b), keeping the pocket opening on the straight grain of the interfacing. Catch lightly down just to the inside of the seam line. Reinforce corners with two lines of straight machining. The simplest order of work is then to attach the pocket pieces to the extensions, trim and finish the seams and press open, and then stitch garment and pocket bag seams in one operation, (c). The pocket is turned to lie towards the front of the garment, so the turnings on the back piece of the garment must be clipped (d) before the seams can be opened and pressed. For extra strength bar tacks may be worked on the right side of the garment through all thicknesses at the top and bottom of the pocket opening.

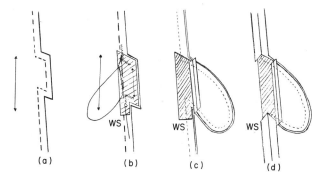

Figure 255   Seam pocket

Patch pockets

These can be almost any shape or size but should always be cut double or lined and should, unless the fabric is very firm, be interfaced. The method

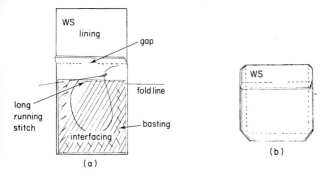

Figure 256   Interfacing and lining a pocket, 1:

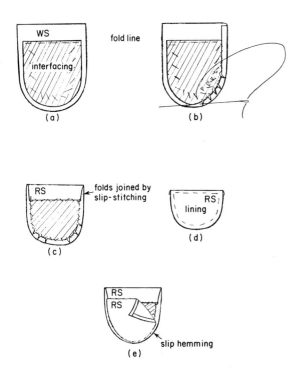

Figure 257   Interfacing and lining a pocket, 2:

illustrated in figure 256 shows a rectangular pocket and that in figure 257 a round one, but both can be adapted for any shape, except that the shape of the top of the pocket may be such as to require a separate rather than an all-in-one facing.

Method 1 (figure 256)

(a) Interface the pocket, attaching lightly through to the right side slightly inside the fold line. Seam on the pocket lining, leaving a gap in the middle. Press the seam towards the lining.

(b) Fold the pocket right sides together and stitch round the three raw-edged sides. Trim the edges and mitre the corners. Turn through the gap, work the edge seam to the inside and press. Hand stitch the gap together.

Method 2 (figure 257)

This is more suitable for tailored garments and thicker fabrics as it ensures the invisibility of the edge seam, but is not really secure enough for garments that are to be washed.

(a) Cut the interfacing to seam lines only at the sides and lower edge and with a small turning at the top. Baste in position and attach near the fold at the top as for method 1.

(b) Fold the turning over the interfacing, notching out where necessary the *exact amount* needed to make it flat. Catch stitch to the interfacing.

(c) Fold under the facing and slip stitch the sides together, making the seam fall to the wrong side of the pocket. Catch stitch the raw edge of the facing to the interfacing.

(d) Notch and fold under the turnings all the way round the lining and tack, making the finished lining a little smaller than the pocket.

(e) Slip hem the lining into place.

Attaching a patch pocket

On firm fabrics fix a strip of interfacing to the ws of the garment along the top edge of the pocket line, extending about 2cm ($\frac{3}{4}$in) over at each end. On loosely woven or stretchy fabric stabilize the whole pocket area. Use diagonal basting to place the pocket, keeping the stitching well away from the edges. Slip-stitch the pocket into position by hand, making sure that the stitches fall *just underneath* the pocket edge in such a position that they cannot be seen from the right side (figure 258 (a)). To strengthen the top corners, turn the work to the ws and cross-stitch through interfacing, garment and under layer of the pocket as in figure 258 (b), making sure the stitches do not come through to the right side.

If a top-stitched effect is desired, the pocket is machined in position, making triangles, rectangles or other shapes at the top corners for strength (figure 258 (c)).

Machining on a pocket often gives a bulky, pulled effect, especially in thicker fabrics. This can be avoided by top stitching the pocket first, before applying to the garment, then sew in position by stab-stitching through the machine stitches, not pulling the thread too tight (figure 258 (d)). Alternatively the pocket without top stitching may be sewn into position with stab-stitch or pick-stitch, using buttonhole thread (see p. 147), which will complement other similar top stitching on the garment.

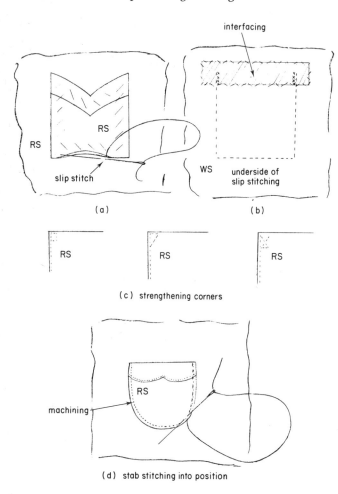

(a)

(b)

(c)   strengthening corners

(d)   stab stitching into position

Figure 258   Methods of applying patch pockets

Bound, piped or slot pocket

This is worked exactly as for a bound buttonhole. The method is shown in figure 259 (a) to (c). Apply interfacing to the garment first to reinforce the proposed slit.

(a) Cut the pocket and pocket facing all in one and apply to the garment as for a bound buttonhole, with about 2cm ($\frac{3}{4}$in) more above the slit than below.

(b) Stitch, cut, turn and complete the binding. Fold the pocket piece in half on itself and stitch and neaten the edges.

(c) Turn to the RS and strengthen by machining through all thicknesses along the seam line at the sides and top of the slot, and stab stitch through the seam and first pocket thickness at the lower edge.

Figure 259 (d), (e) and (f) shows a useful variation for a slanted pocket. Bind the opening with straight grain fabric as for a bound buttonhole, but cut separate pocket bag pieces as in (d), applying as in (e) and (f). Strengthen as for a straight pocket. A curved slot pocket is another variation – work as for the slanted one, but cut the pocket slot binding on the true cross.

As with bound buttonholes, the binding may be corded for emphasis.

Welt pockets

There are many methods of constructing these, most of them equally correct, but the method outlined here in figure 260 (a) to (h) is about the least complicated. As with all pockets, reinforce the garment area first, and mark out pocket position as for a buttonhole.

(a) Cut the welt, welt facing and pocket facing all in one.

(b) Interface the welt, fold RS together and stitch the sides, trim, mitre and turn out.

(c) Apply upside down just below the pocket line and machine. The pocket piece can be cut from lighter fabric and should be the same width but a little (1–2cm ($\frac{1}{2}$–$\frac{3}{4}$in)) longer than the pocket facing.

(d) Fold the pocket facing down out of the way temporarily and machine the pocket piece to the garment, making the line about 5mm ($\frac{1}{4}$in) shorter at each end than the welt.

(e) Turn to the WS and cut the slit, pressing back the small triangles at the ends of the slit. Pull the pocket and facing through to the wrong side and press into position, opening the seam along the top of the slit.

(f) Stitch together, trim and neaten the edges of the pocket bag, curving if desired.

(g) From the RS, fold back the welt and top-stitch the diagonal ends of the slit through all thicknesses.

(h) Fold the welt up into position again and fix the ends down to the garment by top-stitching or slip stitching as preferred.

For variation, the welt may be shaped, but it would have to be made with a separate facing, not a fold on top. For thick fabrics the welt only may be made of garment fabric and the welt facing and pocket facing cut in one out of lining fabric. Cut the interfacing to the seam line only and apply as in figure 261 (a). Attach the facing piece by hand (figure 261 (b)) and

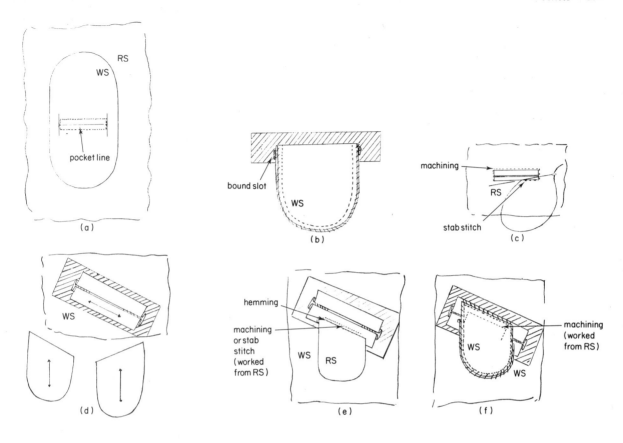

Figure 259   Bound, piped or slot pocket

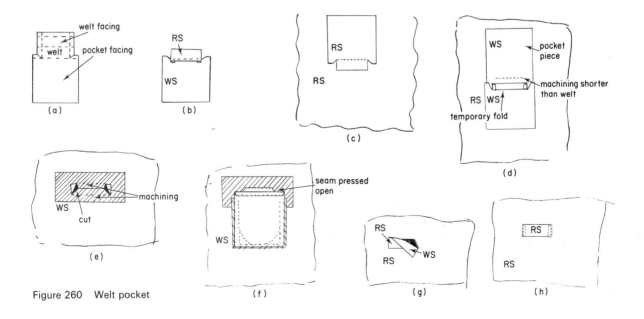

Figure 260   Welt pocket

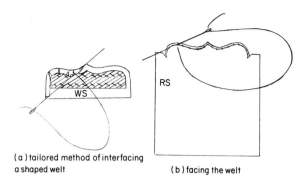

(a) tailored method of interfacing
a shaped welt

(b) facing the welt

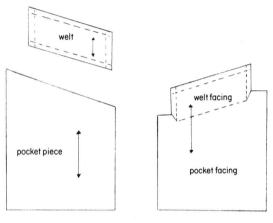

(c) cutting a slanted welt pocket

Figure 261   Welt pocket variations

proceed as shown in figure 260 (c). Slanted welts
are another variation – the construction method is the
same but the cutting is different. Figure 261 (c) is an
example.

Flap pockets

Like welt pockets, there are many correct methods of
construction. The flap may be made by the machined
and turned out method or by the tailored method for
thick fabrics as for a welt, for which the interfacing is
applied to the flap as in figure 261 (a) and the lining
applied as in figure 261 (b). The stages of construction
are shown in figure 262.

(a) Stitch the flap to the garment just above the
pocket line.

(b) Cut the pocket and pocket facing all in one as for
the bound pocket and apply right sides together over
the garment and flap with the pocket line placed just
below centre.

(c) Turn to the WS and machine. Cut through all
thicknesses.

(d) Turn the pocket through to WS and press back.
Fold down the pocket and machine, trim and neaten
the pocket bag, curving if required.

(e) From RS lift the flap and machine or slip-stitch
the slanting ends of the slit through all thicknesses for
strength.

As with the bound pocket, of which this method of
flap is a development, a slanted or curved slit is
possible, and the pocket bag may be made of other
fabric. Some workers prefer to fold the pocket piece
through in such a way as to leave a binding on the
lower edge. This is illustrated in figure 262 (f).

Figure 262   Flap pocket

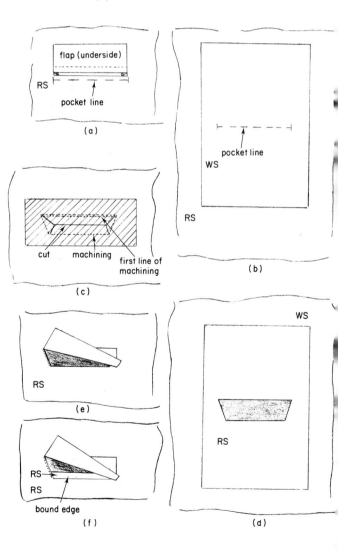

19 Shaping Techniques

Techniques for shaping garments come in and out of use with fashion, and the good dressmaker should be familiar with them whether or not they happen to be in use at a given moment. Those covered in this chapter are boning, weighting, shoulder padding, waist stays, taping interfacing into seams and pad stitching.

Boning

Boning was used extensively in the Victorian and Edwardian eras to prevent wrinkles when dresses were very shapely and tight. It reappeared towards the end of the 1940s with strapless ball gowns and swimsuits, has been used periodically since and no doubt will return again. Occasionally it is seen in skirts either down the seams or round in hoops, but boning has always been more associated with the support of strapless bodices.

Cotton covered steel tape obtainable in several widths is usually used in skirts, while for bodices nylon, whalebone, featherbone and plastic boning are all available. Nylon or plastic are a good choice for washable garments and swimwear, whalebone and featherbone being better for the bodices of strapless evening gowns, where it is desirable to shape the bone.

A strapless bodice is boned in the seams of the lining. Make up the lining, pressing the seams open. For each seam cut a length of feather boning, slightly shorter than the seam length, and a length of lute ribbon or prussian binding about 2cm ($\frac{3}{4}$in) longer at each end. Apply to the wrong side of the seam turnings as shown in figure 263 and machine through all thicknesses up the length and across the top, just below the seamline. (Take particular care not to stretch the binding tightly over curved areas – a little ease is preferable here.) A bone going over the bust must be shaped, so measure and mark on it the bust point, and using the tip of a cool iron gently shape at this point. A gradual curve can also be obtained by

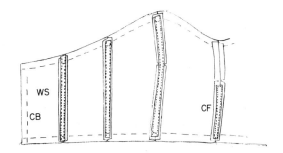

Figure 263   Boned lining for strapless bodice

bending in steam from a kettle. Trim the ends of the bone to a rounded shape and file them to remove the rough edges and insert into the casing. Machine across the bottom just above the seam line. The bone at the centre front seam should reach only up to the top of the midriff and stop short of the bust. Some bodices which are not strapless may also be boned in the midriff area only to prevent creasing.

The boned lining is finally placed in the garment in the usual manner, or it may be used as a mounting for sheer fabrics with the right side of the lining next to the garment fabric, in which case a separate lining is also required.

A boned lining also makes a good foundation for draped styles in chiffon and similar fabrics as it acts as a base for sewing on tucks and gathers.

Weighting

Lead weights are available in sizes from about 1 to 3cm ($\frac{3}{8}$ to $1\frac{1}{4}$in). These must be covered in fabric before inserting into hems or train ends by stitching the covering to seams or hem interfacing. A bead-like type of weighting is also sold on a string by the metre. This is finer and suitable for cowl necks and the hems of jackets. Generally speaking weighting is insufficiently used by most dressmakers – many lightweight garments improve in hang with weighting.

Shoulder pads

These are sold ready made of wadding or foam rubber and vary in shape from the semi-circular to triangular, some being extremely thin and others up to about 2cm ($\frac{3}{4}$in) at the thickest point. Foam rubber ones must be covered so that the stitches fixing them to the garment turnings go through the cover only as they would tear the foam. The wadding ones are usually better for soft tailoring and garments to be dry-cleaned, and the foam ones for garments to be washed. It is not possible to give precise instructions about the best size and shape to use for any specific garment. This depends on fashion and fit. At times when padded shoulders are in fashion it is best to keep a small stock of different types and experiment to find the best at the first fitting. They must be pinned in place for all fittings if it is intended to use them at all.

To fit pads in, hold the garment over the hand or place on the stand. Place the pad in position with its thick edge about 1–1·5cm ($\frac{1}{2}$in) over the shoulder seam, lining up with the seam turnings. The centre of the pad should lie about 1cm ($\frac{3}{8}$in) to the front of the shoulder seam, but the final adjustment is made according to appearance and comfort. In order to preserve the round line of the shoulder it is important to pin the pad in from the right side of the garment, smoothing the fabric into place. (If it is done with the garment inside out the fabric will stretch over the pad in an unsightly way.) Attach the pad loosely to the garment seams or interfacing, taking care to preserve the curve made by the pinning. Figure 264 shows the correct position for the pad. In soft tailoring the hard line which may result from padding at the top of the sleeve can be softened by stitching to the armhole seam from the sleeve side a length of thinned out folded wadding, lambswool or domette as shown. The length and thickness of this wadding is again judged at the fitting of the sleeve.

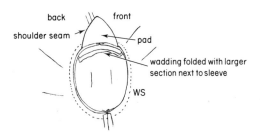

Figure 264   Shoulder pad and sleeve wadding

Staying the waist

When waist seams are in fashion they are greatly improved by taping or staying. Stay tape may be stitched in with the seam either on the bodice or skirt edge, whichever has less gathers or darts, or it may be stitched to the turnings after completion of the seam. Fitted garments without a waist seam, such as the princess line, sometimes benefit from staying at the waist. Cut a length of petersham ribbon with sufficient allowance for turnings at both ends and the desired amount of waist ease and stitch this to the turnings of the dress at each seam. At the CB, CF or side opening, hem the ends of the petersham and add hooks and eyes to fasten before closing the zip. Skirt fasteners may also be used here unless the garment fabric is so fine that the impression would show through.

Taping interfacing into seams

Stabilizing seams with stay tape is covered in chapter 11 but a further use of tape is for minimizing seam bulk where a heavyweight interfacing is used in soft tailored garments. Figure 265 shows the method. Use tape 1–1·5cm ($\frac{1}{2}$in) wide. Cut away the interfacing about 5mm ($\frac{1}{8}$–$\frac{1}{4}$in) short of the seam line and lay the tape over the edge, covering the seam line at one side and the cut edge of the interfacing at the other. Pull the tape firmly so that the garment edge will be firm but not eased to it. Pin in place and run by hand into place along the interfacing edge, taking care not to pick up any of the garment fabric. Keep the work firm with small stitches and occasional backstitches. It may be possible to machine this, depending on the shape of the edge. Press the work well and baste the tape into position down the other edge ready to be stitched in with the edge seam.

Padding collar and revers

Pad stitching is really a tailoring technique and therefore outside the scope of this book, but since it is useful in some types of dressmaker jackets it is outlined here in no great detail. It must be pointed out that pad stitching collar and revers is very far from all that is required to produce a tailored coat or jacket.

The purpose of pad stitching is not only to attach the interfacing to the garment throughout its area but also to shape it into a curve so that the collar and revers will roll rather than lie stiffly or turn up at the corners. Therefore the interfacing must be very

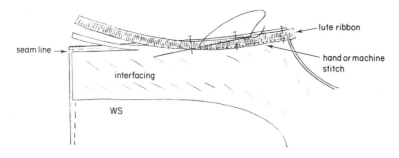

Figure 265   Taping interfacing into front facing edge

loosely basted into position on the flat as it must be free to move against the garment fabric during stitching. It is also essential to hold the work curved in the hand while stitching. Figure 266 (a) shows an under collar with the interfacing basted in. Note the wide turning on the outer edge of the interfacing. Holding the work as in figure 266 (b) pad stitch diagonally following straight grain lines and keeping the stitching well within the seam lines. Push the interfacing gently up with the left thumb to roll it and make sure the stitches take up only a thread of the ws garment fabric. Some experience is needed to achieve this. Turn the collar round to work the right-hand side in the same way. If the worker has curved the work properly the interfacing will have moved down the collar at the outside edge and may jut beyond the collar fabric at the neck edge. This is why it is cut with a large outer edge turning. Trim the

interfacing away to just inside the seam line all round before attaching the under collar to the upper collar and the garment neck (figure 266 (c)).

Revers are similarly pad stitched. Firstly, a stay tape or bridle is hand stitched through to the inter-facing only on the roll line (figure 267). The same rules about curving the work and trimming the interfacing afterwards apply.

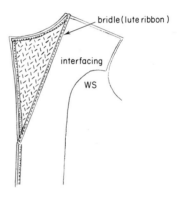

Figure 267   Pad stitching a rever

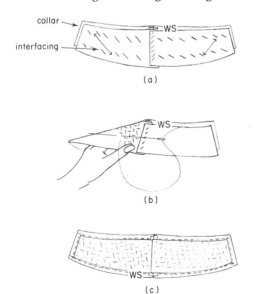

(a)

(b)

(c)

Figure 266   Pad stitching a collar

20 Hems

Many dressmaking techniques remain constant over the generations, but the making of hems is among those which have changed, as standards of acceptability in a hem have changed. If you learned your dressmaking many years ago, you are probably not up-to-date. Hems now are more frequently single than double, hemming is never used, herringbone and slip-hemming rarely used. The stitch you need most often is catch stitch, worked loosely, often under the hem. It is shown in figure 268 (a) and a stronger, but still loose version in figure 268 (b). New techniques constantly appear – recently a designer introduced a 'no turn' hem for jersey, where the raw edge was merely zig-zagged, trimmed and left; a finish not acceptable to all of us, but at least it preserved the fluidity of the fabric.

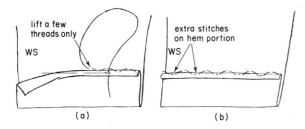

Figure 268   Catch stitching a hem

Standards now rest on the degree of visibility. Unless decorative, hems should be inconspicuous and appear as the edge merely folded under on to the ws. No stitching line should be seen and no impression given from the RS of the depth of the hem. Loose stitching, correct disposal of fullness and sensitive pressing are required. It should be the right depth for the fabric and style. The principle is that the heavier the fabric the less depth of hem is required to ensure the correct hang of the garment, and it must never be so heavy as to distort the hang. Flared skirts need a narrower hem than straight ones to allow them to hang, and to avoid a problem with bulk. The hem must be straight and of an even depth.

Preparation of a hem

Before starting, check that all seams leading into the hem are correctly pressed and graded where they enter the hem. Puckering seams must be corrected, since to leave them until the final pressing would alter the hemline. Allow the garment to hang overnight or longer with bias cuts or stretchy fabric. If it has been hanging during construction this may not be necessary.

(1) The first step is levelling. This may be done on the flat, on the dress stand or on the wearer at the second fitting. Whatever the method no turning is done at this stage. The approximate length will have been decided before cutting out and should have been marked on the skirt. With the garment on the stand or the wearer the method is familiar – marking up from the floor with a long ruler and pins or chalk. However this method is not always satisfactory, for example with very flared garments or when fitting oneself.

An alternative (which some workers prefer in all cases) is to lay the skirt out on the flat and measure down radially from the waist at intervals starting with CB, CF, side seams, any other seams, then at the centre of each panel or gore, and lastly the 'in between' areas.

Improving on this method one can work from hip level. The wearer stands by a table or chair back reaching just below hip level, and turns while pins are inserted around at this level, the measuring following flat on the table as before. This is helpful when fitting oneself.

(2) Adjust the first levelling by altering pins which deviate from the smooth line. Mark the line with trace tacking. Pin up the hem.

(3) Check and adjust the hem length on the wearer. Evening dresses should be about 2cm ($\frac{3}{4}$in) from the floor all round.

(4) On ws, working flat, pin the fold, seams first,

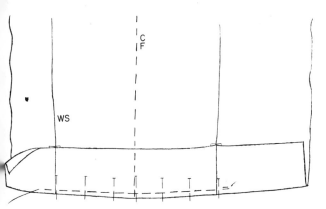

Figure 269   Pinning and tacking the fold

then centres, etc. and tack through both thick-nesses about 1cm ($\frac{1}{4}$in) from the fold (figure 269).
(5) Decide on the hem depth and use a sewing gauge to trim off the excess evenly.
(6) Deal with the problem of fullness if there is one (details below).
(7) Press the hem from the fold to just below the raw edge.
(8) Decide on the method of fixing (details below). Pin vertically as before, tack and stitch.
(9) Press.

Further details of pressing hems are found in chapter 23 and suggestions for techniques for difficult fabrics in chapter 24.

Disposal of fullness in hems

Nearly all skirts have some excess fullness in the hem. Minimize this in flared garments by having as narrow a hem as practicable for good hang. The usual method is by easing. A thread must be run in near the edge by hand or machine (loose tension, long stitch). Place each gore flat on the table, pin up the hem and adjust the easing thread until the edge fits exactly the line along which it must lie. Fasten off (figure 270 (a)). If a zig-zag finish is going to be used for the raw edge, the easing may take the form of a firm thread, e.g. crochet cotton, stitched in with the zig-zag, which may then be pulled up. This saves an operation and is particularly good for those fabrics which tend to stretch while being zig-zagged (figure 270 (b)).

Where a lot of the excess fullness is around the seams, they may be unpicked through the hem and trimmed a little, then slipstitched together again (figure 271). Do not attempt to remove all the fullness by this method or a point at the hem will form below the seam. Combine the method with easing.

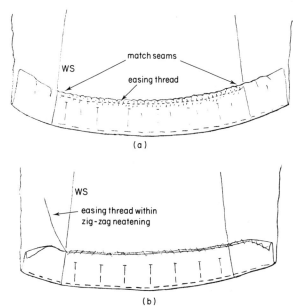

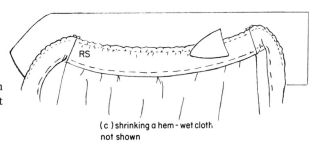

(c) shrinking a hem - wet cloth not shown

Figure 270   Disposing of the fullness in a flared hem

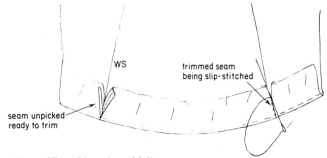

Figure 271   Disposing of fullness at seams

On all wool fabrics the easing procedure is followed by shrinking, (chapter 10). Do not shrink with the hem in the fixed position or the skirt fabric under-neath will shrink also. Fold the hem clearly away from the rest of the garment to shrink (figure 270 (c)).

Avoid if at all possible the commonly used method of pleating away fullness as it causes little points at the hem line and impressions through to the RS when pressed. For these reasons the pleating method is now considered to be out of date.

Methods of fixing hems

Widely used methods for everyday dressmaking include:

The couture or tailor's hem which came into wide use when fashion revived after the Second World War. Neaten the raw edge suitably, probably by the same method as you neatened your open seams, e.g. clean finish, binding, zig-zag, Hong Kong, etc., fold the edge back from the garment and catch stitch underneath 5mm–1cm ($\frac{1}{4}-\frac{1}{2}$in) from the edge. Work loosely and press the hem only as far as the stitches, not the neatened edge (figure 272).

For linings, children's garments and fine fabrics, turn a second fold to make a double hem and slip hem, (figure 273). If the fabric is springy it may be clean finished first, but not too near the edge for easy slip-hemming.

Facing up with bias binding, machined to the edge and slip-hemmed to the skirt (figure 274 (a)). Do not try to use straight seam binding, even on a straight hem, as it cockles when pressed. Treat this method with caution as it requires the cut edge to be pressed flat to the garment and may cause an impression on the right side. In general the couture method is better.

A false hem is a wide bias strip, possibly of lining fabric, applied as above, when shortage of fabric or bulk require it, (figure 274 (b)).

A machine blind hem works successfully and invisibly on thick tweed fabrics (figure 275), and is also satisfactory for children's wear, overalls and linings, where it shows a little but speed may be more important than finish.

Hems for heavier fabrics include:

Loosely worked blanket stitch for the hem of a lined jacket in thick tweedy fabric. The needle skims the top fibres of the jacket but takes a firm hold on the hem. Most of the holding is achieved by firm pressing (figure 276).

To prevent the weight of the hem pulling the catch-stitching, an intermediate row should be worked at about half the hem depth (figure 277), for heavy weight fabrics.

For mounted fabrics the hem can be made invisible by stitching it to the mounting only, not the top fabric. Lightly catch the mounting to the fabric just under the hem line, trim it away, and stitch the hem by a means suitable for the fabric (figure 278).

Very narrow turnings are required for fine or

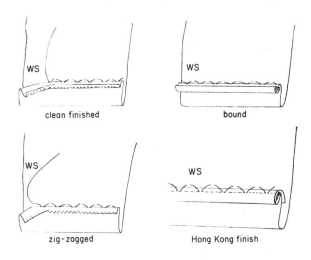

Figure 272   Couture hems

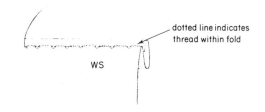

Figure 273   Slip hemming

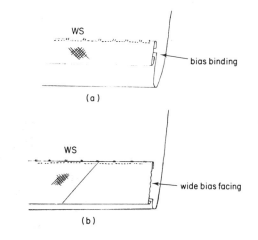

Figure 274   Facing hems with bias fabric

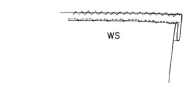

Figure 275   Machine blind hem

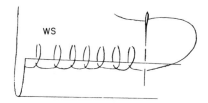

Figure 276   A blanket-stitched hem

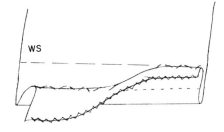

Figure 277   Double catch-stitched hem

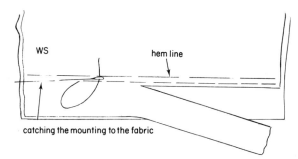

Figure 278   Hem on a mounted fabric

Figure 279   Double machine hem

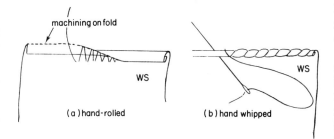

Figure 280   Rolled hems

sheer fabrics on hems of circular skirts or the edges of frills and flounces. Methods include:

Double machine hem   Clean finish the raw edge, trim very closely to the stitching, turn as narrow as possible and machine again right on the fold. The fuller the edge the better this looks and it requires accurate stitching and exactly matching fine thread, (figure 279).

The rolled hem is a less visible version of the above, but very time consuming. Machine a row of stitches as close to the edge as the fabric allows (tissue paper may be used to prevent stretching), trim to about 3mm ($\frac{1}{8}$in), and press under with the machining on the fold. Without pinning or tacking but using a fine long needle and fine thread, work the stitch shown in figure 280 (a), picking up alternately a machine stitch and a little of the fabric. Every few stitches pull up the thread gently, not tightly, to form the roll.

The rolled and whipped hem (see photo no. 33) adds a little decoration to the above. When rolling, work whip stitch instead over the roll (figure 280 (b)). A deeper coloured thread looks attractive.

The machine picot edge is to be highly recommended for its speed and decorative appearance, and is especially suitable for frills and ruffles (note the evening blouse, photo no. 51). The photograph of the lingerie seam, photo no. 34, also shows the working of picot. Fold the edge, work a fine, closely spaced, narrow zig-zag over the fold and trim away the excess.

Sheer fabrics cut on the straight hang better with a deeper hem. The usual slip-hemmed double hem gives an unsightly appearance as two layers of fabric are seen at the fold, then three layers, before the single layer. Avoid this by making two equal folds to make three layers throughout the depth of the hem.

Two special effect hems have occasional use:

The soft unpressed hem for mounted garments is sometimes called for with a soft flowing style and fabric. With loose catch stitches attach a bias strip of interfacing or lambswool to the mounting at the hem line (figure 281) before turning as you would for mounted fabrics. Do not press the final hem – merely steam it.

The stiffened hem is used mainly for long bouffant style evening dresses and is achieved by making a kind of false hem out of horsehair braid. If the braid is creased, steam it first, and then apply by topstitching just above the raw edge, folding underneath to form a hem and catch-stitching lightly to garment or mounting (figure 282). Being sheer but stiff it is a suitable finish for lace.

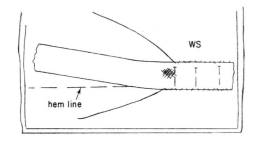

Figure 281   Soft unpressed hem

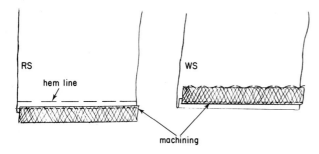

Figure 282   Hem stiffened with horsehair braid

Decorative hems can be made by many of the techniques suggested in chapter 22, but two structural ones should be mentioned:

Scalloped hem, which is really a shaped facing catch-stitched to the garment on its free edge (see chapter 12).

Topstitched hem, particularly effective on flared skirts requiring a narrow finish, and most striking when worked in contrasting buttonhole thread on firm fabrics such as denim, flannel or gaberdine. Work the first row about 3mm ($\frac{1}{8}$in) from the fold and two or three further rows equidistant from the first. Trim the turning closely on ws.

21 Lining

Unless they are summer weight and frequently washed, most fashion garments benefit from being lined. Lining helps to prevent creasing, especially in trousers and tight fitting garments, and stabilizes shape, particularly at the seats of skirts and trousers and trouser knees. It improves the hang of skirts and dresses adding body and firmness. Sheer garments can be lined for modesty and garments of man-made fibres do not cling if lined with an anti-static fabric. Rough fabric needs lining for comfort. All garments last longer if lined as it preserves the garment fabric from perspiration and abrasion. Lining tidies up the inside of a garment and avoids the need for elaborate neatening, particularly with coats or jackets. It can be a fashion feature, made of contrasting or patterned fabric to match another part of the outfit, and may be decorated with machine stitching, piping or braiding.

Fabrics

Usual fabrics are sold under the name 'lining' and are made of tricel, polyester, acetate or rayon. Tricel lining has a tendency to split in wear. Other fabrics include taffeta for a stiff effect, crêpe for softness, and satin for heavyweight coats and jackets as it allows the garment to be slipped on and off easily. Jap silk is a fine lining for wool dresses as it adds no weight or bulk but prevents irritation. Anti-static lining is required for man-made fibres. Cotton lawn is suitable for cotton and linen garments, while knitted or stretch fabrics require nylon tricot. To add warmth to winter coats, quilting and fur fabric are suggested. For fashion effect choose almost any regular garment fabric provided it is smooth, light, firm and fairly crease-resisting. Ranges of linings in retail shops are sometimes very limited, but a simple solution is to send a sample of garment fabric to a mail order supplier for matching.

Cutting linings

General principles are to delay cutting out lining until the garment has been fitted so that the pattern may be altered accordingly and the lining cut and made without further fitting and alteration. For dresses, skirts and trousers the lining should be cut exactly the same as the garment, except that no hem allowance is required because a lining must be several centimetres shorter than the garment. Jackets require a pleat at the CB for movement, so place the CB of the jacket pattern about 2cm ($\frac{3}{4}$in) from the fabric fold to cut. Tack up the CB line before removing the pattern (figure 283 (a)). For the front 'deduct' the width of the facing by placing the facing pattern over the front pattern and marking the inner edge. Mark the cutting line for the lining about 4cm ($1\frac{1}{2}$in) out from this line (figure 283 (b)).

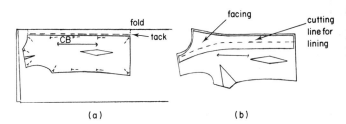

Figure 283   Cutting jacket linings

Lining a dress

(1) Complete the dress except for the neck edge (and armholes if sleeveless).

(2) If there is a waist seam, make up bodice and skirt linings separately. With raglan or kimono styles make the whole lining up, but make set-in sleeve linings separately.

(3) Insert the constructed lining in the dress before adding the collar or neck facing. Baste to the dress up CF or CB, whichever does not have an opening.

(4) Work a large running stitch to join the side seam turnings of the lining to those of the dress (figure 284), stopping about 10cm (4in) short of the hem line. Baste the lining to the dress around the neck and armhole, down the sides of the opening and along the shoulder seams.

(5) Try on to make sure the lining does not pull or drag.

(6) Fractionally to the outside of the stitching line, run or machine together through all layers around armhole and neck. If there is a waist seam, run the skirt lining in with the skirt turnings at the waist, overlapping the bodice lining and hemming this down later (figure 285). Hem down the sides of the opening.

(7) Set the garment neck facing and/or collar, treating the lining and garment as one fabric around neck edge (also armhole facing if a sleeveless dress). Catch the inner edge of the facings down to the lining only.

(8) Finally line the sleeves, running lining and sleeve turnings together down the length of the seam as in figure 286. Turn the lining out over the sleeve, fold under the sleevehead turning and hem it to the seam line. (Some workers machine the sleeve linings into the main garment lining at stage 2. Although quicker than the method described here, it has the disadvantage of being less firm round the armhole and lends less support to the garment.)

(9) At the lower edge of the sleeve proceed as in figure 287.

(a) Baste layers together a few centimetres above the hem.

(b) fold the lining edge under and pin to the garment hem.

(c) Pin around a second time, pushing the lining fold up the hem a little (5mm–1cm ($\frac{1}{4}$in)) to prevent dragging.

(d) Tack and slip hem.

At the skirt hem, the lining is finished separately and left to hang free. It may be attached at the side seams with a French tack or tapes, but some people prefer it left completely free to make pressing easier during the life of the garment.

Lining skirts and trousers

This may be done after completion or before the addition of the waist finish and the two fabrics treated as one at the waist. Treat skirt hems as for dresses but slip hem lining down for trousers by the method given above for sleeves.

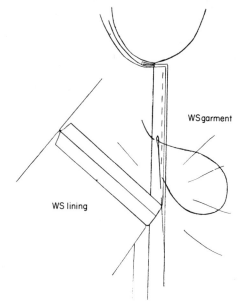

Figure 284   Running in a lining at the side seam

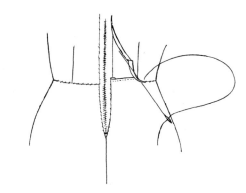

Figure 285   Lining a dress with a waist seam

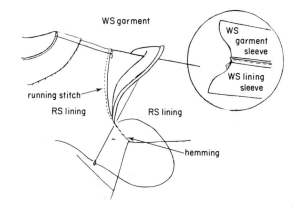

Figure 286   Lining a sleeve

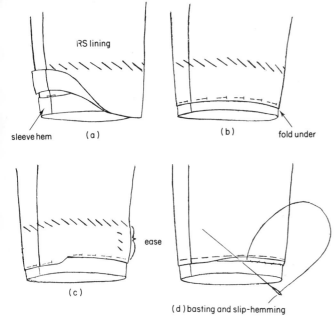

(a) sleeve hem RS lining (b) fold under

(c) ease

(d) basting and slip-hemming

Figure 287   Attaching lining to hems

Lining should be a very little tighter (about 5mm ($\frac{1}{4}$in) on each of front and back) around the hip area to prevent the garment seating. Fit this carefully so that the tightening is not so overdone as to create pulls. Linings of tight skirts may have slits of several centimetres left open in the seams at the hem line. It is possible to half-line a skirt or line the back only, but the proportionate saving in time and money is so little that it is a dubious economy as fully lined garments look better, wear better and are more comfortable.

Lining jackets

Jackets may be lined in the same way as dresses (dressmaker method), but as it is visible a jacket lining ought to be more firmly attached in all areas and should fit precisely to prevent unsightly sagging or creasing. Constant putting on and off of a jacket also disturbs the lining, another reason for preferring the tailor's to the dressmaker's method. There are, of course, many variations and the two methods can be combined. Here is one simple basic tailor's method, for which a stand is essential. The main part of the garment, including the collar and facing, is completed and lined before the sleeves are set in.

(1) Machine waist darts from the bottom to about 2cm ($\frac{3}{4}$in) above the waist and leave free at this point.

(2) Machine front shoulder darts down for a few centimetres only and leave free.

(3) Machine CB pleat from waist to hem and down from neck for 5–10cm (2–4in) and leave free. (Optional – this pleat may also be left unstitched for its entire length.) All these folds may be later supported by bar tacks at other places in their length if they seem too slack and a great deal of ease for movement is not needed.

(4) Machine side seams and sleeve seams only of the jacket lining.

(5) Apply the lining to the jacket by laying it flat on the table and basting down the CB. Keeping weft grain straight with the garment, baste down midway between CB and side (further lines if required). Stop about 10cm (4in) or more short of the hem.

(6) Stitch the lining and jacket turnings together at side seams (figure 284).

(7) Place the jacket on the stand wrong side out, collar and revers turned up. Smooth the back lining over the shoulder seam and catch it permanently into position along the garment turnings. Keeping weft grain straight over the bust, temporarily support the lining at front edge with pins and then arrange the front shoulder over the back, turning under the raw edge and pinning (figure 288).

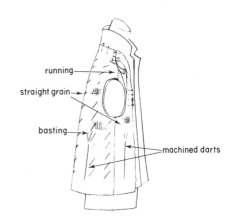

running straight grain basting machined darts

Figure 288   Lining a jacket (tailor's method)

(8) Pin the layers together around the armhole and while still on the stand turn under and pin all the edges except the hem and armhole, clipping turnings where necessary.

(9) Pin the hem as for the sleeve hem, p. 142 and figure 287 (a), (b) and (c), removing the jacket from the stand to work if preferred. Replace on the stand to check.

(10) Remove from the stand, baste all edges, remove pins. Fit and adjust if necessary.

(11) Run the armhole turnings together as in dress step (6).

(12) Slip hem the edges and hem as in figure 287 (d).

(13) Line the sleeve before it is set in. Catch lining and sleeve seams together as in figure 286, turn out by putting the hand down the garment sleeve from the top, grasping both layers and pulling the sleeve out over the lining. Baste layers together around the top arm while holding in the hand (figure 289). When the sleeve has been fitted and stitched in, the lining is hemmed over the seam at the sleeve head as in the dress method.

An attractive finish is to insert piping or cording between the garment and lining under all the slip stitched edges except the hem, which is left to fall loosely for ease. Otherwise the joins may be covered with decorative braid as a final stage.

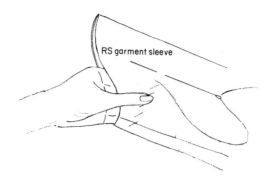

Figure 289   Basting lining and garment together at top arm

22 Dress Decoration

This chapter aims to set out the broad principles of garment decoration, specify some of the possibilities, and give a little practical help on working certain types. To cover the subject exhaustively would need a separate volume and it is suggested that for further information specialized books on, say, embroidery, quilting or smocking should be consulted. The enthusiastic reader will observe, research and experiment for herself.

Principles and practical considerations

Decoration should not be added as an afterthought and is quite definitely not for the purpose of covering up poor workmanship or inadequate fitting. Every garment should have some sort of decorative feature, otherwise it will not look finished. This does not mean that it has to have trimmings – the decorative feature may well be in the use of fabric or grain. When planning the garment decide on the decoration at least in outline, but not necessarily in detail, e.g. the size and depth of scallops can be determined at the toile stage or fitting.

The decoration should emphasize the line of the garment, possibly accentuating the seams. Repetition creates a unified effect, as in the sleeve tucking on the georgette blouse shown in photo no. 51 which is repeated on the jabot. Harmony in shape is required; scallops, for example, do not look well on striped fabric because of the conflict between curves and straight lines. The amount of decoration should be in scale with the garment and should preserve the balance and position of the undecorated parts also. Decoration is meant to show and if it is so subtle that it is not noticed, then it has failed. Without being timid, therefore, learn at the same time to be moderate, for over-decoration cheapens a garment.

If you are adding trimmings, consider practical matters such as laundering and comfort in wear, and match them for fibre and weight as far as possible. As a general rule self fabric trimmings harmonize better than bought ones and are always in good taste.

Decoration falls into two broad types – structural and applied.

Structural decoration

This includes the planned use of patterned fabric. Photo no. 52 shows a well-planned cross cut check dress needing no additional trimming, while photo

Photo no. 52   Using checks

Photo no. 53   Using stripes

no. 53 shows the use of stripes. The use of two or more fabrics together and clever cutting to show up unusual grain lines and seaming all provide interest. Decorative seams are included in chapter 11, but further ideas are suggested here.

Topstitched seam

Topstitching must be absolutely accurate. It may be very close to the seam line or up to 2cm ($\frac{3}{4}$in) away. Keep straight by using the graduations on the needle plate or a strip of masking tape stuck to the machine base as a guide. The machine foot may act as a guide for narrow widths or the quilting guide for wider spaces. On some fabrics the edge of a strip of adhesive cellophane can be used as a guide, providing the tape does not mark the fabric. Several close rows can be worked with the twin or triple needle and the ordinary sewing foot, or by varying the needle position. Lengthen the stitch and work slowly so the fabric feeds evenly. Any thread may be used, but topstitching thread is appropriate on medium and heavy fabrics. A tighter tension and looser pressure, if adjustable, make for a good stitch. If this fails to show up work a second row on top of the first or hand whip over the machine stitches for a cable effect.

When regular sewing thread is used the seam may be decorated by inserting lace, bias folded piping, corded piping, ruffles, ric-rac, self fabric trimmings and so on (see photo no. 54). To make corded piping, cut a strip of fabric on the cross, wide enough to wrap around the cord leaving about 1cm ($\frac{3}{8}$in) turnings. Machine the cord in (no tacking required) using the piping foot (figure 290 (a)), then machine the piping to the under layer of fabric (figure 290 (b)). Place the folded top layer over and topstitch (figure 290 (c)). Machining each step separately saves basting and ensures accuracy. A piped seam is made in the same way with the omission of the cord and using the ordinary machine foot.

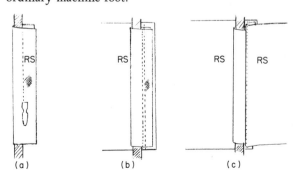

Figure 290   Corded overlaid seam

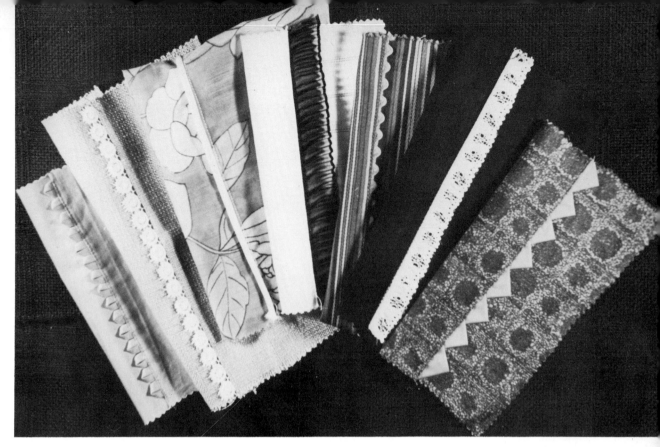

Photo no. 54   Decorated overlaid seams

Topstitching may be done by hand, using a thick thread and either saddle stitch or pickstitch. To preserve the smooth raised effect do not stitch through all layers – skim the needle across the top layer only. Saddle stitching should have longer stitches than spaces, while pickstitching is non-continuous backstitch, worked loosely to leave 'beads' of thread (figure 291).

Handworked decorative seams
These are especially useful for fine blouses and lingerie. Prepare both edges by edge stitching the first and pressing the second fold and tack the sections to a strip of typing paper, using silk thread,

with folded edges meeting or slightly apart if faggoting is to be worked, (figure 292). Use buttonhole or embroidery thread to work faggoting (figure 293) or bar faggoting (figure 294). Photo no. 55 shows an interesting hand buttonholed seam, worked in silk twist on a silk crêpe-de-chine slip, but many different hand embroidery stitches such as feather stitch could be used. Remove the paper before pressing.

Faggoting may be worked on the machine using a long, wide zig-zag or better still the three- or five-step zig-zag (see chapter 5, photo no. 24 (c)).

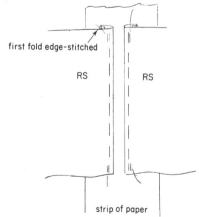

Figure 292   Preparation of seam for faggoting

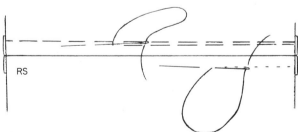

Figure 291   Saddle stitch in parallel rows (upper) RS pickstitch (lower)

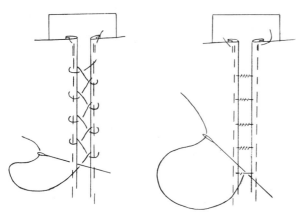

faggoting (left) and bar faggoting (right)

Figure 293   Faggoting   Figure 294   Bar faggoting

Decorative edges

Other areas for structural decoration are edges and hems. (For decorative facings, see chapter 12.) All the types of trimming used for insertion in seams may be inserted around garment edges between garment and facing or between layers of collars and cuffs (photo no. 56).

Other edge decorations:

Rouleau strips and lace edging may be applied by tacking to paper and faggoting in place by hand or machine. The edge of the garment is first finished with a facing or suitable small hem.

Shell edging is popular for soft, delicate and jersey fabrics, and may be worked by hand or machine (photo no. 20). An ordinary binding can be varied by working shell edging over it. The binding needs to be narrowed and the stitching should cover the whole depth of it.

Faced scallops (see chapter 12) are planned after fitting. They may be varied by being graduated in size or alternately one large and one small and so on. A couture touch is the padded scallop with half moon of wadding or lambswool inserted between garment and facing after stitching, and a row of topstitching to hold it in place. In photo no. 57, an idea for an evening dress, the fabric is white rayon crêpe and the topstitching is in gold lurex thread. (In this example the padded scallops also form a topstitched overlaid seam.)

Hand-worked scallops are made by buttonholing round the drawn-out shape and trimming away the excess later (figure 295). They need firm fabric to hold the stitches as they are worked on a single layer. They may be raised by the insertion of another thread under the buttonholing while working. Many machines have a scallop in their range of stitches, which looks particularly effective if corded with crochet cotton (see photo no. 21). Machine over

Photo no. 55   Slip with hand buttonholed seams and rouleau trimming

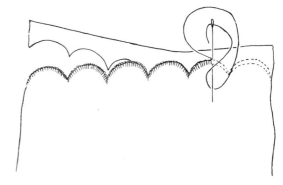

Figure 295   Buttonholing and trimming hand worked scallops

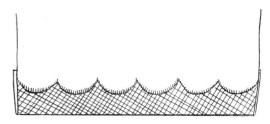

Figure 296   Hand worked scallops with net edges

Photo no. 56   Decorated collar edges

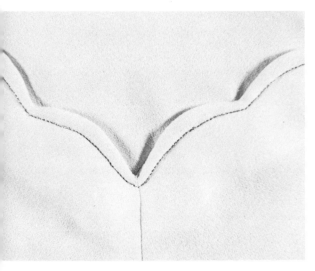

Photo no. 57   Padded scallops set as overlaid seam,
lurex thread

typing paper and tear away afterwards and, as with
hand scallops, trim the edge after stitching.
Net edges   Strips of net, sheer nylon tricot or firm
sheer fabric such as organza, cut on the cross and
folded double may be placed under the edge before
scalloping (or working other satin-stitch based
machine stitches) and both fabrics trimmed after
stitching. This is more decorative and stronger than
plain worked scallops (figure 296).

Applied decoration

This is mostly applied to the surface of the garment as
opposed to the seams or edges and may be a purchased
trimming, made from self fabric or hand or machine
stitchery.

Smocking
The method of inserting the drawing threads is
described on p. 72. When they are all drawn up and
tied off slide the fabric first to one end and then to
the other to make the deep creases necessary to work
on. Then even out before embroidering. Embroidery
stitches for smocking are all simple and mostly based
on stem stitch, and can be found in many embroidery
books. (See photo no. 33.)

Tucking
Use a sewing gauge to mark out evenly, making a
tailor tack or small nick in the fabric at the top and
bottom of each tuck. If the fabric is suitable threads
may be drawn as guide lines. Tucks should be worked
on straight grain and may be any width from pin
tucks to about 3cm ($1\frac{1}{4}$in). There are many types:

Figure 297 Pin tucks – machine down as close to the
            fold as possible; these may be regularly
            spaced or in groups or clusters with
            spaces between.
Figure 298 Cross tucks.
Figure 299 Shell tucks, worked as shell edging by
            hand or machine.
Figure 300 Shadow tucks in sheer fabric with a
            coloured thread inserted afterwards.
Photo no. 58 'Air' or twin needle tucks using the
            special machine foot.
Figure 301 Unspaced tucks, often wider than regular
            tucks.

   Since it is very difficult to estimate the amount of
fabric required, it is usual to cut a tucked section
roughly, work the tucks and then cut out with the
garment pattern. Press tucks all the same way or
symmetrically about the centre line.

Hemstitching and drawn threads
Details can be found in embroidery books. This is
worked by hand or machine on fabric with clear,
even grain, e.g. linen. It is usual to work the stitching
first and draw the threads later, but it can be done
the other way round. Photo no. 59 shows a machine-
worked sample on fine linen suitable for a summer
dress.

Applique
This can vary from the bold, colourful style associated
with children's wear to the delicate subtly coloured

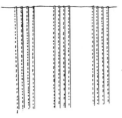

clustered pin tucks

Figure 297   Clustered pin tucks

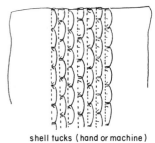

cross tucks

Figure 298   Cross tucks

shell tucks (hand or machine)

Figure 299   Shell tucks (hand or machine)

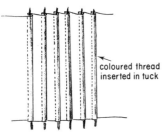

coloured thread inserted in tuck

shadow tucks

Figure 300   Shadow tucks, coloured thread inserted in tuck

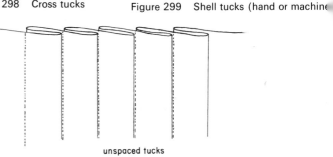

unspaced tucks

Figure 301   Unspaced tucks

Photo no. 58   Twin needle 'air' tucks

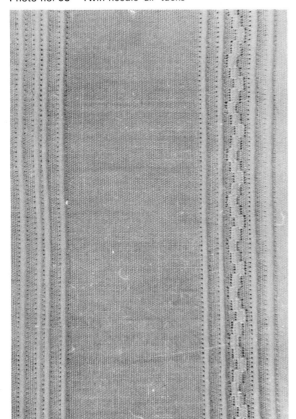

Photo no. 59   Machine hemstitching (Elna Supermatic)

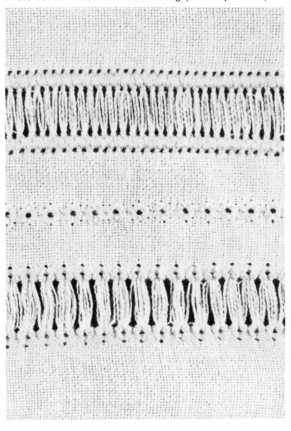

work found on lingerie and evening wear. There are several methods of working, depending on the amount to be done, the fabric and the method of designing the pattern.

Method 1   Attach lightweight iron-on interfacing to the WS of the garment fabric and draw out the design on it in pencil. Taking one piece of the decorating fabric at a time, baste a roughly cut shape on the RS garment, covering the appropriate part of the design. Work a narrow, spaced, zig-zag from the wrong side, turn to the RS and, holding the work in the hand, trim the applied piece closely to the stitching. Working from the RS, cover the stitching and raw edge completely with close satin stitch, wider than the first zig-zag. Decorative stitches may be used or the edge raised with cording. Add further pieces in the same manner. The two designs in photo nos. 60 and 61 were worked by this method, the fish being suitable for adult beachwear and the cockerel for a child's garment. Both designs show additional stitching and beads and were developed from ideas in the Bernina Sewing Machines pamphlet on appliqué.

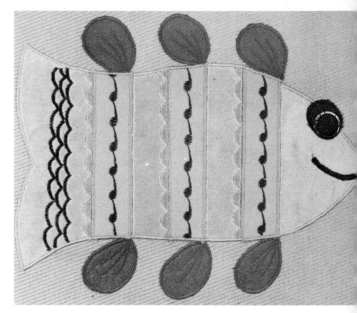

Photo no. 61

Photo no. 60

Method 2   For larger designs (possibly stylized flowers round the hem of an evening skirt) where pieces are bolder and the amount of stitching is proportionately less, the interfacing may be omitted provided the fabric is firm, or vanishing muslin may be used and pressed away later. The designs are drawn on paper, tacked to the RS of the decorative fabric and stitched around with straight stitch. The paper is torn away, the shapes trimmed closely to the stitching, and arranged around the skirt. This gives the advantage that the worker may develop the design as she goes. When all are in place, baste or attach with strips of adhesive cellophane tape and topstitch as before. For badly fraying fabric, place the pieces uncut on the garment with the patterns attached, and zig-zag over the outlines through all thicknesses before tearing away the paper and trimming the shapes. This is a firmer method, but the paper is tedious to remove. Topstitch with satin stitch as usual.

Method 3   Inverted appliqué is shown in photo no. 62. A leaf motif for an evening dress was drawn on paper and basted to the WS garment. The decorative fabric was organza in a lighter shade decorated by rows of zig-zag worked with the wing needle and lurex thread, (photo no. 63). The decorated fabric was applied as in method 1 and the garment fabric cut away underneath after all the stitching (in lurex thread) had been completed. This method is very suitable for delicate work and net is often used for the shapes.

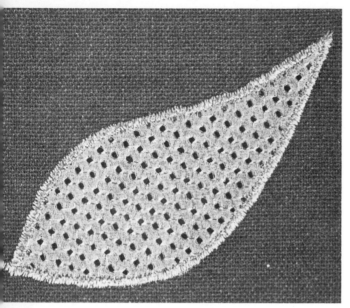

Photo no. 62   Inverted appliqué
Photo no. 63

Beading

One of the earliest forms of dress decoration known to exist, beading has always been extensively used in royal, ecclesiastical and national costume, and enjoyed great popularity in Victorian times and again in the 1920s. Figure 302 shows some of the beads now used: seeds (tiny glass beads), bugles (long thin glass tubes), cabochons (larger beads with holes in the back or bored through their width), round sequins, sequin shapes, pendants, crystals and rhinestones.

Beading may be worked flat before the garment is made up. The design should be simple and is often

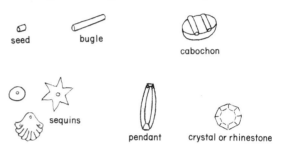

Figure 302   Types of beads

built up on the fabric rather than drawn out in detail first. The decoration in photo no. 64 was evolved in this way.

The techniques of working are shown in figure 303 (a) to (e). Apply vanishing muslin, mull or light-weight lawn to the ws fabric first and attach the beads with silk thread and a beading needle. Sew each bead on separately with a backstitch. Bugles look better if sewn on at a slant rather than end to end (a). Several seeds may be threaded on to the needle at a time (b) and couched down with stitches between them. Single sequins should be attached with a small seed in the middle so that no thread shows (c), and rows of sequins are backstitched one over the other (d). To make long loosely hanging fringe effects (e), take the thread over the last bead and thread back through the rest.

Beading can be very effective on patterned, possibly floral, fabric, picking out the motifs on the fabric and building them up.

Braiding

Braiding was used extensively in Victorian times and was revived in this century by Coco Chanel, who used the decoration to enhance her very simply cut garments. Braids are now made in all fibres, including lurex, and have a plaited or twisted construction which makes them pliable enough to work around

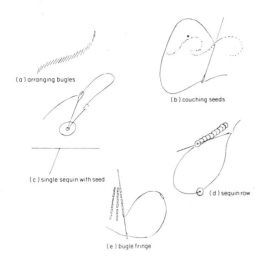

(a) arranging bugles

(b) couching seeds

(c) single sequin with seed

(d) sequin row

(e) bugle fringe

Figure 303   Arranging bugles

Photo no. 64   Decoration with round rouleau and beading

curves. Military braid is flat, up to about 3cm ($1\frac{1}{4}$in) wide and occasionally sold folded down the centre. Round braid is a fine tube, usually rayon, and Russia or soutache a double tubular braid, covered in threads – make sure it is well-covered when purchasing. Jersey cord is a soft braid, often in a scalloped design or hanging as fringing, while gimp braid is firm and wiry. Ric-rac comes in many widths. For washable garments select washable, dye-fast braids.

Designs should be simple, and other forms of decoration such as beading can be combined with it. It is usually better worked out on the garment before or after construction. Soutache may be machined down the middle using the braiding foot, or hand stitched flat (photo no. 65) or on one end to give a raised effect. Designs may begin and end in the middle of loosely woven fabric by pushing the braid through to the ws between fabric threads. Ric-rac should be caught down with a small hand stitch on each point, both sides, not machined down the middle as this makes it curl up in wear. It may be inserted in seams or edges (photo nos. 54 and 56). It combines well with machine or hand embroidery. Military braid needs careful handling when used for binding edges because of its elasticity and should be applied taut. Corners should be mitred. The right side should be stitched first, preferably by slip hemming or running stitch, and the ws hemmed in place underneath. When used as an edging for a garment with interfacing and facing, remove the turnings and machine stitch the three fabric layers together at the edge to give a flat effect before applying the braid. Allow ample for turnings, as military braid unravels easily, and try to arrange for the ends to be stitched in with the garment seams.

Photo no. 65   Soutache braiding, fly front opening

Quilting

Quilting takes up a lot of fabric and so should be worked before the garment pieces are finally cut out. Sections only may be quilted, such as the hems of skirts especially for evening wear, or the whole garment. The latter use is generally for warmth as in housecoats and has a thicker layer of wadding than the former. Trapunto or Italian quilting is an art on its own and outside the scope of this book, but there are many publications dealing with it in detail.

To prepare for machine quilting, lay the backing fabric right side down on the table, cover with the wadding (if it is necessary to piece this overlap it, thinning out both edges to maintain regular thickness), and then the outer fabric, right side up. Keep flat on the table and baste in rows, working from the centre out to the edges along the four straight grains. Add other rows of basting also on straight grain. Only the first lines of quilting in each direction need to be marked and these should be the centre ones. Subsequent lines are machined equidistant from each other by use of the quilting attachment. Squared or diamond patterns are the most usual. Work one vertical and one horizontal row alternately, using straight, zigzag or embroidery stitches (not satin stitch type). Use a lengthened stitch and adjust tension as necessary. Curved designs must be marked out on the fabric first, possibly on the backing fabric, which then goes uppermost under the machine. The general principle is to cover the fabric evenly and not to leave too big spaces without stitching or the wadding layer will move in wear.

Application of purchased trimmings

Trimmings not so far mentioned include ribbons, lace edging, insertions and frilby, woven Dobby and Jacquard trimmings, fringing, bead and sequinned motifs, *broderie anglaise* trimmings and fake fur. Use all these with caution, as they do not fit so naturally with the garment fabric as decoration designed and made by the dressmaker for the particular garment.

Self fabric trimming

Skill and originality in dressmaking can be shown through the making of trimmings which can be used structurally or applied as surface decoration.
Rouleau strips have many uses – a few are suggested here but the reader will be able to devise many more. Rouleau is made by cutting strips of fabric on the true cross. It is assumed that the method of making it is familiar to the reader, but it may not be realized that there are two types – flat and round. Flat rouleau

is made by trimming away nearly all of the turnings before turning through and pressing the completed strip flat with the seam to the underside. Round rouleau requires a large amount of turning to be left to fill it when turned, roughly twice the width of turnings as the measurement from the stitching line to the folded edge, but samples should be tried for effect. It is more difficult to turn and can only be made in smooth fabrics. The bodice of the evening dress in photo no. 64 is decorated with round rouleau and beading. Round rouleau can also be used instead of cord for frog fastenings and Chinese ball buttons.

Flat cross cut rouleau can be applied to edges by faggoting, or several strips can be faggoted together side-by-side to form a wider insertion for a midriff or down the front of a blouse. Long strips can be plaited together three or more at a time to form an attractive braid for surface application or for belts or sleeve bands. Long, narrow, single strips can be applied like tubular braid in surface decoration in flowing designs. Insertion trimming for seams and edges may be made from short lengths. The left hand sample in photo no. 54 was made by folding pieces as in figure 304 (a). Many other designs can be worked out, as the ideas in figure 304 (b) and (c) illustrate. The top of the slip in photo no. 55 is trimmed by

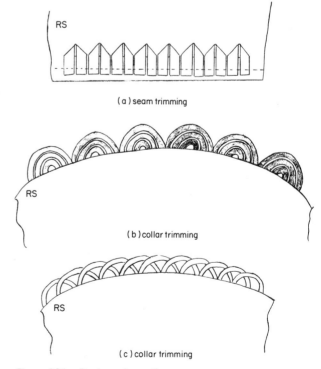

Figure 304   Rouleau decoration

Photo no. 66   Decoration by self fabric strips

Triangle trims (see photo no. 54, right hand sample) are made by folding and interlocking cross cut squares as in figure 306 and inserting them in seams or edges.

Ruffles are made with wide cross cut strips folded double ws together and gathered along the raw edges before inserting.

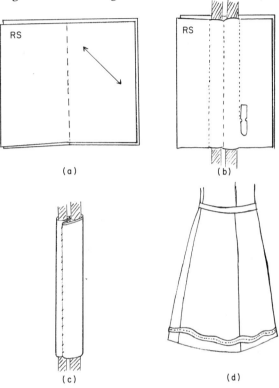

Figure 305   Double cording

inserting small rouleau strips between garment and facing at one end and in a bias strip at the other. All this delicate work needs to be tacked through to paper while being positioned and stitched.

Straight cut strips may be made and turned the same as for rouleau where stretch is not required. The wild silk evening dress in photo no. 66 is decorated around the midriff and floating back panel with 200 interwoven straight cut strips. Whole sections of a garment may be made in this way.

Double cording is made by placing together a piece of cross cut fabric and a piece of lining as shown in figure 305.

(a) Stitch down the middle.

(b) Insert cords and use a piping foot to machine down the outsides of them, trimming the turnings to sufficient to fold back and overlap on the lining side.

(c) Fold one edge under and hem to the other.

(d) Apply to the garment surface by hand in gradual curved shapes.

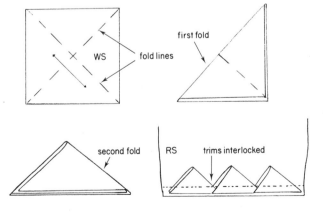

Figure 306   Self fabric triangle trims

Frills can be cut any width on straight grain, single thickness, with an appropriate narrow hem (see chapter 20) and the other edge gathered.

Circular flounce can be made out of any sheer fabric by cutting a large circle, diameter about 50–70cm (20–27in), and then cutting one continuous strip any width from about 6cm ($2\frac{1}{4}$in) starting from the circumference and working in. Strips may be joined together as for bias strip joins. Experiment with paper or calico to determine how much flounce can be cut from a given circle. This flounce is very flared.

Home-made fringing is made by cutting a straight grain strip, width and length as desired, from easily fraying fabric and machining a close zig-zag the length of the strip about 2cm ($\frac{3}{4}$in) from one long edge. Leave this edge intact as it is the insertion edge, but fray off the wider part up to the zig-zagging.

Self fabric ruching can be made of single width weft cut strips neatened along both long edges or doubled, stitched and turned through with the seam pressed along the middle of the underside. It may be any width from about 4cm ($1\frac{1}{2}$in) upwards, depending on its use. Figure 307 shows some of the ways of gathering it:

(a) Gathering along the middle by hand or machine.
(b) Shell gathering – mark out evenly first, placing points each side mid-distance from those on the opposite edge, gather and pull up evenly.
(c) Knife pleating.
(d) Box pleating.
(e) Box pleating with the edges of pleats caught together over the centre line.

Double ruching can be achieved by modifying any of the ideas above with a narrow ruching strip stitched down the middle on top of a wider one, identically pleated or gathered.

Use of the machine in decoration
Chapter 5 and the manuals of the various makes of machine contain many suggestions for getting the most out of a machine. In general if much surface decoration is being done, the fabric should be interfaced with lightweight iron-on interfacing and the work done over typing paper, especially for satin-stitch effects. The insertion of cord, lace or lacet tapes into machine embroidery adds another dimension (see photo no. 26) and much interesting work can be done with the specialized needles and feet. Thick

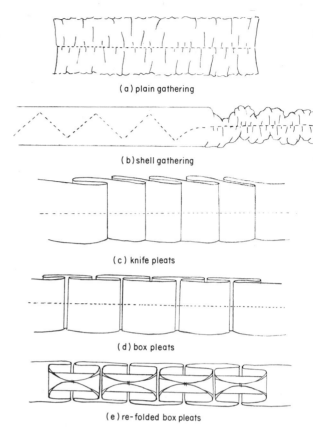

(a) plain gathering

(b) shell gathering

(c) knife pleats

(d) box pleats

(e) re-folded box pleats

Figure 307   Preparation of self fabric ruching

Photo no. 67   Shadow decoration with twin wing needle

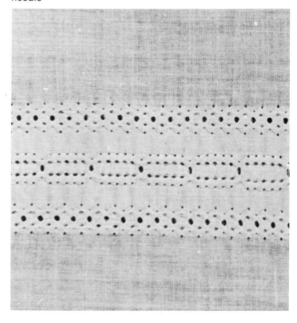

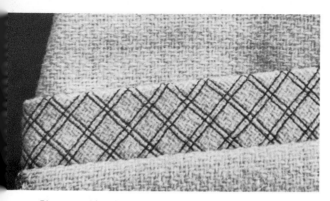

Photo no. 68   Twin needle topstitching on pocket welt

Photo no. 69   Machine shell tucks and scroll design on dress

cords may be couched on or wound in the bobbin and the work placed wrong side up through the machine. Machine manuals give more details, but it must be remembered that adjustments to tension, stitch length and so on are necessary.

Photo no. 67 shows the use of a twin wing needle. Another layer of fabric was sewn through underneath and trimmed after stitching to give a 'shadow' effect. Photo no. 68 is simple topstitching with twin needle and ordinary foot. The jersey dress in photo no. 69, of which a detail is shown in photo no. 70, was decorated with shell tucks and a scroll design stitch in rows, the section being worked before it was cut.

Photo no. 70   Machine decoration enlarged

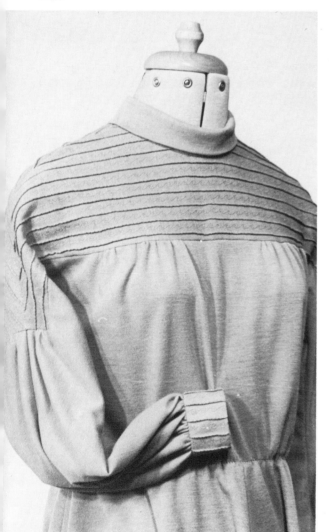

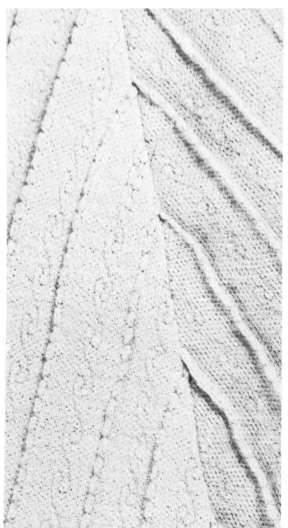

23 Pressing

Pressing has two functions, to flatten and to shape. It is as important to dressmaking as stitching. Chapter 1 considered the elements which separate the amateur from the professional and I doubt whether there is one reader who would not have put the quality of pressing on her list. It needs time, time and more time, as many a sewing operation is completed with three or four separate pressings. Three elements do the job: heat, moisture and pressure. The correct combination of these must be used according to the fabric and the sewing operation being completed. While an attempt is being made to do so in this chapter, it is not possible to lay down in writing hard-and-fast rules for success, as there are far too many variables in obtaining the correct combination of the three elements. Experience develops the skill of handling the iron correctly, seldom completely flat, frequently using the tip alone or the side or holding it above the work without touching at all. The usual error in pressing is using too much pressure, so develop the practice of using as little as possible and increase it later if necessary.

'Overpressing' is a term frequently used to describe the flat, shiny, used look of a garment, but *it is not caused by too much pressing*, but by too much moisture, heat or pressure. It is almost impossible to press too often – amateurs press too little as a rule. What is needed is the sensitive development of skill in handling the cloth and the tools. Pressing is a light 'lift-and-lower' operation, not a sliding one. An understanding of both the fibre content and structure of fabrics is essential, as is the safety precaution of always trying out pressing operations on a sample piece of fabric before touching the garment. Any rules given here must be generalizations, subject always to the worker's discretion after trying the sample.

The first essential is the right equipment, and quite a lot is needed to cover every operation. Most of it is obtainable cheaply, but some items such as a needle board and tailor's ham are fairly expensive. Unfortu-nately there is no guarantee of success without them. Dressmaking requires the right tools for a professional finish. Essential items (some illustrated in figure 308) are:

Boards Standard skirt board, rigid, well-tapered, well-padded with several layers of old blanket or plastic foam, covered in drill which must be easily removable for washing.

Sleeve board.

Wire needle board for pressing velvet and pile fabrics.

Steam iron with sole-plate in good condition.

Cloths A selection of different sizes, including long narrow ones for seams. Suggested fabrics are drill, calico, lawn. They must be boiled to remove dressing. A well-worn cotton sheet serves the purpose well. Some transparent cloths, e.g. muslin or cheesecloth, to enable the work to be seen through them. A piece of wool flannel cloth or similar wool with a matt finish for preserving the dullness on the right side of woollens. A cover to fit over the iron plate, drawn up by a cord, is useful for some operations. Note that damp cloths should not be too wet – soak the cloth in water, wring out, then press lightly all over to remove excess moisture.

Paper Tissue for protecting delicate fabrics, and brown for avoiding seam and hem imprints.

Pressing mitt Preferably purpose-made, but an oven glove kept specially for the purpose serves adequately.

Tailor's ham or cushion For pressing curved areas, side seams, darts, etc.

Padded roll Made from tightly rolled blanket or broom handle covered with blanket, with washable cover, for pressing seams without impressions.

Pounding block Specially made, or any piece of thickish wood with a handle or means of grasping firmly. This is used to apply pressure on several thicknesses of cloth where heavy pressing with the iron would cause the fibres to flatten and shine.

Pressing pads One of terry towelling (a towel will

do) and one sheet of plastic foam about 1cm ($\frac{1}{2}$in) thick.

Clothes brush   For restoring nap.

It is also useful to have available a large table, blanket covered, for pressing and shrinking fabric lengths. For points, collar edges, etc. a point presser (sometimes called seam board or edge presser), which is a piece of hardwood about 2cm ($\frac{3}{4}$in) thick, pointed at one or both ends. It should be covered by drill, but not padded. This is not absolutely essential as a covered pencil may be used.

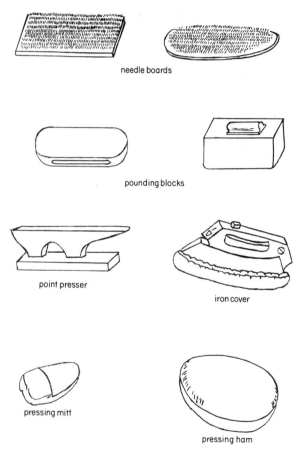

needle boards

pounding blocks

point presser

iron cover

pressing mitt

pressing ham

Figure 308   Pressing equipment

General procedures applicable to most operations

(1) Test everything first on scraps.

(2) Press with the grain, never across weft or bias. Directional pressing for fraying seams. Special care not to stretch bias seams and bias cut garments.

(3) All constructional pressing on the WS if possible, but if RS pressing is essential, cover the area with tissue paper.

(4) Press as you go during construction, i.e. each seam or dart before it is crossed with another. Allow the area to cool before moving off the board.

(5) Avoid touching other parts with iron by using tip, side etc.

(6) Use tailor's cushion for shaped parts.

(7) Arrange garment to press it in the shape it will have when worn, e.g. press seams in correct curves, facings from inside.

(8) Double thickness, e.g. collars, underside first.

(9) To avoid imprints, place garment against hard surface when pressing from WS and padded surface when pressing from RS.

(10) Shine and basting marks are removable by covering with damp cloth on RS and holding iron above to steam. Brush if suitable for fabric. Very lightly steam press if suitable. Avoid deep basting marks by pressing very lightly over them in the first place, then removing them for heavier press. Pure silk thread marks least.

Seams

Several pressings are always required. Press the stitching line first to remove pucker or crinkle. If it does not come out at this stage, restitch the seam. Then press to give direction to the turnings. Press again after neatening. With some seams e.g. the underarm part of armscye, backs of pleats, the first press and the after-neatening press only are required as seams do not have a flat direction. Avoid seam imprints by pressing over a padded roll or slipping strips of brown paper between the garment and seam turnings. If they do occur remove by slipping the side of the iron under the turnings.

Keep scissors handy to clip through the turnings on inward curves and corners, but the minimum amount only. On one edge eased to another be careful not to shrink the part below the ease. If pressing appears to have shrunk seams a little, press the area between the seams afterwards.

Darts

Press the stitching line without direction first. Press horizontal darts down, vertical towards the centre, thick fabrics with darts slashed open. Use a tailor's cushion to achieve a curved shape at the end or lift the work up at the pointed end. A rotary motion with the tip of the iron gives good shaping.

Gathers

Press before gathering to avoid pressing the gathers. Steam by holding a steam iron above the work if necessary. Part below the gathers – work the tip of the iron into gathers, lifting the gathered part from the board. Shirring and smocking are also steamed only.

Zip openings

Press on RS over a padded surface, inserting paper between the teeth and fabric for sheers. Be careful of the iron heat with nylon zips.

Skirt hems

Never press around a hem as the edge is on the bias. Press in short motions up from the crease to the stitching line only. Never press the edge down to the fabric. Should a ridge appear (possibly during wear or after dry cleaning) remove by sliding the side of the iron under the hem. Brown paper may be used to prevent imprints. Soft hems should be steamed and patted into place only.

Necklines

To avoid stretching, place a small piece at a time on tailor's cushion. Place RS of the garment to the cushion and press with the facing uppermost but holding the neckline in the curve it will have on the body. Press collars from the outer edge towards the neck and keep curved. Completion of a tailor's collar – place the garment on a stand and steam into shape.

Pockets

Avoid imprints of flaps, pocket bags, etc. by placing brown paper under. If heavy pressure is required, use a pounding block.

Pleats

If necessary baste to press, press lightly, remove the basting once the fold shows for a harder press. A pounding block may be used. Press the back folds first, then the top folds. If it is vital to press flat, insert brown paper strips to avoid imprints on other pleats.

Cowls and drapes

Press small areas at a time. Be careful not to press in unwanted folds. Allow to cool before moving each area.

Facings

If understitching, do this immediately after pressing the stitching line. If not, press the stitching line, trim etc. edges, press the turnings open before pressing the facing with the seam to the underside. Press from the facing side. With front opening and revers mark the lower end of the rever fold clearly, so that the facing seam below it may be pressed to the underside, but the seam above to the garment side so it will be underneath when the revers are open. Baste to press if necessary.

Sleeves

Give no direction to the lower half of the armhole seam. Press the upper half with the tip of the iron as figure 309, then over the shoulder area from RS using a pressing mitt to support and tissue paper to protect the fabric.

Press the lower edge to avoid stretching by slipping the iron inside the sleeve to press the hem or facing. As shown in figure 310, work a little at a time and rotate the sleeve.

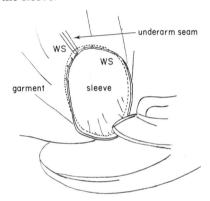

Figure 309   Pressing a sleevehead

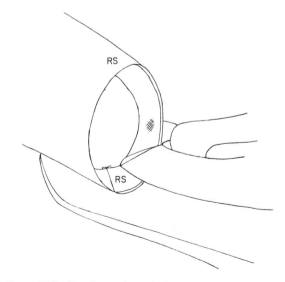

Figure 310   Pressing a sleeve facing

Finished garment

A garment should need no more than a touch up if properly pressed during construction. Press double parts first, then sleeves and neckline, bodice and skirt last. Move the completed parts away from your body as you work. Leave the warm garment on a dress stand to set and cool.

Fabrics

All the above directions are subject to alteration if the method does not suit the fabric. Awareness of the fibre and construction of fabric and its behaviour under the iron is the priority. Techniques for various fibres are as follows:

Cotton   High temperature, pressing dark colours on WS to avoid shine. Press dry to avoid puckering and possible mildew. To add moisture use a damp cloth and press the garment till dry, or dampen the pressing board with a wet cloth and hot iron first.

Linen   Press on WS to avoid shine. Steam press, then press till dry.

Wool   Fibres are pliable under a combination of heat and moisture and then set in the position in which they were pressed. The permanence of the shaping depends on the amount of pressure and the time for which it is applied. Hence tailors use heavy irons. Once shaped, keep the areas away from steam or they will return to their original shape. If the fabric shows during tests that it is likely to shine or flatten, use the pounding block to press the moisture in. Napped surfaces lose surface under heavy pressing, so use a wool press cloth to cover the board and protect RS of face cloth, flannel, etc. Try hard worsteds over a plastic foam pad as they may look fresher this way.

Silk   Most silks watermark, therefore if moisture is needed use a slightly damp cloth with a dry cloth between it and the fabric. On RS use tissue paper. Press white silk very little to avoid yellowing. Wild silk – press dry. Test all silks carefully.

Rayons   Medium hot iron, test to determine shine.

Nylon   Very cool iron, press damp or dry.

Other thermoplastics (acrylics, polyesters, acetates) Cool iron – test – if shine develops it is a layer of melted fibre and is not removable. Press with light pressure on WS. Some synthetic jerseys respond well to a damp cloth, but test first. Crimplene jersey steams well.

Suede or leather   Dry iron, warm only, no cloth but brown paper. Work quickly on a thick pad. Brush suede nap while still warm.

Mohair   Generally better with a dry iron as it may flatten and matt.

Vinyl and plastics   Cool iron over a dry cloth.

Metallics   Press very little, dry iron over tissue paper.

Fibre blends   Press as for the weaker fibre (e.g. cool iron for wool/nylon blend).

The construction of a fabric also has a bearing on pressing:

Knitteds   Press in the direction of lengthwise ribs, never across them. Lift the iron or glide gently. Press on WS, not too much moisture to prevent stretch.

Pile, fleecy and napped fabrics   Place RS fabric to needleboard. Steam or dry iron according to fibre. Lift the fabric gently over board, do not drag. For facings, lay a piece of self cloth RS down over the facing, with a needleboard under the garment. It is also possible to press small areas without a needleboard by standing an iron on end and pulling WS fabric over it. For pressing during wear hold over a steaming kettle or hang for a long period in a steamy bathroom.

Fur fabric   If little pressing is required because of rich pile, a finger press may suffice. Seam edges may be catch-stitched back to fabric. Test for reaction on needleboard or terry towelling with light pressure and cool iron.

Lace   Press on WS on layers of towelling. Avoid damaging patterns by covering with tissue paper. Press the point of the iron into scalloped edges.

Poult, grosgrain, brocade, embroidered and quilted fabrics, beaded fabrics   Test for very cool iron, light pressure on WS, on the plastic foam pad. Possibly catch seam turnings back to underlining. Take care of loose threads on WS fabric, as they may catch in the iron point.

Satin   May watermark with steam pressing. Never press with basting in as marks will remain. Warm, dry iron, gentle touch on WS. Aim for a soft look – do not overpress – seams need not be quite flat. Be careful of imprints.

Soft, gauzy woollens   Light pressure, steam iron, may be better dry, over a pad of self fabric.

Embossed, seersucker, plissé, textured fabrics, crêpe WS, dry iron, very light pressure on plastic foam or terry pad.

Foam-backs   Cool iron, damp cloth or light pressure with a steam iron.

24 Special Techniques for Difficult Fabrics

Since fabric is the raw material of dressmaking, an understanding of its manufacture, behaviour and characteristics is essential at every stage, from the choice of a suitable style to the final pressing and even beyond to the correct storage and care of the completed garment. Fabric qualities affect marking, choice of haberdashery items, selection of machine tension, pressure, stitch, needle and foot, choice of techniques, for example type of hem or opening, and pressing methods. Choices can be made only in the light of both knowledge and experience, but this chapter is intended as a short cut for those still acquiring experience.

Two factors about every fabric must be known and understood – its fibre content and its construction, including finish. The latter is usually obvious but it is not so easy to ascertain the fibre unless one does so at the time of purchase. Experience and fibre tests help, but these can be difficult and inconclusive and it is better to buy from a reliable source and make a note of the manufacturer's fibre content tag rather than buy fabric the fibre content of which is unknown.

Broadly speaking, the fibre content affects only the choice of thread and haberdashery, the pressing methods and the wearing and care potential, while the construction of the fabric affects all aspects of dressmaking. The notes that follow therefore are concerned mainly with fabric *construction*, but the reader should remember to weigh the advice given with what she knows about the fibre.

Other references are found in many sections of the book, especially chapters 7, 8, and 23.

Bulky fabrics

This heading includes a wide range of fabrics all of which present making-up problems entirely on account of their thickness, in addition to any caused by their specific structure, such as double-cloths, quilted and embroidered fabrics, fur, leather and their imitations. The specific characteristics are dealt with in later sections – this section deals with the bulk aspect only.

Suitable styles Avoid fullness in style or fit. Gathers are unsuitable and so, in many cases, are pleats. In the areas where the pleats are stitched down, the underlayers should be removed and replaced by support fabric (see p. 75).

Double areas such as welt or flap pockets, fold-back cuffs and facings should be avoided, as should bound buttonholes unless they are essential because the fabric frays. Sometimes the problems of having two layers of fabric may be avoided by reducing the thickness of the fabric itself, e.g. removing a layer of double cloth, or by replacing it with a thinner one for facings, pockets and linings.

Flared skirts are unsuitable not only because of bulk on the figure but because the hems present difficulty (chapter 20). They must be narrowed, bulk reduced, and possibly replaced by false hems.

Cutting Single cutting may be necessary.

Machining Loosen the pressure and tension and use a long stitch. Possibly a roller foot.

Seams Grade thoroughly, neaten appropriately, i.e. no edge stitching. Graded edges should be neatened separately where necessary. Understitching is required to make enclosed seams lie correctly, although this cannot be done with pile fabrics. Topstitching, except for pile fabrics, produces flat seams and edges. In some thick fabrics it may sink in and not show. A second row should be worked over the first in regular or topstitching thread or a machine triple stitch employed. See also chapter 11.

Darts Trim, press open and neaten as seams.

Pressing Seam imprints may occur with the firm pressing needed. Methods of avoiding these are given in chapter 23. A pounding block is helpful.

Double cloth

The advantages of double cloth are that it is very warm, having an air layer between two cloth layers, and it is thick without containing thick yarns. It is usually coat weight.

True double cloth (as opposed to laminated or bonded fabrics) may be made by weaving two layers of cloth at the same time with two warps and two wefts, arranging occasional interweaving of these threads between the two layers in such a way as to join them. Fabric which appears to be double cloth should be carefully examined by cutting a small piece and attempting to separate the layers by snipping the connecting threads. Fabric made in the way described will be damaged by separation since its threads are cut, and must therefore not be separated into layers while being made up. It needs to be treated as a bulky fabric, but while it may be made up on either side, cannot make a really satisfactory reversible garment.

Double cloth is more frequently manufactured, however, by interweaving a *fifth* thread between the two layers of cloth which may then be clipped apart without damage, an advantage which may be utilized in many construction operations and enables the garment to be made reversible. It is this type of fabric to which this section applies.

Suitable styles Since some seams can cause difficulties it is advisable to have as few as possible, avoiding those with ease on one edge. Set-in sleeves are possible but tricky, and raglan or kimono styles often suit the bulk of the fabric better anyway. More scope in styling and construction is given if it is remembered that while reversible garments may be worn either way out, the two sides do not have to be identical. Some of the suggestions here produce such variations.

General principles of construction There are two main differences between conventional and reversible garments, firstly that no interfacing, lining or facings are possible, and secondly that much of the construction work is easier to do by hand as the machine cannot easily reach all parts. As double cloths are usually thick woollen coatings, skilful hand stitching sinks invisibly into them. Experience and imagination will produce new ideas and processes, but few are given here as guidelines to the type of thinking which must be employed.

Darts Separate the layers around the dart sufficiently to machine one layer. Trim and press open; neatening is unnecessary. The other dart may be similarly stitched, but accuracy is difficult and it is better to trim it, turn the edges under and slip-stitch (figure 311).

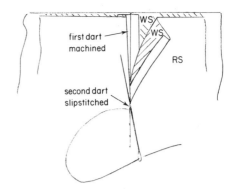

Figure 311 Darts on double cloth

Seams Methods include:

(a) The conventional double-stitched seam, with all four layers machined together on the stitching line, and three trimmed away to about half width while the remaining layer is folded under and machined down flat over them (figure 312). This produces a similar but not identical seam on both sides.

(b) A special overlapped seam which is very flat and identical on both sides. On each piece, separate the layers for the depth of the turning and cut one away (a different one on each piece) exactly to the stitching line (figure 313 (a)). Fold over the long layers to meet the cut edges and tack down (figure 313 (b)). Overlap the two edges on the stitching lines, tack and machine close to the fold. Turn the work to the other side and machine the second fold (figure 313 (c)).

(c) An open seam may be finished and topstitched to show contrasting turnings on one side and ordinary topstitching on the other. Trim away the two under layers of turning, fold the top layers over them and topstitch (figure 314).

Set-in sleeves These may be attached by a double stitched seam or by separating the layers around the sleeve head, turning in the edges to face one another and slipping the armhole edge, with turnings trimmed to half width, in between the two layers. Topstitch on the folded edge through all the layers (figure 315). This is difficult to do with equal accuracy on both sides. To avoid the topstitching, lay the armhole on top of the sleeve, machine through both layers of armhole and one layer of sleeve, turn out flat. Turn under the second sleeve layer and slip stitch the fold down (figure 316).

Similar methods may be used for mounting collars.

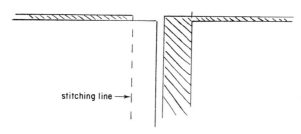

Figure 312   A double-stitched seam on double cloth

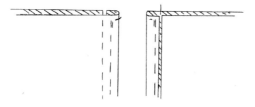

(a) trimming both layers

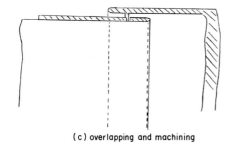

(b) folding both long edges

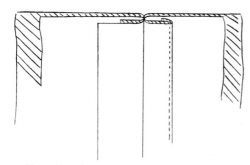

(c) overlapping and machining

Figure 313   Identical overlapped seam for double cloth

Figure 314   Topstitched open seam for double cloth

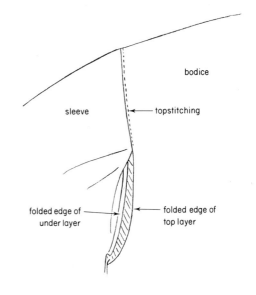

Figure 315   Application of sleeve between layers of fabric (double cloth)

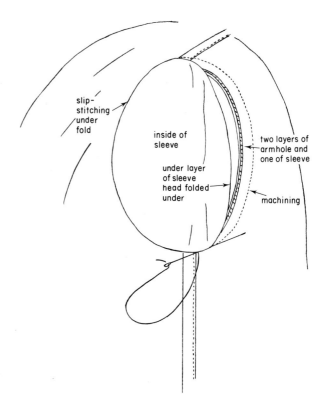

Figure 316   Application of sleeve to armhole in double cloth (method without topstitching)

Edges

(a) The layers may be separated, turned in to one another, graded and the folds slip-stitched together.

(b) Purchased corded piping may be inserted between the layers in (a).

(c) A flatter method is to bind the edge with military braid.

(d) A method with different appearance on each side, suitable for straight edges only, is to trim away one layer to the stitching line, fold the other over it, turn under the raw edge and topstitch. Corners treated in this way should have the long layer mitred (figure 317).

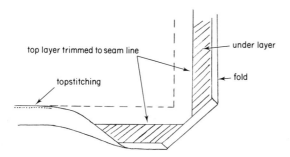

Figure 317   Mitred corner for machined hem in double cloth

Fastenings   These can produce a problem since there must be a set on each side. Worked buttonholes are possible, also piped ones made by the following method as shown in figure 318:

(a) Cut the slit first and insert fine scissors to snip away a few connecting threads.

(b) Turn in the edges on each other to leave a box opening, tacking each fold firmly to keep the turnings in position. Press.

(c) Make the pipings by folding in half lengthwise strips cut from one layer only of the double fabric.

(d) Insert these between the layers of the buttonhole, tack and topstitch into position.

Reversible coats are often fastened with a hook and worked loop and a tie belt. Press studs and novelty clasps, provided they are flat, are also suitable.

Patch pockets   A patch pocket on each side of the fabric can be weighty and cause strain as it cannot be reinforced. A possible variation, giving a different appearance on each side, is to make a horizontal slit

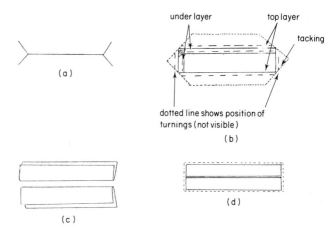

Figure 318   Reversible buttonholes for double cloth

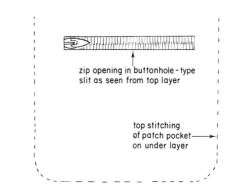

Figure 319   Patch pocket for double cloth coat

and insert a zip on one side (or arrange a button and loop fastening to draw the slit together) and a patch pocket on the other, positioned as shown in figure 319. Keep the zip closed when wearing the coat pocket side out. On the other side the zip forms an opening to an inside pocket.

This last suggestion is typical of the ideas which can be designed for this unique fabric.

Bonded or laminated fabrics

These are types of double fabrics but are not reversible, since the under layer acts as an interlining or lining. Almost any fabric can have another layer bonded. Common examples are jerseys, lace, suedettes, crêpes and woven acrylics. Linings may be woven or knitted and nylon tricot is frequently used. Bonded linings make the fabric more stable and in effect produce pre-mounted fabrics. Plastic foam is the most usual bonded interlining, its great advantage being that it adds warmth out of all proportion to its weight, making lightweight fabrics suitable for winter wear. Laminated fabrics enjoyed great popularity in recent years but their use is declining possibly because of their main disadvantage – the impossibility of obtaining flat well-pressed seams and the rather balloon-like appearance they give to a garment. They interfere with a fabric's draping qualities in a way which imparts stability to loose weaves and jerseys but detracts from their appearance. There are several methods of production:

(a) one layer is coated with adhesive, the other superimposed and pressed.
(b) both layers contain a proportion of heat sensitive fibres (e.g. foam-backs) to which heat and pressure are applied.
(c) three layers of fabric are used, the top fabric, a layer of fine foam, and a lining.

Layers of laminated fabrics should not be separated, but the fabric is constructed into garments as for a mounted fabric (see chapter 8) and also as a bulky fabric. Do not purchase off-grain fabric as it cannot be straightened. The lamination stabilizes the garment sufficiently to allow it to hang well but the pattern or grain will look unsightly.

Cut out right side uppermost so that the grain or pattern can be seen. Machine with tissue paper next to the foam to prevent damage.

Quilting

Purchased or home quilted fabrics are another type of double fabric, the main element in their handling being their bulk. They combine well with other fabrics, e.g. satin, or with unquilted sections of the same fabric. Any type of fine fabric, knitted or woven of any fibre, may be quilted. Garments must be mounted or lined to protect the wadding. The mounting fabric may be applied before the quilting is worked so that the stitching goes through all three layers. In general they are treated as bulky fabrics (p. 162) and simple styles are required.

Stitching Protect the wadding with tissue paper when machining. Finish off raw edges securely with binding or machine overcasting to prevent the wadding from tearing away.
Bulk The wadding may be removed from double thicknesses. Garments of heavy quilting should have facings and hems of other fabrics.

Fur fabrics

Fur fabrics can be made to imitate real fur or can have a character of their own. Man-made fibre is used for the pile, but the backing may be of a different fibre, mostly cotton. The length of the pile is variable. Mostly it runs in one direction, when it should be cut pile down, but sometimes it has a left and right as well which should run the same way all round the garment. Jersey-backed fur fabric is more flexible than woven.

Suitable styles Styles should have as few seams as possible, no double pieces if they can be avoided, and no pleating or gathering. Alter the pattern to reduce the ease to the minimum. Raglan sleeves are more suitable than set-in styles.
Pile Directional working is important both for cutting and stitching. When cutting do so singly with small scissors which will snip just through the backing, not the pile. Pull the pieces away gently to separate the pile from the remaining fabric.
Marking Thread marking may fall out and chalk marking not show, so it is permissible, since all fur fabric garments must be lined, to mark in ball point pen.
Edges Facings are best avoided – garments may be lined to the edge. If self-fabric facings are, however, used, a good way to prevent bulk at the edge seam is to lay the facing on the garment ws together, baste down the edge, remove turnings and bind the two edges together with leather strips.
Fastenings Leather strips make excellent bound buttonholes. Other methods of fastening are buttons and cord loops, frogs, toggles, button and chain fastenings, buckles and leather straps, fancy clasps and furrier's hooks and eyes. Zips can be used only on short pile fabrics and even then the pile should be sheared away from the turnings of the opening and the zip inserted by hand in the conspicuous (i.e. teeth showing) method.
Stitching Use a long machine stitch and loose tension and pressure. After stitching, trim pile away from the seam allowances and the slashed and trimmed darts, and because the fabric will not press well, catch the seam allowances back with catch stitch to the fabric backing only. Any pile hairs caught in the seam on the right side should be eased out with a bodkin or stiletto and stroked over the seam to cover it.

In other respects treat the fabric as a bulky fabric. As they cannot be understitched, facings may be made to lie flat by lifting them from the garment and working a loose catch stich in lines 2–3cm ($\frac{3}{4}$–1$\frac{1}{4}$in) apart parallel to the stitching to join together the backings of the facing and the garment (figure 320).

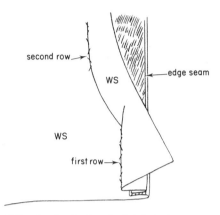

Figure 320   Catch stitching fur fabric facing to garment

Photo no. 71   Sun dress and jacket in suede, leather by Barrow Hepburn, outfit designed by Caroline Charles (hat by Edward Mann). Photograph by Christopher Moore, by permission of Barrow Hepburn

Leather and suede

Leather, once used only for motoring coats and trimming clothes to make them wear longer, has now been in the front of the fashion scene for several years, and is used for all manner of clothing from dresses to bikinis. The simple cut of the sun-dress and bell-sleeved jacket by Caroline Charles in photo no. 71 shows what can be done. Modern machines cope so well with leather and suede that they have come well within the scope of the average dressmaker, providing a few basic rules are observed.

Most leather clothing is made from sheepskins, but goatskin, cattle-hide and pigskin are also used. Leather is made up of bundles of fibres which interweave in a three-dimensional way, making it porous, flexible and strong. It 'breathes' much like conventional fabrics and has excellent insulation because of the air pockets between the fibres. The skin of an animal is not of uniform strength, quality or thickness. The centre area of the skin (figure 321) is from

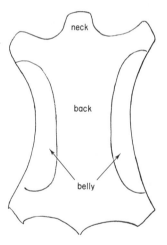

Figure 321   Centre area of animal skin

the back of the animal and has the firmest texture, so the centre fronts and backs of patterns should be placed in this area, while the belly areas at the sides of the skin are more flabby and elastic and should fall at the sides of the garment or be used for facings, etc. Leathers suitable for the home dressmaker include:

Calf   Soft and pliable.
Nappa   The split outer layer of cattle hide or sheared sheepskin, which is glossy on one side.
Suede   The under layer of split cowhide, pigskin or sheared sheepskin, which is brushed up

to give a pile running upwards in a garment.
Buckskin Suede from the deer.
Chamois The inner layer of sheepskin, very fine and soft, also from goatskin.

Skins are sold by the square foot. Take the pattern pieces with you when purchasing and try them on the skins for maximum economy. Buy sufficient of the same batch at one time, as tanning and dyeing may vary from batch to batch and the difference may not show until the garment is dry cleaned.
Suitable styles Choose styles cut in small pieces rather than large for economy. Avoid gathers, pleats or too much ease. Reduce the amount of ease in a sleevehead to about 1cm ($\frac{3}{8}$in), depending on the flexibility of the leather. For economy and fashion effect, leather can be combined with fur, fur fabric, wool fabrics, knitting and crochet. Make a toile first, preferably from thick fabric (felt is ideal) to check cut and fit. Alterations cannot be made in leather.
Cutting Examine the skin carefully and mark imperfections on the wrong side with chalk. Lay the pattern pieces singly in a balanced way so that the same quality of skin occurs identically on the left and right of the garment. Secure the pattern by pins in the turnings only (if they will go in) or by weights. For economy, facings may be cut of other fabric or omitted altogether and the garment lined to the edge. If the design seems wasteful, cut it into smaller pieces (known as 'piecing') by introducing yokes or panels, but plan to make the cuts part of the style. Irregular joins in facings are acceptable. Cut with very sharp shears or a Stanley knife and keep straight edges immaculate by using a steel rule. Mark on the ws with tailor's or blackboard chalk, whichever proves more satisfactory on a particular skin.

Because the skin is lightly stretched during tanning, the direction for laying the pattern, cutting, stitching and pressing is from top to bottom (the neck end of the skin being the top).
Interfacing Use iron-on interfacing, checking first that it withstands dry cleaning, or woven interfacing of a weight suitable to the leather, e.g. hair canvas, glued into position with a rubber based adhesive.
Gluing Rubber based adhesive may be used sparingly to secure hems, seam turnings and darts after trimming. Hammer these areas into place after gluing with a hammer covered in leather to prevent damage. This helps them to fold firmly and presses the edge while thinning out the leather in areas of double thickness.
Topstitching Hems, seams, etc. may be topstitched for decoration and extra hold after gluing.
Seams Seams should be taped where the leather is flexible. They may be orthodox open seams or lapped by removing the seam allowance from the top layer, laying the cut edge over the other layer and topstitching with straight, zig-zag or decorative stitch.

Decorative seams may be made by removing both seam allowances, punching holes in a regular sequence with a rotary punch, and joining together with lacing or leather thonging. It is better to use purchased thonging than strips cut from the skin as it is stronger. Eyelets may be applied to the holes for extra strength and decoration.
Fastenings Zips look well hand-stitched in place, but use a semi-concealed setting to reduce bulk. Hammered in snaps and fastenings are suitable. When working bound buttonholes, do the first stage in the normal manner, but after applying the facing topstitch around the buttonhole just outside the stitching line of the binding, right through to the facing. Trim away a rectangle of facing (figure 322). A shorter method is to cut away a rectangle from the garment, glue behind it strips of leather folded double to make pipings, apply the facing, topstitch and trim the facing as before. Reinforce buttons by stitching through to a small button underneath.

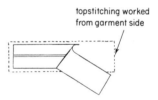

topstitching worked from garment side

Figure 322   Trimming away facing from bound buttonhole in leather; topstitching worked from garment side

Pockets Welt, bound, flap and patch pockets are all suitable.
Decoration According to fashion, leather may be stencilled, painted, appliquéd, embroidered, especially by machine, braided, beaded, plaited in strips and quilted, especially chamois. A traditional decoration is to cut lines of small slits, straight or in patterns, and thread contrasting thonging through. Photo no. 72 shows thonging and fringing decoration on a tabard.

Lining Leather garments should be lined for ease of taking on and off and to prevent dye colour rubbing off on other garments. Anti-static lining is advisable as leather builds up static electricity. It can be applied in several ways, including the following:

(a) In garments with no facings, cut the lining to the same pattern and make up separately. Attach as a normal lining to turnings, but at the edges turn under a small hem on the garment to cover lining edge. Top stitch through all thicknesses.

(b) In garments with facings, sew bias tape to the inner edge of the facing and slip-stitch the lining to this.

(c) Lining may be glued in place under the loose edge of the facing.

Leather-look plastics and suedettes are handled as leather. Some of the techniques advised for vinyl also suit these fabrics well.

Vinyl

Vinyl fabrics come in several types. Transparent vinyl has no backing. Opaque vinyl is a fine layer, coloured or printed, laminated to a knitted fabric backing. This is a fashion fabric. Also fabrics of various fibres and patterns may be coated with transparent vinyl. The fabric is inflexible and sticks to itself, qualities which make it rather difficult to handle. Simple styles with no gathers and almost no ease are demanded. The 'A' line gives about the right amount of flare. The knit-backed versions are easier to handle and can have set-in sleeves.

Pinning and tacking All types show permanent holes where pins or tacking have been, so patterns should be pinned in seam allowances only or held in place with weights, and tacking should be replaced by paper clips or adhesive cellophane tape for fitting.

Cutting Because layers stick together, place backing sides together when cutting double.

Stitching Little paper clipping is needed while machining, but difficulties arise in passing the fabric smoothly under the machine foot. A roller foot helps, as does dusting the fabric with talcum powder or French chalk or spraying with silicone spray. If the machine foot or feed dog leave marks when tested on a scrap of fabric, machine the garment with paper to protect it. Lightweight typing paper works well. Finish machine ends by hand as backstitching leaves another set of holes. Long stitches and light pressure and tension are required.

Avoid hand sewing if possible. Hems and turnings can be stuck down or topstitched. Welt or lapped seams made by trimming away some of the seam allowance, overlapping the edges and topstitching one or more rows, are suitable as they are both flat.

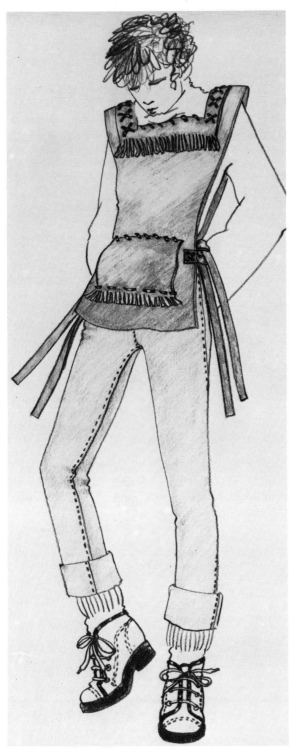

Photo no. 72   Leather trousers and tabard by Barrow Hepburn

Fastenings   Suitable fastenings are machined-on Velcro and hammered-in snaps. To apply a zip, use a semi-concealed setting, fold back the turnings and topstitch, finally inserting the zip by hand, taking an occasional backstitch through the same holes made by the machine topstitching. Buttons should be stitched on with a small supporting button underneath to prevent tearing a hole. Buttonholes are made as for leather.

Pressing   No pressing may be done unless the vinyl is backed or a cloth used.

Sheers

The term 'sheer' is the fashion term now given to any diaphanous fabric no matter what its construction, fibre or texture. It includes laces, voile, open patterned jerseys, crisp organdie or organza, and fluid fabrics such as chiffon and georgette, all of which must be worked with consideration for their transparency. Many have other problems also, being slippery and fraying, for example.

When sheers are mounted (the two fabrics being made up as one) the limitations cease to exist and they are treated as normal fabrics. Mounting hides seams more effectively than loose lining, but loose lining preserves the sheer effect of the fabric. It is possible to combine both methods, for example by making up the sheer with gathers and the lining with darts before combining the two by mounting to join the seams. Mountings and linings may be of regular fabrics or of more exotic fabrics such as satin or lace.

Suitable styles   These include all types of fullness, drapery and tucking, and all manner of delicate decoration such as shadow work, picot edging, smocking, and so on. Seams should be as few as possible as they show up so much, kimono styles being ideal. Fullness should not be too skimpy – slash and spread pattern pieces to add more fullness if the style is not designed for sheers.

As seams are not strong, never aim for a tight fit.

Handling   Handle the fabric as little as possible, making a toile for fitting from muslin as it is also sheer. Avoid tailor's chalk or tracing paper. Use only fine pins and needles and very sharp scissors to avoid pulling the fabric. Tacking and marking should be done in silk thread and removed cautiously. Do not interface.

Machining   To prevent damage to delicate fabrics, machine with tissue paper over the feed dog and under the presser foot. Keep pressure regular but loosen both tensions. Machine slowly to prevent puckering.

Processes   Substitute gathers for darts whenever possible, as darts show through in an unsightly way. To avoid finishing off thread at the points of darts, 'bobbin stitching' is often advised. Thread the top thread as usual as far as but not through the needle. Thread the bobbin, pull up the thread through the hole and thread the needle. Pull out about three times the length of the dart and tie the end to the spool end. Rewind the spool of thread to draw up the bobbin thread until it is tight. Stitch the dart from the point to the wide end. The problems with this method are that is is not easy to stitch a dart accurately from the pointed end and fine fabrics may bunch up under the needle. Always test out the method first. Darts should be trimmed and finished like seams.

Seams   As they show through they must be neat on the ws and as narrow as 3mm ($\frac{1}{8}$in) when finished. French seams, lingerie seams and mock French seams are suitable, but not open seams nor any seam requiring topstitching. Hems must be very narrow or if straight may have two wide even folds, (p. 139).

Edges   Facings are not possible because they cast an unsightly shadow. Possible methods include:

(a) cutting the part double, using one piece to line the other fully, e.g. bodices.

(b) binding or, better still, French binding.

(c) adding frills or flounces of double or single fabric, with the raw edge picoted.

Fastenings   Use only lightweight hand-sewn zips or invisible zips. Avoid buttonholes, bound because the binding shows through and worked because it makes too much strain on the fabric. Buttons and worked loops are suitable, also invisible press studs, hooks and eyes and self fabric rouleau ties.

Loosely woven and fraying fabrics

Most badly fraying fabrics are made of man-made filament fibres or silk, e.g. synthetic twills, satins, crêpes, velvets and metallic fabrics, but others may fray because of the looseness of their weave, mohair being an example.

Cut out with extra wide seam allowances and arrange not to have the garment too tightly fitting or seam slippage will occur. Mounting helps to stabilize the fabric and seams should be reinforced (see p. 76). Iron-on interfacings can help to preserve weak areas, but should be used in small strips or patches as required. If interfacing shows through the loose weave, apply it after mounting.

Work directionally, particularly when machining or pressing. Loosen tensions, both top and bottom, but maintain the balance. Machine slowly. Bulky loose weaves require a roller foot or tissue paper to protect them.

Neatening should be firm and close. Binding or Hong Kong finish are good, and if machine overcasting is used it may be necessary to work one row over the edge and another alongside it to give a depth of neatening. If not too thick, edge stitching is by far the firmest method.

Avoid clipping turnings wherever possible as in sharply curved seams, 'slash-to-dot' operations, cut openings and worked buttonholes. If buttonholes are essential make bound ones with the binding cut on the cross and the cut well supported by iron-on interfacing. Buttons and rouleau loops are a possible alternative.

Handle sensitively and as little as possible.

Satin and sateen

Satin Satin may be made of silk, rayon, acetate, nylon or terylene. It varies from heavy crêpe-backed satin, double satin and duchesse satin to the lighter weight slipper satin. The sheen is produced by using filament yarns of low twist, and weaving with long, loose warp floats, the warp passing over four and under one weft or over seven and under one for more luxurious types. The warp threads are so tightly packed that the weft threads scarcely show.

Problems Stitching shows, pinning leaves marks, flat pressing is impossible, machining puckers, slippage occurs in seams, long floating threads are subject to wear by abrasion and can be caught in the machine, and the fabric is both fraying and slippery. It is about the most difficult a dressmaker ever has to handle.

Sateen This is a cotton fabric made similarly by leaving weft instead of warp floats. It does not have such a high sheen as the staple fibre is not so lustrous. Its problems are similar but not nearly so severe.

Techniques Advice on handling slippery and fraying fabrics is given separately, and pressing is dealt with in chapter 23. Because of its lustre, satin may need cutting as a one-way fabric. Pin and stitch marks are avoided by using fine pins or pinning in the seam allowances only, using pure silk thread and fine needles for tacking, and mounting the fabric for support and to take inside stitching, e.g. hems. Do not handle with rough hands or fingernails. The machine needs careful adjustment and testing for pressure, tension and stitch length to avoid pucker. Hand sew zips or apply invisible ones.

Since areas of ease look awkward, adjust the pattern either to reduce it to a minimum or to increase it to make true gathers.

Slippery fabrics

All woven fabrics which are slippery, such as satin and foulard, also fray badly, and a separate section has dealt with this problem. Certain synthetic fibre tricots and jerseys also slip badly. Most of the problems arise during cutting. A cutting board is a great help if the fabric is pinned to it before the pattern is placed. This will help to keep the grain straight. An alternative is to cover the table with a sheet before laying the fabric. Use frequent, fine pins.

Fabric will slip less under the machine if tissue paper is placed between layers, tacking is small and firm, possibly diagonal basting, and pins are placed at right angles to the edges while machining.

In general work on a large cloth-covered surface for support.

Crêpes

Crêpe is an inclusive term for several types of crinkle-surfaced fabric and includes fine crêpe-de-chine, originally a silk fabric, crepon, with tree-bark irregularities, and georgette which is sheer. It is manufactured by several methods:

(a) In fibres which swell with moisture, i.e. silk, wool, cotton and rayon, extra hard twist yarns with alternate Z and S twists are used in the weft or occasionally both warp and weft. After weaving these shrink and snarl when the fabric is treated with heat and moisture.
(b) Thermoplastic fibres are used for heat-set crêpes.
(c) A combination of embossing and resin treatment on rayon.
(d) The random crêpe weave gives an irregular effect to fabric of any fibre.

Crêpes may be slippery, fraying and/or sheer and should be handled appropriately.

They present a cutting problem as the grain does not show up. To detect crosswise grain a thread must be pulled. Some fabrics show stitches through and should therefore be mounted. Styles should be fluid and draping. Pleats do not hold but folds, cowls and flounces are ideal. Interfacing is not usually used in these styles unless support or reinforcement is needed for specific parts. Zips should be hand-sewn or invisible.

As the fabric tends to stretch, care should be taken while cutting out and handling and on account of this hems should be left to hang as long as possible before stitching. A soft unpressed hem is suitable.

Crêpe garments should be folded to store, not hung, to prevent loss of shape.

Metallic fabrics

These fabrics contain some proportion, usually a small one, of metallic filament threads. The range includes brocades, jerseys and lace. Metallic threads are made of aluminium foil in thin strips covered in clear plastic and come in a variety of colours. Although reasonably flexible, they are not resistant to abrasion and tension. They are also manufactured as hand or machine sewing threads. Entire garments made of these fabrics can be overpowering, particularly if there is a high proportion of metallic thread, and the fabric combines well with satin, velvet and the taffetas. Fabrics may often be made up on either side, or a combination of sides used.

The two most difficult characteristics to handle are the extreme fraying encountered in woven metallics, due to the smoothness of the threads (see *Fraying fabrics*) and their tendency to show up hand-stitching badly. The latter problem is best overcome by mounting the fabric. Metallic fabrics are scratchy against the skin and snag stockings and tights, so false hems and facings of other fabrics may be called for. An alternative is to bind or pipe the edges in velvet or satin.

Sharp new needles and pins are required as the fabric blunts them and scissors may require sharpening after use.

Metallic brocades have long loose threads which may easily catch in the machine or damage during fitting. Fit with seams overlapped or pinned or tacked very loosely and machine with tissue paper. Never unpick and take great care when removing tackings.

Press with a cool iron and light pressure over tissue paper. Continual pressing breaks threads, which is why pleated styles are unsuitable and alterations cannot be made. Garments should not be folded.

Knitted fabrics

There is no fibre which cannot be knitted although some, such as linen, are very rarely processed in this way. Knitted fabrics vary from the fine and fluid to the heavyweight and stable, depending on the fibre, yarn and knitting method. They are nearly always made much wider than woven fabrics, up to about 170cm (66in).

Weft knitteds are made flat or tubular and have one continuous yarn across the fabric, as in hand knitting. Fabrics thus made may be very stretchy, unstable if thin and will ravel. They include:

(a) Single jersey (like hand-knitted stocking stitch)
(b) Double jersey, which is made with two sets of needles and two yarns, looks very similar on both right and wrong sides, and is reasonably stable. If it is pulled across the width it curls to the right side.
(c) Jacquards, made similarly to double jersey with coloured patterns
(d) Interlock, a double knit rib fabric with smooth texture.

Warp knit fabrics are more complicated and made differently, principally for fine fabrics in man-made fibres. They will not unravel and are more stable than weft knits, stretching mainly in the weft direction. In production several yarns at a time run the length of the fabric parallel to each other. Fabrics include:

(a) Locknit or tricot, a stable fabric, with or without pattern, frequently used for lingerie and lining, sometimes light and open, the wrong side being more matt than the right side.
(b) Raschels – vertical rows of chain stitches holding loose crosswise yarns. Many types of net, lace and mesh fabrics are included in this category.

Jersey fabrics may be the basis for other types, e.g. fur fabric, stretch towelling, ciré (a wet-look fabric produced by applying hot rollers to the surface of nylon knit) and panne velvet.
Suitable styles   The more fluid knits require styles with drapery, gathers, etc. or can have a slinky clinging fit. Stable knits tailor well and can be pleated, and when made into tailored styles should be lined, possibly with tricot. Very flared skirts and bias cutting should be avoided since they do not look well and drop out of shape. Bound edges are ideal as the binding is simply cut from straight across the fabric instead of bias.

Fabric to be avoided is that with a strongly noticeable centre fold as it may not press out, causing cutting complications. Fabric printed 'off-grain' or badly shaped should not be purchased since it cannot be straightened.

The handling of knitted fabrics is dictated mostly

by their stretch qualities and is therefore dealt with in detail in chapter 25. Modern aids to sewing are ball point sewing and machine needles and pins, serrated edge shears, stretch interfacing and synthetic threads which must be used for their elastic quality whatever the fibre of the knit.

Cut edges will not fray and do not need neatening unless they ladder. To test for laddering, cut a small square of fabric and pull the edges in turn holding the ends, when any laddering will become apparent. These edges should be bound or closely zig-zagged. Neatening may be performed on non-laddering edges simply to improve the appearance or to help prevent curling.

Both bobbin and spool tensions should be loosened but balanced. In a machine with a removable bobbin case, the bobbin tension is right when the case and spool slide slowly down the thread under their own weight when suspended by the end of the thread. The top tension must then be loosened to balance this. Some knitted fabrics are very slippery and need to be treated accordingly.

Lace

Lace has been made by hand for hundreds of years in many different ways including knitting, crochet, embroidery on handmade net with needle and thread, and with bobbins on a pillow. The first mechanically produced lace appeared in the latter half of the eighteenth century when the Rev. William Lee found a method of varying the patterns on a simple knitting machine to leave evenly spaced holes. Patterns became more complicated and were sometimes outlined by hand afterwards. Before the end of the century a warp lace machine for knitted lace had supplanted the earlier invention and this machine, with modifications, is still in use today.

The twisting method of lace production was introduced in 1800 when Heathcote invented the bobbin net machine producing lace of considerable strength and stability. The most famous name in the history of lace making is John Leavers, who developed Heathcote's machine to produce many kinds of laces still known as Leavers lace. The basic principle is the twisting together of two sets of warps instead of the weaving process involving warp and weft. The design is produced by Jacquard cards, named after their inventor, which are punched with a series of holes to represent the pattern and which control the levers making it. A modern Leavers lace machine uses 15,000 threads and can reproduce many types of traditional lace such as Honiton, Brussels, Limerick,

Valenciennes, and so on which were originally made only by hand.

Fibres now used are cotton, linen, wool, silk, nylon and terylene, but cotton and nylon form the bulk of laces produced.

Leavers lace with the design extending to a straight edge is known as 'allover' and varies from fine filmy laces for lingerie to sturdy 'suiting' laces.

Flouncings are usually about a metre (36in) in width and made in standard lengths of five to six metres or yards. One edge is scalloped, sometimes deeply, and the fabric is used as a border pattern fabric. Sometimes the other edge has an identical scallop or a smaller one and can be used to repeat the hem pattern on another part of the garment.

Guipure is a heavy open-work white cotton nylon or wool lace with very pronounced motifs. Decorative edges are easily cut by clipping away threads around the motifs. These do not need finishing and make beautiful edge finishes for 'V' necks, centre fronts, sleeve hems, etc. Long strips or separate motifs can be cut this way to appliqué to any part of the garment.

Chantilly lace has similar well-spaced floral motifs on a net background, usually outlined in heavier thread, and is used cut and clipped for edges like Guipure.

Ribbon lace is very expensive as the patterns are outlined in fine ribbon.

Suitable styles There must be minimal seams and darts to avoid breaking up the pattern. Gathers should not be so full as to distort the pattern, and lace does not drape softly in very full gathers. Avoid intricate processes such as buttonholes, fancy openings, as the background of the fabric is not strong enough to support them. Lace has no grain and may be cut in any direction, the aesthetic placement of the motifs being the only consideration. It must be used imaginatively – the dress stand helps to plan and modelling is a good method of designing all or part of a garment. Lace combines beautifully with satin, velvet, taffeta and other plain fabrics which serve as a foil to it.

Cutting To match motifs, cut singly with the pattern pieces under the fabric so the design can be seen. The mounting fabric may be cut first and basted underneath the lace ready for sewing before cutting the lace. This makes it easier to handle.

Mounting   Lace is usually mounted to add strength or to hide turnings and darts which otherwise show through. If strength without loss of sheerness is desired net or marquisette can be used. Organdie and organza give a slightly less sheer effect. Opaque fabrics for mounting include taffeta, satin, fine jerseys, linings and lawn. They can be flesh-coloured, self-coloured or a complete contrast. Fabrics should be applied as mountings not linings, and the garment may be both mounted and lined. Consider mounting some parts, e.g. cuffs and collars to hide the turnings, and leaving the rest of the garment sheer.

Machining   A loosened tension is required for heavier laces. Place tissue paper both under and over the work to protect it.

Neatening   None is required since the fabric does not fray.

Seams   If not mounted, keep both edges together, stitch a second row of machining 3mm ($\frac{1}{8}$in) inside the first and trim closely. Seams on certain parts of the garments may be arranged so they can be appliquéd together, e.g. a straight CB seam. This must be borne in mind when cutting. Overlap one edge over the other matching the pattern exactly and oversew closely by hand or zig-zag with a carefully adjusted stitch width down a prominent line of the design (figure 323 (a)). Trim raw edges close to stitching on both sides.

Darts   On unmounted lace stitch with two rows of machining and trim closely as for seams, or appliqué, but the pattern will not of course match as in a straight seam. Trim along a well-marked motif line as near as possible to the dart stitching line, lift this and arrange it at a fitting to overlap the other edge in the best way available for fit and preservation of the pattern. Appliqué it into place as for seams.

Edges, including hems, may be dealt with in several ways:

(a) cut around motifs, especially in Chantilly and Guipure lace and leave. If there is a mounting it can either be cut away level with the inner points of the design and finished with an appropriate fine hem, or it may be cut to the shape of the lace edge and finely whip-stitched to it

(b) a lace border trim, purchased separately or cut from the fabric may be appliquéd around the edge (figure 323 (b))

(c) mounted lace may be faced with the mounting fabric in the regular way

(d) unmounted lace may be faced with net, cut as shaped facings or a doubled strip, stitched with

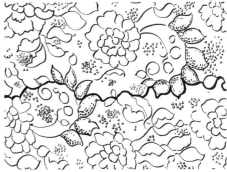

(a) Invisible appliquéd lace seam

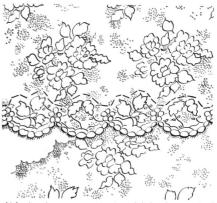

(b) trimming away surplus lace fabric after appliquéing a scalloped edge, cut from spare fabric

Figure 323   Working with lace

two rows of machine stitching and trimmed closely

(e) the whole section of garment may be lined with net, stitched around the edges and turned through

(f) edges may be bound in satin or other suitable fabric

(g) for hems, edge stitch or finish with horsehair braid (chapter 20). Bobbin net may be left straight cut.

Fastenings   Lightweight zips sewn by hand or invisible zips are possible if the fabric is mounted, but would be unsightly on laces left sheer. Mounted fabrics support most fastenings, but unmounted lace is restricted to tiny buttons and worked loops, hooks and eyes or invisible press studs. Bound openings are suggested.

Pressing is dealt with in chapter 23.

Velvet

Velvets come in many types, some delicate luxury fabrics and some quite serviceable. They are made of silk (ring and chiffon velvet) these being the most delicate, luxurious, lustrous and expensive types; of acetate or rayon, sometimes with a cotton backing, also expensive and luxurious with rich deep pile, or of nylon with cotton backing to prevent slipping. The last is more serviceable but the pile is thin and lacks richness. The type used for millinery is traditionally known as 'mirror' or Lyons velvet, and that for coats as 'street' velvet. In recent years the term 'trouser' velvet has appeared. Hollow-cut velvet has a corded effect, while sculptured effects are known as 'embossed' or 'figured' velvet, both of these being delicate. Panne velvet has a long pile, flattened by pressing and with very high lustre, and may have a woven or knitted base. It is not delicate.

Velvet is made by weaving in an extra warp thread to a plain or twill weave base, inserting wire blades among the weft threads. These are withdrawn, cutting the warp pile as they go. More rarely it is woven as a double cloth, with the backings on the outside layers and the extra warp thread running between the two layers. The two layers are cut and separated after weaving.

Velveteen is a cotton fabric similar to velvet, but with a weft pile. Corduroy and needlecord are also weft pile, mostly of cotton, but nylon needlecord exists. They have pile in ribs only. All the weft pile fabrics are hardwearing, mostly washable and can be pressed without the use of a velvet board.

Velvet and velveteen are cut with the pile running upwards to produce a rich colour and corduroy may be cut this way also, but when used for skirts or trousers it is more usually cut pile down for harder wear and to enable clothes to be 'brushed down' for everyday wear. Panne velvet is cut pile down. Velvet shades attractively when cut on the cross, but is unsuitable for larger figures because of the sheen.

Suitable styles Velvet garments should have few seams and feature gathers, folds and cowls. Combinations of velvet with other fabrics such as tweeds, chiffon, metallic brocade and satin in one garment are effective and can reduce sewing problems. (Seams joining two fabrics should be machined with the velvet underneath.) Only needlecord or panne may be topstitched.

Special considerations The fabric must be handled as little as possible and with a very light touch. Reduce handling by fitting a toile first. Avoid self-facing where possible by using lining or similar lightweight replacement. Fraying is a problem.

Knitted panne must also be treated as a knit.

Cutting A single lay is best as two layers creep upon one another. Secure the pattern with very fine pins or needles in the turnings, darts or other inconspicuous places. Sharp shears are needed to prevent damage to the pile.

Marking If mounted, the marking can be confined to the lining fabric. If the velvet itself must be marked use a fine needle and pure silk thread, taking care to trace tack backing threads only.

Machining Lighten the pressure, use a long stitch and silk or polyester thread with a fine needle. Guide the fabric firmly and lift the presser foot as often as necessary. If the layers of fabric creep too much on one another stitch with a layer of tissue paper in between. Tacking needs to be very firm, and must be outside the stitching line so that it does not leave a mark. Pins may be left in the seam allowance while machining. Stitch in the direction of the nap rather than with the grain. Tape bias and horizontal seams, especially in soft silk velvet. Take great care when removing tacking as velvet both marks and tears easily.

Neatening Problems are excessive fray, bulk and curling edges. Good methods are machine stitch and overcast by hand or binding with jap silk or net or the Hong Kong finish. Necklines and armholes look well bound if the fabric is not too thick.

Fastenings Avoid machine or hand-worked buttonholes as they mark the fabric and bound buttonholes are frequently unsuitable because of bulk and fray. Consider decorative clasps or buttons and hand worked loops. Zips must be lightweight and hand-sewn or invisible.

Hems These must be very lightly sewn as the fabric stitch marks, and hanging the hem is one of the main reasons for mounting velvet. Soft hems are possible.

Pressing See chapter 23.

Storage Hang on a padded hanger, stuff with tissue and place in an uncrowded cupboard. Do not fold.

Towelling (Terry cloth)

Dress towelling is nearly always made of pure cotton as it needs to be absorbent. Basically it is a plain weave with an extra warp thread, as for velvet. The extra thread is raised to leave loops on both sides of the fabric. It must be handled carefully while cutting and machining since it damages easily and a loop catching on a sharp object will pull out for many centimetres, disturbing the pile. The weave is loose and slippage is a problem, therefore terry garments must never be too tight. Seams fray very readily, particularly those cut across the fabric from selvedge to selvedge. Edges must be securely finished. Three special seams exist for terry cloth:

First method

(a) allow turnings of about 2cm ($\frac{3}{4}$in) when cutting. Cut one edge to half this width after fitting.

(b) Place RS together, seam lines touching and fold long edge over short one. Tack (figure 324 (a)).

(c) Fold up the top layer as in figure 324 (b) and topstitch close to the fold on RS fabric.

(d) Turn garment and topstitch the other folded edge (figure 324 (c)). This encloses both edges securely but is a little bulky.

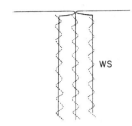

Figure 325   Finishing an open seam on terry cloth

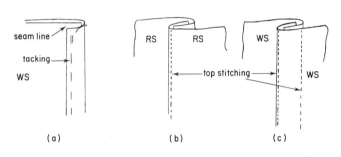

(a)   (b)   (c)

Figure 324   Seaming terry cloth

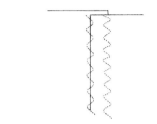

Figure 326   Overlap seam for terry cloth

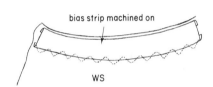

Figure 327   Bias facing for terry cloth

Second method

Construct a regular open seam, neatening the edges by stitching them down flat to the garment with three- or five-step zig-zag. This stitching shows through to the right side a little but is an attractive finish if the cotton is well-matched. To reinforce, a further line of machining may be added over the seam line (figure 325). This modern finish replaces the old-fashioned 'flannel seam', now outdated, in which turnings were herringboned to the garment.

Third method

Cut turnings to about 1cm ($\frac{3}{8}$in). Overlap on stitching line and work three- or five-step zig-zag over both raw edges (figure 326).

Zips   Do not try to conceal the zip as the towelling loops will catch in it. Fold the edges back and apply to the zip tape leaving the teeth showing. Work a three- or five-step zig-zag from the RS over the folded edge to attach it to the tape. This stitch will prevent the loops coming into contact with the zip.

Edges   These can be bulky if faced with self fabric. A good replacement is purchased bias binding in narrow or wide width and used as a facing. The free edge should be stitched through to the garment with three- or five-step zig-zag (figure 327). Narrow hems and edges may be finished by a single hem sewn with the same stitch. Another attractive finish is to bind the edges with bias strip cut from contrasting or matching plain woven cotton fabric, e.g. poplin or cambric, or with folded military braid (cotton or rayon) topstitched in place.

For other processes treat terry as both a bulky and a fraying fabric. Stretch towelling is handled as a stretch fabric (chapter 25).

Beaded fabrics

Fabrics of all weights and types may be embroidered with beads, sequins or rhinestones, but usually only fairly heavy satins, taffetas, foulards and the like are thus decorated. Beading adds still more weight, so plain styles without too much fullness are called for. The fabrics must be mounted for support and to prevent wear to the loose threads on the WS and damage to skin or lingerie from the prongs of rhinestones etc. Some beaded fabrics are also border designs.

Cut heavily beaded fabric singly and be prepared for blunted scissors.

Tack up loosely for fitting to prevent damage to the beads, and if heavily encrusted overlap turnings for fitting instead.

After fitting, thread-mark new seam lines and remove all beads from facings, dart folds, turnings and hems before tacking firmly for machining. When removing beads leave long ends of the attaching threads to sew in to secure the remaining beads. Stay-stitch all edges where there remains any possibility of losing fine beads.

Matching self-coloured fabric may be used for facings and false hems.

Dry press on a foam rubber pad as steam may damage the trimmings.

Fabrics requiring matching

Fabrics which have to be matched are those with regular patterns of any type, whether floral, geometric, striped, check, and so on. Most of the difficulties are encountered during cutting out and these are dealt with in chapter 7. A few extra considerations to bear in mind when planning are that:

(a) side seams interrupted by an underarm dart will not match throughout their length and should do so below the dart as the seam above the dart is concealed by the arm

(b) shoulder seams interrupted by a back shoulder dart should match from dart to shoulder as the neck to dart section may be covered by a collar or hairstyle

(c) the armhole seam should match at the level of the balance marks and downwards, but the top of the sleeve head may not necessarily do so

(d) collars in striped or irregular check fabric should not be cut on the bias

(e) buttonholes in striped or checked fabric should be spaced according to the pattern so that they fall on the same stripe or check each time.

Pinning Patterns can be matched by inserting pins by a stabbing method, placing the pin in upright and making sure it goes through both layers to match them before turning it to lie horizontally and take up fabric.

Seaming Slip-tacking is the best method for tacking. See p. 85.

25 Stretch

Stretch fabrics, which can now be said to be causing a minor revolution in the clothing and fashion industries, are by no means new. We have long been accustomed to rubberized elasticated fabrics, used for swimwear, corsets, etc, to knitted fabrics, which are in a sense stretch fabrics, and to woven fabrics with some degree of stretch due solely to the method of fabric construction such as crêpes. The real revolution began, however, in the U.S.A. in the 1960s with the introduction of the first elastomeric fibre, 'Lycra'. Every year since has seen growing use of stretch fabrics and it is the forecast of the textiles industry that at some future date a very large proportion of the fabrics used for clothing will be of this type. Modern life demands that clothing be comfortable, durable and easy care as well as of pleasing appearance, and the pursuit of leisure and the active life which are now so much a part of our age demand such fabrics. Along with the development of these new fabrics has come the development of new techniques of sewing. Swing needle machines are essential to their proper handling and their introduction to the sewing public in general has been hastened by the need to find adequate methods of sewing stretch fabrics.

What are stretch fabrics?

Almost all fabrics stretch to some degree, even if this involves only a little less stability in the weft direction. Two qualities are generally considered necessary, however, to enable a fabric to be defined as 'stretch'. Firstly the fabric must have an extension when stretched of at least 10 per cent, and secondly it must return to its original dimensions quickly after being relaxed. Most knitted fabrics fall into this category because of their construction, and woven fabrics may be stretch because of the nature of the yarns used. These are of two distinct types, (a) bulked thermoplastic yarns and (b) synthetic elastomer fibres made from a polymer consisting of segmented polyurethane, a product of the petro-chemical industry.

Type (a), bulked thermoplastic yarns, are produced on the principle that such fibres as nylon, polyesters, etc. are softened by heat and may be moulded by various methods into different crimped shapes, which are retained on cooling. 'Agilon', for example, is filament nylon yarn heated and pulled over a sharp edge giving a coil-like springiness, 'Banlon' is nylon yarn tightly packed in a heat stuffer box and set into a zig-zag form, while such yarns as 'Helanca' and 'Fluflon' are produced by twisting nylon yarn tightly, heat setting and then untwisting. Sometimes these yarns are then doubled with yarns twisted in the other direction, and thus highly stretchable yarns are produced.

Type (b) the synthetic elastomeric fibres, known in the U.S.A. under the generalized name of 'Spandex', were developed to replace rubber because rubber has these disadvantages:

(i) poor tensile strength – threads need to be bulky to obtain sufficient strength
(ii) it perishes under conditions of moist or dry heat
(iii) it will not dye
(iv) it deteriorates with acid (perspiration)

Elastomeric fibres therefore have these properties:

(i) greater recovery power (400–700 per cent stretch will return to normal)
(ii) can be dyed
(iii) high resistance to chemicals, sunlight and other disintegrative influences
(iv) light weight – yarns can be sheer
(v) greater strength than rubber
(vi) they may be bleached, finished and heat-set
(vii) softness and suppleness of handle.

The reason for their elastic quality is that the crimp is at the molecular level. Polymer molecules are coiled or folded on each other and may be straightened out. No fabric is ever made out of 100 per cent elastomer yarns. They may be used bare in conjunction with other fibres, mostly in knitted fabrics, or form the basis of a yarn made by the 'core-spun' or covering methods in which they are covered or wrapped by other fibres. Trade names are Courtauld's 'Spanzelle', and 'Lycra' and 'Vyrene' (U.S.A.).

Categories of stretch garments

The clothing trade is generally agreed on these categories:

(a) Comfort Stretch

Not necessarily close fitting – almost any garment may have this property if made of stretch fabric. Extensibility is designed to reduce resistance to body movements and thus give comfort and better wear. For example, ski-pants would otherwise lose shape and wear out at seat and knees.

(b) Stretch-to-Fit

Designed to fit body contours closely without exerting any figure shaping pressure, for example, swimwear, tights, leotards, body stockings and bras.

(c) Power Stretch

These exert control over body shape by compressive pressure on the surface, and include such garments as medical support stockings and girdles.

Classification of stretch fabrics for dressmaking
Standards of classification have now been agreed upon by the major pattern companies for use with their patterns to grade the degrees of stretch required in materials for their patterns. An example is Simplicity's 'Pick-a-Knit' Rule (figure 328).

When testing fabrics for stretch, it is advisable to note rapidity of relaxation and its completeness, in order to detect suitability of fabric for purpose and the amount and type of interfacing, stay-stitching and support needed.

A summary of the characteristics of stretch fabrics in wear

(a) They fit well and set perfectly
(b) They are crease resistant
(c) Easily washed and quick drying
(d) They keep shape and thus wear well.

Place crosswise grain of knit fabric below the PICK-A-KNIT Rule™, away from the cut edge of fabric, as shown.

Hold fabric with thumbs at each end of the 4" area.

Keeping left thumb anchored firmly, stretch fabric gently with right hand to end of rule.

If fabric stretches to at least the end of the rule, your knit is suitable for the pattern. Your knit may stretch slightly beyond the rule and still be suitable.

Figure 328

Fabrics available in the woven range include stretch towelling, stretch denim, Moygashel Expando (with the appearance of linen) stretch repp, stretch twills, stretch nylon lace, stretch brocades, and co-ordinated stretch banding for cuffs, neck bands, etc, widely available in the U.S.A. but difficult to obtain in Britain.

Dressmaking techniques for stretch fabrics

Preparation of fabric   Test for shrinkage in the warp direction by steam ironing a measured piece of fabric, then re-measure. If shrinkage is noted, pre-shrink the entire length. Fabric should in any case be allowed to relax from its rolled or folded state for some hours before cutting. Grain must be straightened as on other fabrics and tubular knits should be cut and opened with careful attention to 'grain'.

Designing   Pattern companies take care of this aspect, but for the dressmaker designing and cutting her own pattern, the following guide lines are worth noting:

(a) Use as few seams as possible as they inhibit stretch
(b) Use as few buttonholes as possible
(c) The amount allowed for ease may be reduced or eliminated altogether, according to the purpose of the garment and the type of fit required
(d) It is possible to eliminate darts altogether for moderate, very stretchy and power stretch fabrics. A suggested adaptation of the basic

block to eliminate bust, back shoulder and front and back waist darts, reduce width measurements to exact body measurements and maintain length measurements is given in figure 329. It is also possible by this method to reduce the block to less than body measurements for a clinging fit for swimwear, body stockings, etc.

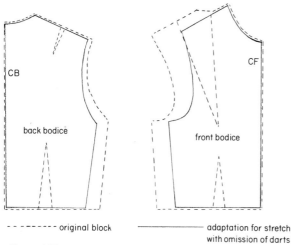

- - - - - - - original block
————————— adaptation for stretch with omission of darts

Figure 329

Cutting   Very sharp or serrated scissors are required to prevent snags and pulls. Knit fabrics do not generally run or ladder on cutting, due to the matting effect of manufacture and finishing.

Lining   Jersey or tricot fabrics must be used.

Machine adjustments   These will vary according to the machine used. In general automatic tension machines will not require adjustment. Other machines may not produce a satisfactory result unless the tension of the bobbin thread is reduced and the stitch balanced by the adjustment of the top thread tension. Should the fabric not feed through evenly the presser foot pressure may have to be reduced. Needle size should correspond to that normally used for the weight of fabric, and a ball point needle is preferable to avoid puncturing threads.

Machining   Only a swing needle machine is able to cope really adequately with stretch material, and many of the more advanced machines have several special stitches devised solely for working on stretch fabrics. Details of some of these follow later. If a straight stitch must be used, the fabric must be stretched while sewing and the number of stitches to the centimetre increased above normal to allow more thread to work into the seams. There are problems here, as fabrics do not always return to normal dimensions after being stitched in this way, and tests should be carried out on scraps first. Even when the seam reverts to normal, it will not be really satisfactory as sufficient stretch cannot be imparted in this fashion. All seams which need to retain stretch should be stitched with a zig-zag stitch or other special stitch designed for the purpose on the particular machine being used. Ideally the amount of extensibility of the seam should be equal to that of the fabric so that the fabric may be stretched in wear to its limit without the seam breaking out. The special stitches provide for this and in general the more thread in a seam the greater the extension. When starting to machine, pull fabric very clear of the throat plate to prevent its being drawn down by the needle. Seams where stretch is not required, e.g. shoulder seams, pockets and front edges, should be taped. Seams with a great deal of stress, such as armholes and centre front and back seams on trousers may require reinforcement with a second row of stitching. Very firm tacking is required.

Thread   Polyester sewing thread is required because it is slightly elastic.

Interfacings   Special stretch interfacings should be used on all parts of the garment where the stretch quality of the fabric needs to be allowed to 'give', e.g. centre front facings. Ordinary interfacing may be used where stretch is not required, e.g. collars and cuffs. When using stretch interfacing it must be cut as though it had 'grain' to allow the stretch to run in the desired direction.

Other processes   If fabric tends to roll on cut edges seams may be trimmed to 7mm ($\frac{1}{4}$in) wide and edges machine neatened together.

Some machines provide a special stitch for buttonholes, but if using conventional zig-zag, open it out more than normal satin stitch length.

When easing in, stretch the smaller piece to fit the larger one and place the edge to be stretched *on top*; for example, if setting in sleeves, contrary to normal practice, the bodice armhole will be on top.

A quick method for finishing edges without trim or facing is to turn the edge under and topstitch with straight stitch, twin needle or zig-zag, according to taste and the position of the edge on garment.

Self-fabric trimming for necks and edges can be quickly and neatly applied by cutting strips double the finished width required, plus turnings, and only $\frac{3}{4}$ of the length of the edge to be finished. The stretch should of course be on the length. Fold the strip in half lengthways, place all three raw edges together, stretching the strip to fit the garment. Pin or tack or both, and stitch with trim on top, (figure 330). This seam is best accomplished with one of the special

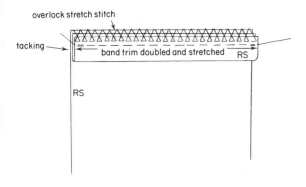

Figure 330

stretch stitches that seam and overlock in one operation, but it may also be neatened with conventional zig-zag stitch. The seam should be pressed toward the garment – it will be found that it falls naturally this way.

Pressing Take care not to stretch by sliding the iron too much or too heavily. The heat of the iron should be adjusted to the fibre, but in general should not be too hot or heat-set crimped fibres may lose their spring. Steam may be used and may be necessary. Do not allow a newly pressed part of the garment to hang over the edge of the board while still warm.

Stretch and the sewing machine

It has already been suggested that the great advances in sewing machines over the last 20 years have been very largely due to the need to develop techniques which would adequately deal with modern fabrics. Figure 331 illustrates some of the stitches which have been developed for stretch sewing. Some are common to various makes of machine, while some are unique. The naming of stitches also varies with different manufacturers.

Stitch (a), zig-zag, may be worked at different widths. Worked at width $\frac{1}{2}$ and the normal length for the fabric, it scarcely appears to be zig-zag at all, but does in fact give reasonable limited stretch. It is used for general seaming. Worked at width 1 and shortened length, about 1, the stitch sinks well into the fabric and has more stretch while still giving a flat seam.

Stitch (b), the three- or five-step zig-zag or serpentine stitch, is used for applying one layer upon another, for example when applying a reinforcement over specific areas of a power stretch girdle. The reinforcement piece is applied, machined and then trimmed off close to the stitching. Elastic may also be applied with this stitch.

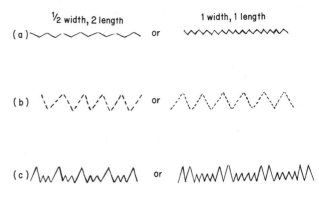

(d)

(f)

Figure 331

Stitch (c) worked at width $1-1\frac{1}{2}$ and length $\frac{1}{2}-\frac{3}{4}$ makes a very elastic stitch for fabrics with a great deal of stretch and sinks well into the fabric. It serves as a blind hem stitch for elastic fabrics, sewing only every so often on the garment part. It may be used for shell hems on stretch fabrics and makes more satisfactory buttonholes than the normal zig-zag.

Stitch (d), triple stitch, can only be made by machines with reverse feed action and stretches about

75 per cent of its own length. It is very good for seams that must bear especial strain, such as crotch seams on ski pants, and is the only method of producing a traditional straight topstitching on stretch fabrics.

Stitch (e) seams and overcasts in one operation and produces a fine, firm but very stretchy seam for armholes and other places where turnings should be kept narrow. It is used for appliqué on stretch fabrics, for setting elastic and for setting neck bands and cuffs of doubled strips as in figure 330. It can be adjusted to stretch more than 100 per cent of its own length. This is another reverse feed stitch.

Stitches (f) and (g), again of the reverse feed type, also sew and overlock in one operation and are suitable for power stretch fabrics. They are often successful on delicate fabrics which tend to pucker with stitch (e). They are ideal for swimwear and set elastic quickly and decoratively around edges.

Stitch (h) makes a good decorative flat joining seam of the double stitched type, while the ladder stitch, (i), seams, overcasts and decorates in one operation and is most effective worked in contrasting thread.

While it is not possible to describe the full range of stretch stitches here, nor to outline all the possibilities they present, these examples will serve to show the great variety of stitches and methods available and, it is hoped, will encourage the reader to experiment with her own machine and discover the exciting possibilities of this relatively new art of stretch sewing.

26 Lingerie

The principles of making successful lingerie are a little different from those of outerwear as an undergarment must always complement the fashion garment with which it is worn rather than create its own image. For this reason bows, ruffles and so on, so beloved of lingerie manufacturers, may often be quite unsuitable as they spoil the flat smooth line and can show through in bulges to the outer garment. Even seams in slips, if not flat and delicate, or if misplaced, can spoil the line of a closely fitting dress. Clinging or sheer dresses need slips designed specially for them, complementing them in line, colour and fit.

That having been said, lingerie should be decorative as well as functional, and it is the traditional ground for much delicate hand and machine work, so long as the decoration does not interfere with the purpose of the garment. Easy-care properties are important and comfort is essential, which is why knitted fabrics do so well as lingerie. The purpose of a bra may be to give support and control, to provide modesty or to give a 'no-bra' look, and its cut and fabric will vary accordingly. A slip should provide a good basis for a dress, possibly creating a smooth surface for the dress to fall on or providing stiffness and support, say for a gypsy style dress, when flounces would be in order and the fabric might well be taffeta or a stiff cotton.

A variety of fabrics may be used, plain or patterned, and of cotton, silk or man-made fibres. Crêpes, satins, lace, lawn, chiffon, georgette, tricots (40 denier opaque or 15 denier sheer), seersucker, power nets and stretch fabrics all have a place. Fabrics should be non-static to prevent 'cling', and if not purchased as such a fabric conditioner should be applied to all man-made fibre fabrics.

Patterns

Nightwear needs to be cut with less ease than outerwear, but depending on personal preference, should be less tightly fitting than slips for comfort. Patterns made from personal blocks require the reduction of bust ease to about 5cm (2in) for an average adjustment, but this will depend on the wearer's taste and the style of the garment. Slip and bra patterns, on the other hand, need a very definite alteration in the basic block or shell, to provide sufficient bust shaping. For slips, increase the size of the bust dart, whether at the side or shoulder, by 50 per cent (figure 332) (up to 100 per cent for bras and bikinis) and lengthen the appropriate seam to restore the length lost. The dart is then ready for manipulation in the usual way. Secondly reduce the bust ease to 1–3cm ($\frac{3}{8}$–$1\frac{1}{4}$in) depending on the elasticity of the fabric to be used. This may be done at the side seam or by taking a tuck vertically through the length of the pattern, or both, the method not being crucial as so little of the bodice block is eventually used.

Slim-fitting slips are more practicable with side seam slits, and all slips in woven fabric fit better if cut on the cross. Avoid facings as they add bulk

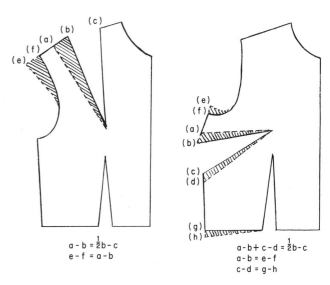

$$a - b = \tfrac{1}{2}b - c$$
$$e - f = a - b$$

$$a - b + c - d = \tfrac{1}{2}b - c$$
$$a - b = e - f$$
$$c - d = g - h$$

Figure 332   Increasing the size of the bust dart

unevenly. Replace them with bound edges, small stitched hems (possibly edged with lace), or double bodices. If facings are unavoidable bias strips should be used rather than shaped facings (see chapter 12).

Slips should be cut sufficiently low under the arm to avoid the possibility of showing under sleeveless garments.

Haberdashery

A number of specialist items are available. The smallest possible fastenings should be used, and if press studs are required the transparent ones are best. Other useful items worth searching for are ready-made adjustable shoulder straps, elasticated shoulder strapping by the metre, bra back fastenings (usually sold as 'repair kits') and fancy elastics, lace edged and/or plush which are more resilient as well as more attractive than cord elastic.

Techniques

Many of the special techniques required for lingerie making are covered in other sections of the book. See chapter 24 for the handling of sheers, satin, crêpes, slippery fabrics, quilting, lace and knitted fabrics, and chapter 25 for detailed procedures for stretch fabrics.

Chapter 12 deals with the application of bias strip facings, binding and French (double) binding. A further method of applying strip facings is shown in figure 333 (a) and (b), all stitching being by machine, which is an acceptable, firm and attractive finish for lingerie edges.

(a) Apply to the RS, stretching or easing to curves as appropriate, and machine.

(b) Turn to the WS and topstitch along both sides of the strip.

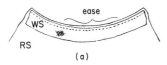

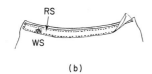

Figure 333   Bias strip facing

Figure 334   Stretch lace as a right side facing

Figure 334 shows the application of stretch lace to the RS, a simple but attractive edge finish.

Seams must be finely finished with small turnings and must lie flat. Open seams are not generally suitable for lingerie. Better choices are the fine French, mock French, lingerie, overlaid and flat felled seams detailed in chapter 11, together with the hand- or machine-worked decorative seams, such as the faggoted seam in chapter 22. A useful seam is the strap seam, particularly for bras. Turnings are cut very small and the strap may be a bias or straight strip or lace, ribbon or braid, provided it has bias or stretch qualities if curves are involved.

Hems must be delicate and free from bulk and on slips should be about 2cm ($\frac{3}{4}$in) shorter than the garment. Several possibilities are detailed in chapter 20, the double machined, rolled, rolled and whipped, machine picot, scalloped and topstitched all being suitable for lingerie. Lace is frequently added to a hem, (see chapter 5 for methods). Corners should be mitred where necessary (figure 335).

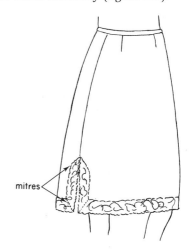

Figure 335   Mitred lace edging corners

Lingerie ought to be delicate and decorative, the principles of decoration being that it must be flat and lightweight. Machine embroidery and monograms are ideal as fine threads are used, and other machine techniques which are especially suitable for lingerie are twin needle work, hemstitching, air tucks, machine faggoting, shell edging, broderie anglaise, inverted and net appliqué, details of which are given in chapters 5 and 22. Rouleau may be used as in photo no. 55, and many similar designs can be evolved, but the rouleau must of course be the flat, not the round, variety. Hand processes include shell edging and tucks, shadow work, scallops and smocking.

Fastening and elasticizing

Techniques for applying elastic by machine are given on pages 41 and 42. When making an elasticized waist it is easier to apply it before closing the last seam, so that the work is flat and may be more easily divided into proportional sections. Apply plush elastic to the WS of the slip, the plush side next to the body. Fancy or lace-edged elastic is usually applied to the RS of the garment.

An adjustable hook and eye fastening for the back of a bra or bikini may be made as in figure 336, steps (a) to (e). Several sets of loop eyes are used, machined in place in tucks as in (a). The eye strap needs reinforcing with ribbon (b) and is finally faced by topstitching the facing round the three edges as shown in (c). Insert a few centimetres of elastic into the fourth side to join the fastening to the bra. The hook side is similarly constructed, except that the hooks are stitched to the ribbon interfacing by hand and the hook end must be hand-sewn to the facing as it is not possible to pass it under the machine foot (d) and (e).

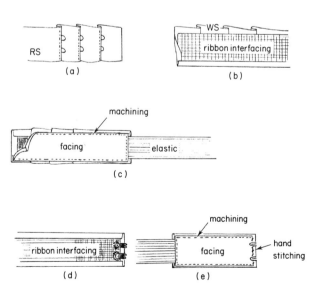

Figure 336   Adjustable bra closure

Shaping and reinforcing

The best bra forms are foam rubber as they launder well and keep their shape. The thin ones are mounted on to the facing of the bra cup with three- or five-step zig-zag. The stitch design depends on the design of the bra cup but a few suggestions are illustrated in figure 337 (a), (b) and (c). Always work from the centre outwards. Apply the padded facing to the bra cup afterwards, turning through in the usual manner. Alternatively, apply the facing to the cup leaving the lower edge open and insert the bra form between the layers, stitching it into position through all thicknesses. This makes a firmer finish.

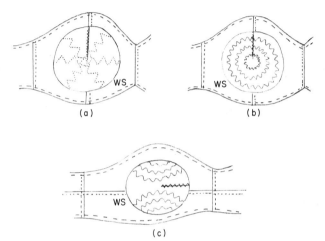

Figure 337   Application of shaping and reinforcement

Areas requiring a second layer of fabric such as a front panel for extra control on a power net girdle are treated in a similar way (figure 338). Crotches of girdles, panties and swimsuits may be lined by the same method, using cotton jersey.

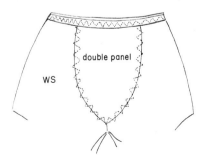

Figure 338

Straps

Stretch and adjustable straps may be purchased or
fabric ones made, affording scope for individuality,
particularly in nightwear where wide fancy straps
can be used to effect. Bra straps are better if they
include a small length of elastic, usually replacing
part of the strap at the back where it joins the bra.

The simple narrow tube, cut on the straight of the
fabric, stitched and turned as for rouleau, forms a
basic bra strap and the basis for decoration for night-
dresses. It may be decorated with a wide double-
edged lace stitched up the middle flat or gathered, or
be centred over a double-edged ruffle. Two narrow
straps look effective when joined with faggoting,
making a wider strap suitable for a slip. Another
attractive wider strap is made by folding a strip of
fabric as in figure 339 (a) and basting both narrow
hems before fixing them with a machine embroidery
stitch or hand hemstitching.

Straps in nylon tricot may present a problem as
they need stabilizing. As this fabric also makes

excellent shell edges a good solution is to treat as in
figure 339 (b). Baste a length of nylon ribbon up the
centre of the strap piece and tack down side hems
which just cover the edges of the ribbon. Use machine
blind stitch to attach the ribbon, make the hem and
the shell edge in one operation.

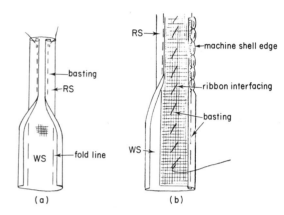

Figure 339   Lingerie straps

List of Suppliers

Bead Merchants
Ells and Farrier
5 Princes Street
Hanover Square
London W1
(personal callers only)

Creative Beadcraft Ltd
Unit 26
Earl Howe Road
Holmer Green
High Wycombe
Buckinghamshire
(mail order)

Belt and button making
from customers' own materials
Harlequin
258 High Street
Epping
Essex
CM16 4AW
(mail order)

Dress Forms
Leisure Arts Ltd
18 St Ann's Crescent
London SW18 2LY
(Form-O-Matic)

A.E. Arthur Ltd
Unit 6, Oldmedow Road
Hardwick Industrial Estate
Kings Lynn
Norfolk
(Diana) (Venus) (Twinfit)

Fibres
British Enkalon Ltd
PO Box 62
Enkalon House
Regent Road
Leicester
LE1 9AF

Courtaulds Ltd
22 Hanover Square
London W1A 1BS

Hoechst
Hoechst House
Salisbury Road
Hounslow
Middlesex
(Trevira)

ICI Fibres
Hookstone Road
Harrogate
Yorkshire

International Institute for Cotton
10 rue de Commerce
Brussels 1040
Belgium

Monsanto Ltd
10–18 Victoria Street
London SW1H 0NQ

Haberdashery Manufacturers
and Suppliers
Aero Zipps (Textron) Ltd
Aero House
Ealing Road
Wembley
Middlesex

J. & P. Coats Ltd
Domestic Marketing Division
16–25 Bastwick Street
London EC1P 1BA

Lightning Fasteners Ltd
Kynoch Works
Witton
Birmingham B6 7BA

MacCulloch & Wallis Ltd
25–6 Dering Street
London W1R 0BH

Henry Milward & Sons Ltd
Studley
Warwickshire
B80 7AS

Newey Goodman Ltd
PO Box 277
Robin Hood Lane
Birmingham 28

Scovill Dritz Sewing Aids Division
Whitecroft
Lydney
Gloucestershire
GL15 4QG

Interfacing and Lining
Manufacturers
Lantor UK
St Helens Road
Bolton
BL3 3PR

Milium Promotion Centre
St Ann's House
St Ann's Place
Manchester
M2 7LP
(insulated linings)

Vilene Information Service
Bondina Vilene Ltd
Greetland
Halifax
Yorkshire

Interfacing and Lining
John Lewis & Co. Ltd
Oxford Street
London
W1A 1EX
(mail order)

Lace
A.C. Gill Ltd
Lace Manufacturers
Warser Gate
Nottingham
NG1 1PA
(Witchcraft Lace)

The British Lace Federation
Chamber of Commerce and
Industry
395 Mansfield Road
Nottingham

Leather
(garments, skins, tools,
patterns, etc)
Barrow Hepburn Leathercraft Ltd
205 Kensington High Street
London W8

Gomshall and Associated Tanneries
Queen Street
Gomshall
Guildford
Surrey
GU5 9LE

Permanent Pleating
(Customers' Materials)
J.V. Landers & Co.
21/2 Colebrook Row
London N1
(mail order)

Sewing Machines
Bogod Machine Co. Ltd
50–2 Great Sutton Street
London EC1
(Bernina)

Elna Sewing Machines (GB) Ltd
180–2 Tottenham Court Road
London
W1P 9LE

Husqvarna Ltd
High Lane
Stansted
Essex
CM24 8LG

Necchi (Great Britain) Ltd
69/85 Tabernacle Street
London
EC2A 4BB

Pfaff (Britain) Ltd
22 Croydon Street
Domestic Street Industrial Estate
Leeds
LS11 9RT

The Singer Company (UK) Ltd
255 High Street
Guildford
Surrey

Sewing Threads
J. & P. Coats Ltd
Domestic Marketing Division
16–25 Bastwick Street
London
EC1P 1BA

Perivale-Gutermann Ltd
Wadsworth Road
Greenford
Middlesex
UB6 7JS

Index